ON SILVER WINGS

RAF BIPLANE FIGHTERS
BETWEEN THE WARS

ON SILVER WINGS

RAF Biplane Fighters Between the Wars

Alec Lumsden And Owen Thetford

OSPREY
AEROSPACE

First published in Great Britain in 1993 by Osprey, an imprint of Reed Consumer Books Limited, Michelin House, 81 Fulham Road London SW3 6RB, and Auckland, Melbourne, Singapore and Toronto

© Alec Lumsden and Owen Thetford

ISBN 1 85532 374 5

Edited by Tony Holmes
Designed by Mike Moule

© Cutaways by *Aeroplane Monthly*
© Scale Drawings by Alf Granger and *Argus Publications*
© Colour profiles by Charles Hannah
Origination by Mandarin Offset, Hong Kong
Printed in Great Britain by BAS Printers Limited, Over Wallop, Hampshire

Title page *Classic formation of Fury Mk IIs of No 25 Sqn up from Hawkinge in mid-1937. The three aircraft with solid black fins were assigned to the squadron OC and the two flight commanders respectively. The unit passed its beloved Mk IIs onto No 41 Sqn at Catterick in October of 1937, receiving decidedly pedestrian Demons in their place*

Acknowledgements

Alec Lumsden is greatly indebted to many friends who have helped in the preparation of this book. In particular, thanks are due to the Commandant of the Aeroplane and Armament Experimental Establishment, Boscombe Down, and to Sherri Carnson, the Librarian. Peter Elliott, Librarian of the Royal Air Force Museum at Hendon has dug out long forgotten technical manuals from the archives and invaluable help, gratefully acknowledged, came from noted aviation historians J M Bruce MA, Alec Harvey-Bailey, Derek N James, John Heaven and the late Ray Cook, with their contributions on Sopwith, Armstrong Whitworth, Gloster, Hawker and Bristol aeroplanes and their engines.

The verification of dates and other historical data is a massive undertaking in a study such as this, and Owen Thetford gratefully acknowledges the help he received by regularly consulting some key reference works which find an honoured place in his aviation library. The shortest possible bibliography would have to include James Halley's works published by Air Britain and Wg Cdr C J Jefford's invaluable *RAF Squadrons* which was published in 1988. Thetford also found of the greatest interest Francis K Mason's *The Gloster Gladiator* (1964) and David Luff's *Bulldog* (1987).

Finally, the editor would like to thank Richard Riding, Editor of *Aeroplane Monthly*, for his tireless enthusiasm for this project, and of course for having the foresight to commission the original articles in the first instance. Phil Jarrett also deserves a word of thanks for digging out many of the excellent photographs that illustrate this volume.

CONTENTS

FOREWORD

To a pilot of my age and vintage – I was born in 1913 – the aircraft described in this book, Snipe, Woodcock, Grebe, Gamecock, Siskin, Bulldog, Fury, Demon, Gauntlet and Gladiator, are magic names which conjure up a golden age of early experience and youthful excitement. I flew all but the first four.

The Snipe was left over from the First World War, being the last of the Sopwith fighters to serve in the fighter squadrons on the Western Front and the first of the newly-formed Royal Air Force after 1918.

In 1922 the Air Ministry issued a specification for a new fighter, the Hawker Woodcock; the first post-war design, it entered RAF service in May 1925. When I first served in an RAF fighter squadron (on Bulldogs) in 1932 there were still some pilots and many NCOs who remembered the Woodcock.

The RAF was formed on 1 April 1918 by the amalgamation of the RFC and the Royal Naval Air Service as the first independent air force in the world. Initially, the whole concept was opposed politically by the Navy and the Army, who disliked the idea of a third fighting service which would no doubt claim a share in the rapidly decaying National Defence Budget, and a voice in the formulation of national strategy. So, the early years of the RAF were not without problems, in addition to those of post-war organisation and administration of a brand new fighting service; and that service was in itself an act of faith in an unproven future based upon a technology – aviation – which was still in its infancy.

The RAF was based upon the idea that the aeroplane was essentially an offensive weapon and that one day there would be such a thing as air power, which would complement the long-established elements of sea and land power.

The RAF's founding fathers believed that such power would need to be developed and nurtured, and that it should be in the hands of a single independent fighting service. It has not been achieved easily, nor without sacrifice.

In 1923, not much more than four years after the Armistice, a situation of grave political antagonism arose between Great Britain and France over the payment of German war reparations, which alarmed the Cabinet of the day. France had 600 aircraft capable of raiding Britain and it was decided in June 1923 to expand the RAF

Clutching the appropriate paperwork pertaining to the Siskin IIIA parked behind him, Flg Off Jeffrey Quill stands by as Flg Off Dick Reynell tests his oxygen mask prior to performing a weather check sortie with the Duxford Met Flight in the early 1930s (Photo by Charles E Brown)

to a 52-squadron force. The Air Staff believed that the best air defence would come from the deterrent effect of a counter-force of bombers – so the new total of 52 squadrons was to comprise 35 of bombers and only 17 of fighters, which determined the size of the Fighting Area of ADGB (Air Defence of Great Britain) for years to come.

This book is about the aeroplanes of the early days of the Fighting Area, which in 1936 became Fighter Command, of immortal memory. The aeroplanes of the Fighting Area, and the men who flew them, maintained them and commanded the force, thus built up between 1923 and 1936, a system and tradition of air defence which, with the timely and decisive aid of British science in providing radar, enabled the great commander of Fighter Command, Air Chief Marshal 'Stuffy' Dowding, to win the Battle of Britain in 1940.

JEFFREY QUILL OBE AFC

AUTHOR'S PREFACE

Most of the biplane fighters of the period between the two World Wars wore the various bright heraldic colours adopted as uniform by fighter squadrons allocated to the Air Defence of Great Britain. In addition to the roundels and rudder or fin stripes of the Royal Air Force, they were painted or sprayed with silver dope over the taughtened fabric with which most were covered. In wartime, the colours of all aircraft tend to be subdued in order not to draw the attention of other aircraft, particularly marauding fighters from above. It was not so after hostilities ceased. From the end of World War 1, until the late 1930s when there was an uneasy peace, a brief, bright flash in the sky was probably an indication of a wheeling fighter, its silver wings reflecting the sunshine. To the pilot, the dope finish was like varnish and could be quite dazzling. Fighters were often called interceptors and, before radar was invented, had to be able to climb rapidly, with little or no warning, to defend the target they were there to protect.

Not all fighters were equipped for night flying, but those that were tended to be given the inelegant name of 'day-and-night-fighters'. Sight and colour are just as emotive in surrounding darkness. Anybody living near an RAF aerodrome would sometimes have the added drama of night-flying. The first indication, towards dusk, would be one of the station tenders, trundling at a walking pace across the landing ground as the officer in charge of night flying – 'Paraffin Pete' – supervised laying the flare-path of goose-neck flares into the wind in the form of a letter L. The one or two aeroplanes detailed for flying were wheeled out, their engines given a preliminary run-up and then there was silence until dusk. Next, the engines started again and navigation lights were switched on. Lacking steerable brakes and with panting airmen running at the wing-tips, slowly the fighters taxied to the beginning of the flare path, red and green wing-tip and white tail lights shining in the darkness. After another run-up, they took-off and disappeared, usually for practice 'circuits and bumps'. A red light on a left-hand circuit showed an approaching fighter, the green slowly appearing as well, as it turned in to land.

Suddenly, and most dramatically, an electrically-fired magnesium Holt flare on a bracket beneath a wing-tip would burst brilliantly into light, illuminating the ground

Flg Off Alec Lumsden models his favourite cap whilst attached to No 118 Sqn, flying Spitfire IIAs from Ibsley in May 1941

and the silver aeroplane itself. After landing, the fighter, with its flare still burning very brightly (and hotly), had to taxy to prevent the wing catching fire, until the flare suddenly burned out and died. It was certainly dramatic. When a few circuits or local flying was over, the fighters, looking small and fragile, taxied back to the hangars and weary crews dowsed the flares, reloading them onto the transport, and so to bed.

The fighter stations, mostly scattered round London, were, of course, frequently visited by aircraft from other stations. Big twin-engined biplane bombers, sombre in their 'Nivo' green, some with angry-sounding Napier Lion engines, often appeared and day bombers – Harts, Wapitis, Gordons and IIIFs – joined the row of fighters on the grass, tarmac or apron near the hangers, usually for lunch. It was all apparently very relaxed. What was always a matter for discussion, or excitement, according to age, was the row of perhaps eight or nine upper wings in the distance, not quite level on the rough grass. What squadron colours were visible and was there a visitor with an unfamiliar unit stripe? If those small fighters had one thing in common apart from the colour which they portrayed most vividly, it was the atmosphere of clattering engine noise and the smell and blue haze of burnt castor oil. With their ferocious purpose and looks, the little silver-winged biplane fighters bore more than a touch of modern heraldry.

ALEC LUMSDEN MRAeS

AUTHOR'S PREFACE

I have been writing about military aeroplanes, especially those of the Royal Air Force and Fleet Air Arm, for over 50 years but, even today, I never forget the thrill I experienced when, as a schoolboy spotter in 1936, I logged my first Hawker Fury biplane, with its distinctive Kestrel engine note, performing a barrel roll at low altitude over the family house in Cheshire. Judging by its vivid yellow fabric and burnished aluminium cowling glistening in the sun, it must have been a fighter trainer from the nearby FTS at Sealand. I do not know who was flying that magical aeroplane but, whoever it was, I now offer my belated thanks for inspiring what was to become a professional career in aviation authorship and journalism. An equally Proustian moment came in the summer of 1938 when I witnessed nine Gladiators of No 72 Sqn taking off in immaculate formation to perform air drill at the opening of Ringway Airport, closely followed by Gauntlets of No 46 Sqn.

Such golden memories, as can be imagined, were never far from my mind when making my contribution to the present work, which was indeed a labour of love. To my mind, nothing can surpass the fascination and the romantic aura surrounding the RAF's biplane fighters of the 1920s and 30s, and it is to be hoped that something of that enthusiasm is reflected in the words and pictures of *On Silver Wings*, and that it will inspire similar pleasure among the younger aerophiles of today.

Delighted as one is to observe the steady increase in vintage aircraft participating in today's air displays, there is still a dearth of items celebrating the RAF's classic biplane fighter era other than Old Warden's magnificent Gladiator. Every time I watch this old warrior, I cannot help thinking how marvellous it would be if it could be accompanied by the Bulldog (which crashed in 1964) and the elegant Fury replica from the late Patrick Lindsay's collection which, unfortunately, was sold abroad. Even static exhibits are limited to the RAF Museum's Gladiator at Hendon and the reproduction Fury II at Cosford which, it is rumoured, is likely to be transferred to the Tangmere Museum in Sussex. However, hopes are high that a projected Gamecock reproduction will emerge in due course from an enterprising group in Cheltenham.

Dare one expect that more such reproductions of these charismatic aeroplanes will follow? How superb it would be if, one day, there were to be an RAF Fighter

Happily ensconced in his favourite environment (in this case, a Chipmunk),
Owen Thetford takes a break from the typewriter

Museum which incorporated all the historic types (albeit in reproduction form) which led up to the crowning achievement of the Battle of Britain.

I am indebted to such authors as John Rawlings, whose classic work *Fighter Squadrons of the RAF* (1969) is justly celebrated, and James Goulding whose valuable *Camouflage and Markings, RAF Fighter Command* (1970) is indispensable for its sections on the years 1936 to 1939.

Personal experiences recorded by the rapidly diminishing generation of biplane fighter pilots are to be treasured. They can convey a remarkable period atmosphere. The literature of first-person narrative on this subject is surprisingly sparse and predominantly to be found in books now sadly out of print, but the choicest examples have been quoted and are acknowledged in the body of the text. Many of the books thus cited can rank as pure literature and are to be highly recommended as background reading, supplementing more factual reference studies.

OWEN THETFORD

THE SOPWITH SNIPE

THE SNIPE WAS CONCEIVED by the Sopwith Aviation Company in 1917 as a private venture, a direct development of the Camel. The hope was to emulate the excellent handling qualities of the Pup and eliminate the worst tendencies of the Camel. In order to appreciate the characteristics of the Snipe, it is perhaps helpful to recall those of its antecedents. Whatever may be recalled in these days of Battle of Britain nostalgia about the air fighting in the Great War of 1914–1918, it is almost certain to evoke pictures of the snub-nosed little Sopwith F.1 Camel. Possibly, even more vividly, we recall one of its adversaries, the scarlet Fokker Dr.1 Triplane flown by the dreaded 'Red Baron', von Richthofen of the German Air Force, a forebear of his country's former

distinguished Ambassador to the Court of St James's. (We are indebted to the American cartoonist Charles M Schulz for keeping memories of that great air war alive via 'Snoopy' and his bullet-riddled 'Sopwith Camel' kennel).

The design of the Camel was sheer inspiration, largely the work of Harry Hawker and Fred Sigrist working under the guidance of T O M Sopwith in 1916. A properly-stressed affair and one of the first to be designed with due and proper regard for the scientific laws governing structural integrity, it was a

Below A view of the third prototype Snipe at Martlesham. The revised centre section is apparent, as is the delicate inward canting of the beautifully crafted wheels

Above A Sopwith Snipe of No 25 Sqn on police duties over Constantinople in 1922 during the Chanak crisis

strong and pugnacious-looking little fighter. The gyroscopic forces of the Camel's rotary engine, coupled with its other touchy handling qualities and lightning-like responses meant that flying it could be hazardous for a novice, demanding the pilot's close attention at all times, particularly at low speeds and low altitudes with an engine whose reliability was uncertain. This was in strong contrast to its predecessor the Pup, whose handling was exemplary and virtually viceless. However, once its control peculiarities were mastered, the Camel became the most successful Allied fighter of the Great War, and its twin synchronized Vickers .303 in machine guns set the standard for fighter armament for nearly 20 years.

Built in large numbers, the Camel was powered by various types of rotary engine, including the 100 hp Gnome Monosoupape, 110 hp Le Rhone 9J, and the rather unreliable 130 hp Clerget 9B (in the case of RFC Camels). The most successful installation of all was the 150 hp Bentley B.R.1 in those flown by the RNAS. The Air Board issued 12 specifications for future aircraft for the flying Services at the beginning of 1917, one of these, Type A.1(a), being for a high-altitude single-seat fighter for the RFC. This required

a speed of 135 mph at 15,000 ft, an average rate of climb of 1000 ft/min, above 10,000 ft and a ceiling of at least 25,000 ft. In addition, three guns, two of them with 375 rounds of ammunition each, together with fuel for three hours were specified. The third gun, with 250 rounds and able to be pivoted upwards, was an option which could be traded for fuel. An armoured shield behind the pilot was required, as well as provision for keeping him warm and supplied with oxygen. Significantly, the aeroplane was to be 'very handy to control' and the flying surfaces to be stiff and strong.

It is by no means certain that the Snipe was actually designed to fulfil the stated requirements, nor that Sopwith knew the relevant details when the design was drawn up. Despite that, the fact that the two requirements coincided fairly closely pointed to harmony in the trend of current thinking.

There was an odd arrangement whereby the Air Board procured the Snipe. If ever there was official hesitancy in considering a new and potentially useful fighter, this was it. In the summer of 1917, the

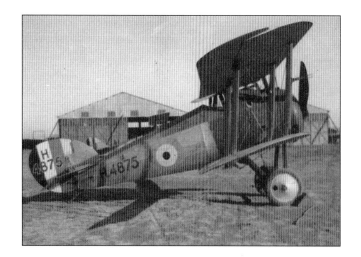

Left Snipe H4875. The curved streaks either side of the fuselage serial are not squadron markings but the shadows of the interplane struts

The Air Board's requirements, when they became known to Sopwith, placed quite formidable demands on a small aeroplane, even with one of the higher-powered rotary engines already installed in the Camel, notably the 150 hp Gnome Monosoupape and the 150 hp Admiralty Rotary, the A.R.1. The latter, a highly successful engine designed by the then Lt W O Bentley, was soon to be renamed the B.R.1, this being selected for the first of two prototype Snipes. Even before the engine had achieved its initial success with Camel squadrons of the RNAS, Bentley felt he had a winner and designed the 230 hp B.R.2. This would be a natural choice for the production Snipe, particularly as the alternative and nominally rather higher-powered 11-cylinder Clerget 11E rotary was far from ready because of teething troubles, keeping it out of the Snipe competition. Much of the design work of the Camel had been the responsibility of Herbert Smith,

unlovely Sopwith Rhino triplane was the subject of official Licence No 14, allowing four prototypes to be built as a private venture rather than under contract. Only two of the four proposed Rhinos were built and there was a lack of precision about the future of the project. The Snipe, not having been submitted officially as a contender to Specification A.(1)a, was conveniently tacked on to this licence, in an arrangement of a kind which had occurred at least once previously. Two prototypes were put in hand.

Below The Snipe's cockpit, with the breeches of the twin Vickers machine guns prominent. The traditional spade grip between the padded .303s appears well used

and when the need for a successor to the F.1 was apparent towards the end of April 1917, he and R J Ashfield shared the design work.

SOLID CAMEL

As a private venture on the part of Sopwith, to be called 'Snipe', the new machine looked like a slightly smaller but rather more 'solid' Camel, with a deeper fuselage. This enabled the pilot to be placed higher, his eyes being roughly in line with the centre section rear spar. The centre section was completely uncovered between the root ribs, giving him a considerably better view than in a Camel. The struts on the prototype were vertically mounted on the upper longerons. There was a slight, but equal, dihedral on upper and lower wings which were, at first, supported by a single pair of interplane struts on each side. The gap was a moderate 4 ft 3 in but, to compensate for any restriction of view downward, there was a substantial

stagger of 17 inches. Although the prototype Snipe had a slightly smaller span (25 ft 9 in) than the Camel, the wing area was almost the same.

The fuselage was slab-sided, with short tapering fairings behind the engine. The vertical tail was closely similar in low aspect-ratio to that of the Camel. The whole structure was of wood, wire-braced internally and externally and covered with fabric. The initial success of the powerful B.R.2 engine resulted in large orders being placed for it in October 1917, output expected in due course to comfortably exceed 1000 units per month. Thus powered, the Snipe seemed to stand a very good chance of fulfilling Spec A.1(a), and an official contract for six prototypes was issued on 10

Below Re-engined with the 320 hp ABC Dragonfly nine-cylinder radial engine, the Snipe was to have been developed into the Dragon. But the engine proved disastrous and, although a few Dragons were built, the type never entered RAF squadron service

November 1917, retrospectively covering the first two airframes at least. The exact date of the A.R.1-powered prototype's first flight seems to have gone unrecorded but it was in the autumn of 1917. The prototypes have been recorded as B9962–67. What is known, by photographic evidence, is that the second of these was B9963 (powered by a prototype B.R.2). The first (which bore no Service identification in photographs of it) is therefore presumed to have been B9962. Lacking a formal contract, the marking of a serial number on it might have been considered improper. Nothing seems to have been recorded about

B9964, and the RFC openly expressed interest in only the last three of the batch. It would appear that the first trio were included so as to cover Sopwith's costs in developing the Snipe and producing the B.R.1 and B.R.2 prototypes, plus seemingly one 'for luck', or to provide spares back-up for the other two. They were going to be needed!

In the stress of wartime production, a somewhat haphazard approach to record-keeping is understandable. Whatever the truth of the matter, the first Snipe ('9965') to go to the Aeroplane Experimental Station (AES) at Martlesham Heath – as the Testing Squad-

ron, formerly Experimental Flight, CFS, was renamed in January, 1917 – was due to arrive in November, but it crashed at Brooklands on 19 November and had to be repaired. It arrived, as B9965 on 18 December, whereupon it crashed again on 23 December and was sent back once more to Sopwith for repair. During its brief stay at Martlesham, it was found to be quite a bit down on its expected performance – top speed 119 mph and ceiling only 21,500 ft. However, the AES report concluded that the aeroplane was not representative of a standard, although exactly what that would be was unstated. A photo-

graph taken at the time showed a Snipe with single-bay wings, which differed from the two previously known aircraft in that it had rounded fuselage sides and splayed centre-section struts, with correspondingly shortened interplane struts. Further, the fin was smaller than before and the rudder had a squared-off horn balance.

TRUE PROTOTYPE

The conclusion drawn, therefore, is that this was the first true prototype B9965, in its early form. The battered but repaired B9965 was back at Martlesham on 25 January 1918. A report dated 18 February made it clear that the aircraft had by then acquired two-bay wings, with a span of 30 ft. Further trails were to be made following more modifications to the mainplanes, and these were complete by 9 March 1918, the Snipe going to France two days later. The extra wing area had given the fighter both better performance and aileron control, and a Lewis gun had been fitted to the rear centre section spar.

It was now a competitor for a revised specification for the Type 1 single-seater fighter, which required provision for electrically-heated clothing for the pilot and a rack for five Cooper bombs. Still it was not ready for a final assessment as it was wrongly rigged, being nose-heavy on turns and had too little rudder control. Further, when flown 'hands-off' and engine 'on', the Snipe was tail-heavy, would stall and then spin. With

Left Sopwith Snipes of No 1 Sqn flying over Iraq. The unit took delivery of its first Snipes in January 1920 and retained them until November 1926, operating from Risalpur, Bangalore and Hinaidi on police duties

Below Wearing the now famous red and white chequers of No 56 Sqn, Snipe E6964 basks in the spring sun at Hawkinge in May 1923

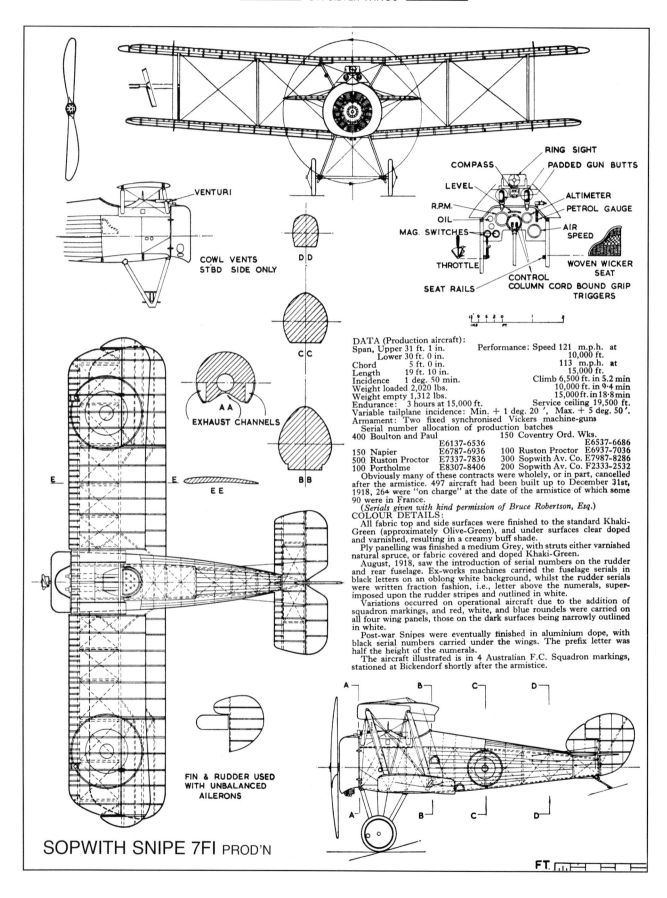

VENTURI

COWL VENTS
STBD SIDE ONLY

D D

C C

A A
EXHAUST CHANNELS

B B

E E

E E

FIN & RUDDER USED
WITH UNBALANCED
AILERONS

RING SIGHT
COMPASS   PADDED GUN BUTTS
LEVEL
ALTIMETER
R.P.M.   PETROL GAUGE
OIL
AIR
MAG. SWITCHES   SPEED

THROTTLE   WOVEN WICKER
SEAT
CONTROL
SEAT RAILS   COLUMN CORD BOUND GRIP
TRIGGERS

DATA (Production aircraft):
Span, Upper 31 ft. 1 in.   Performance: Speed 121 m.p.h. at
       Lower 30 ft. 0 in.   10,000 ft.
Chord   5 ft. 0 in.   113 m.p.h. at
Length   19 ft. 10 in.   15,000 ft.
Incidence   1 deg. 50 min.   Climb 6,500 ft. in 5.2 min
Weight loaded 2,020 lbs.   10,000 ft. in 9·4 min
Weight empty 1,312 lbs.   15,000 ft. in 18·8 min
Endurance: 3 hours at 15,000 ft.   Service ceiling 19,500 ft.
Variable tailplane incidence: Min. + 1 deg. 20´, Max. + 5 deg. 50´.
Armament: Two fixed synchronised Vickers machine-guns
    Serial number allocation of production batches
400 Boulton and Paul   150 Coventry Ord. Wks.
              E6137-6536   E6537-6686
150 Napier   E6787-6936   100 Ruston Proctor E6937-7036
500 Ruston Proctor E7337-7836 300 Sopwith Av. Co. E7987-8286
100 Portholme E8307-8406   200 Sopwith Av. Co. F2333-2532
    Obviously many of these contracts were wholly, or in part, cancelled
after the armistice. 497 aircraft had been built up to December 31st,
1918, 264 were "on charge" at the date of the armistice of which some
90 were in France.
    (Serials given with kind permission of Bruce Robertson, Esq.)
COLOUR DETAILS:
    All fabric top and side surfaces were finished to the standard Khaki-
Green (approximately Olive-Green), and under surfaces clear doped
and varnished, resulting in a creamy buff shade.
    Ply panelling was finished a medium Grey, with struts either varnished
natural spruce, or fabric covered and doped Khaki-Green.
    August, 1918, saw the introduction of serial numbers on the rudder
and rear fuselage. Ex-works machines carried the fuselage serials in
black letters on an oblong white background, whilst the rudder serials
were written fraction fashion, i.e., letter above the numerals, superimposed upon the rudder stripes and outlined in white.
    Variations occurred on operational aircraft due to the addition of
squadron markings, and red, white, and blue roundels were carried on
all four wing panels, those on the dark surfaces being narrowly outlined
in white.
    Post-war Snipes were eventually finished in aluminium dope, with
black serial numbers carried under the wings. The prefix letter was
half the height of the numerals.
    The aircraft illustrated is in 4 Australian F.C. Squadron markings,
stationed at Bickendorf shortly after the armistice.

A   B   C   D

A   B   C   D

SOPWITH SNIPE 7FI PROD'N

FT.

engine 'off', it would dive. Martlesham was informed that Sopwith intended reducing the stagger and altering the tailplane incidence. The undercarriage was rather too 'stalky' and narrow, leading to ground-handling difficulties in strong winds.

The Snipe was not the only contender for the Type 1 production order, the others being the Austin Osprey triplane, Boulton Paul Bobolink and Nieuport B.N.1. The last was destroyed by fire before tests were complete but, with the triplane, was considered the most manoeuvrable; the Snipe offered the best view for the pilot, but engine accessibility was better in the triplane than in the Snipe. The Vickers gun arrangement was equally good in all except the triplane but, for production and maintenance purposes, the Nieuport and Austin triplanes were markedly better than the Snipe and Bobolink.

The Snipe was selected for reasons which are, at this stage in history, rather obscure. It seems that it was the least unsatisfactory of the four(!), added to the fact that the Snipe's design and construction was a direct extrapolation of a well-established airframe

Below Following nearly a decade of frontline service, E6524 ended its days as an instructional airframe at the RAF Cadet College at Cranwell

construction, using a number of common Sopwith components. Clearly, this would contribute to the ease and rapidity of production in a period of widespread sub-contracting. Following the visit to France by B9965 for evaluation by the RFC, it was recorded that the Snipe was very tail-heavy and had a very poor rudder. Otherwise, visibility and manoeuvrability were good and the engine ran well. At least five pilots in No 65 Sqn flew it and concluded that, subject to certain improvements being made, it was 'vastly superior' to any other scout on the Western Front. The Lewis gun was almost unusable and could be removed. Subsequently, it was tested by No 43 Sqn pilots who were less enthusiastic and made similar criticisms of its controls.

CONTRACTS ISSUED

Strangely, even before the RFC's reports were received, no less than seven contractors undertook to build a total of 1700 Snipes, in a contract dated 20 March 1918. Prototype B9965 returned to Sopwith on 1 May for a large spinner to be fitted, and subsequently went to Martlesham and Farnborough for climbing and speed tests with and without it. Snipe B9966, in as nearly as possible production form, went

Above Five Snipes led by Flt Lt J S T Fall performed aerobatics at the RAF Pageant at Hendon in July 1920

to Martlesham on 6 April. A tailplane adjuster, operated by a sliding control, was mounted on the upper starboard longeron. Fuel and oil capacity had been increased and a Badin-type fuel system was installed, a venturi tube drawing fuel from a tank beneath the pilot's seat to a header tank behind the engine. The rudder was only marginally larger than that fitted to B9965. The performance tests made by the AES this time were as disappointing as previous ones. Top speed was 112.5 mph at 15,000 ft and service ceiling only 19,500 ft. Much earlier, a Camel with a B.R.1 engine had returned better figures, although with a lighter fuel and weapon load. The Snipe's performance was certainly not very promising. Directional control was acceptable, but lateral control response needed to be quicker. The elevator control was rather heavy in a dive, but otherwise good.

Following repair after an accident in June 1918,

B9966 was used for testing the Badin fuel system and the two types of carburettor available. The dihedral was altered and tested in August. Soon after it was tested with horn-balanced, inversely tapered upper ailerons and a much larger fin and rudder. More modifications included a two-piece adjustable, triangular-shaped tailplane and horn-balanced elevators with inverse taper, but the latter proved unsatisfactory and were abandoned. It was not until 18 August 1918 that the first true Snipe, E8006, arrived at Martlesham. After extensive testing, its performance was still not as good as initially hoped, and by no means as good as that of the Martinsyde F.4. Several other modifications, built in as a result of operational experience at the very end of the war, included a reinforced wing leading edge, modified tail skid, strengthened rear fuselage and stiffened fuel tank, which had tended to bulge when full. The long-range version of the Snipe, the 7F.1A, Snipe Mk IA, with a 50 gallon main tank and a $1\frac{1}{2}°$ sweep-back (to compensate for the changed cg) and strengthened structure, was intended as a

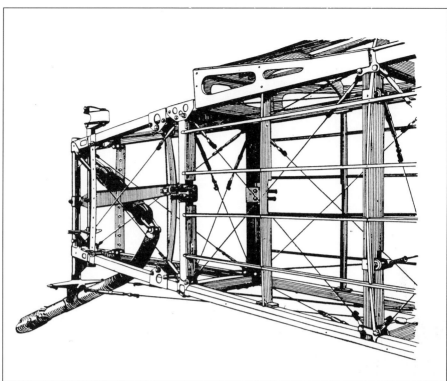

*Two illustrations from the RAF Snipe manual; **above** the rear fuselage **right** the forward fuselage* (Crown Copyright)

bomber escort for the Independent Force. Its strength factor was still lower than desirable and it was 'not for stunting or aerobatics in any sense of the word'.

SNIPE VARIATIONS

The first, E8089, had a Dolphin-type tail unit but this was not continued in production aircraft. In the event the long-range Snipe was not needed before the end of hostilities, and some at least were converted back to the Mk I standard. Another proposal was for a shipboard version of the Snipe with a hydrovane for ditching, but this was not pursued very far. Here it may be helpful to mention the controls of the B.R.2 rotary entine. The fuel-air mixture entered from the carburettor at the rear of the engine into the crankcase itself, and thence into the cylinders, via long induction pipes, to the cylinder heads. There were two controls – the throttle which regulated the amount of mixture admitted in the usual way, and the 'Fine Adjustment', which was a simple but vital mixture control.

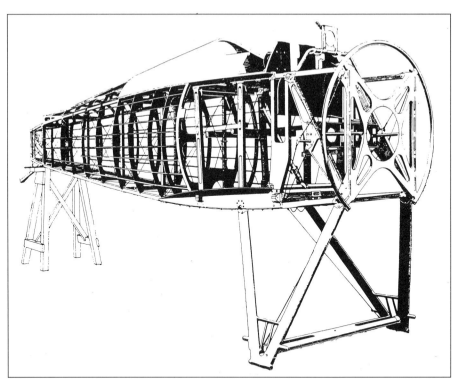

Left *Another illustration from the Snipe manual, showing the bare fuselage frame. The complexity of the airframe ribs and bracing stringers is readily apparent*

Theoretically, a correct position for this could be found and set, after which the engine was controlled by the throttle only. In practice, however, although the engine would run this way, it was better to make small mixture changes as the throttle was varied.

Before starting, sucking-in (switches off) was done with the throttle fully open, fine adjustment a third open (towards rich) and mechanics' hands over the air-intakes. For starting, throttle a quarter open, fine adjustment closed. Once firing, the fine adjustment was slowly opened until the engine ran smoothly for half a minute. The throttle was then opened steadily until the engine misfired. This was the weakest mixture the engine would take. The fine adjustment was then advanced again, and so on up to maximum permitted rpm, the throttle always being advanced first, but run as weak as the engine would take happily. The distance between 'too-rich' and 'too-weak' for all throttle settings was about $\frac{1}{4}$ inch. For take-off, the throttle and fine adjustment were both advanced until maximum rpm was obtained, black smoke indicating too rich a mixture and white smoke indicating too much oil.

For landing, the throttle was closed as far as possible, with the engine running smoothly using the fine adjustment, and then either using the main ignition switch or 'blip switch' on the stick at short intervals to keep the engine ticking over as smoothly as possible, using the considerable inertia of engine and propeller to keep it going until safely on the ground. It had been hoped that the powerful ABC Dragonfly radial engine would be a suitable replacement power-plant for the Snipe but the engine turned out to be a disaster because of severe over-heating, vibration and high fuel-consumption (the Snipe, when fitted with it, became known as the Sopwith Dragon but did not enter RAF squadron service). However, when powered by a Bentley B.R.2, the most advanced rotary engine then available, the Snipe was at the extreme end of its development.

As things turned out, the Snipe was spared the unmitigated disaster which would otherwise have ensued, and it was to become the single-seater on which the great traditions of today's RAF fighter squadrons were built. In total, 4685 Snipe were ordered, but only a little over 1550 were delivered.

Left Although this marvellous collection of Snipes boast not a single unit marking between them, identification is not overly difficult as they were photographed at the 1921 Hendon Pageant, and the only Sopwith fighter participation at the event that year was provided by the Central Flying School, based at Upavon. All the Snipes in this shot wear the wartime P.C.10 drab finish, although two or three aircraft also boast painted engine cowlings

Above *Snipe surrounded by RAF Halton apprentices. It bears the early form of markings for an instructional airframe, 'INST^{R}' followed by the serial number, most of which is obscured*

Right *A Snipe's Bentley B.R.2 roars into life with the aid of a Hucks Starter. Finished in the silver Cellon heat-reflecting aluminium dope finish which began to appear on RAF fighters from 1923 onwards, this aircraft was photographed whilst on strength with No 5 FTS at Sealand*

Although it served primarily during the 1920s with the Royal Air Force, there was always a strong aura of the Western Front and dogfights with Fokker DVIIs about the Snipe. This is scarcely surprising since it was first made famous as the mount of the celebrated Maj W G Barker who was awarded the Victoria Cross for his heroic fight whilst serving in France with No 201 Sqn on 27 October 1918. Piloting Snipe E8102, and flying alone over the lines, he encountered about 15 Fokker DVIIs and contrived to shoot three of them down despite being severely wounded.

This legendary encounter was no doubt uppermost in the minds of many spectators at the first post-war RAF air display at Hendon where Snipes were prominently featured. Then known as the RAF Tournament, this took place in 1920 and subsequently on an annual basis as the RAF Pageant and later the RAF Display. Snipes performed at every show until 1925. As if to reinforce the 1918 image, they appeared in 1920 and 1921 in the original wartime colour of P.C.10

(chocolate-brown dope) and pilots with distinguished World War 1 exploits to their name were featured in the display programmes. In 1921, for example, 'Chris' Draper (popularly known as 'the Mad Major') who had commanded the famous No 208 Sqn until December 1918, headed a formation team of Snipes from the Central Flying School. One Snipe in his team was flown by none other than Flt Lt A Coningham, DSO, later to become Air Marshal Sir Arthur 'Mary' Coningham, Commander-in-Chief of the 2nd Tactical Air Force in World War 2.

Although a rival design was, for a period, considered for the equipment of the infant RAF's single-seat fighter re-equipment programme (the Martinsyde Buzzard), this rapidly faded with the coming of the Armistice and the Snipe emerged supreme as the legendary Camel's successor, and subsequently as the first standard fighter of the inter-war RAF squadrons. If it seems somewhat odd that an essentially 1917 design with an old-fashioned rotary engine should still be fulfilling such a role as late as 1926, it should be remembered that plans to re-engine the Snipe with the radial ABC Dragonfly (producing the Sopwith Dragon) had to be abandoned in about 1921 with the complete failure of that powerplant to meet expectations.

The Snipe's necessarily brief, though very successful, period of service at the end of World War 1 began when No 43 Sqn (who had been re-arming since August) finally flew them into action over the Western Front on 23 September 1918. By 31 October there

Below A rare photograph of a No 43 Sqn Snipe, seen at Bickendorf, Germany, in 1919. Nos 70 and 208 Sqns served alongside the 'Fighting Cocks' as part of the RAF's commitment to the British Army of Occupation immediately postwar

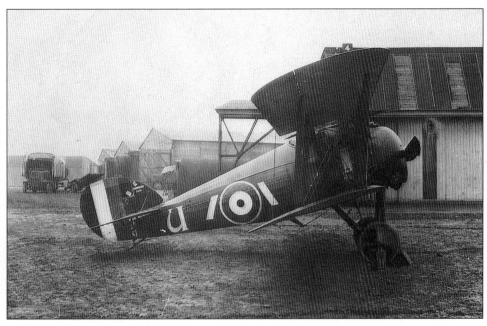

were 97 Snipes with the BEF in France (including two with the Independent Force for bomber escort with No 45 Sqn), and No 208 Sqn was just beginning to convert from Camels when the war ended. A further 45 Snipes in RAF service at home had gone to training units and one had been delivered to No 78 Sqn on home defence duties at Sutton's Farm (later Hornchurch).

Massive production contracts exceeding 4000 Snipes were under way with seven manufacturers

Left The third Snipe prototype, B9965, at Martlesham Heath. The aircraft retained single-bay wings, although the centre-section was widened (note the splayed cabane struts)

when the Armistice came and over half were subsequently cancelled. Deliveries continued until September 1919, by which time about 1567 Snipes had been built. An inventory of RAF aeroplanes in 1921 showed 532 on charge, including 400 in storage.

The Snipe's first peacetime task was to form part of the air elements of the British Army of Occupation in Germany. Snipes served in this capacity with Nos 43, 70 and 208 Sqns, based at Bickendorf and Eil. They returned to the UK during August/September 1919. In June 1919 some Snipes (including E6351 and E6360) were sent to Archangel to join RAF forces fighting the Bolsheviks.

Meanwhile, some units of the wartime Home Defence force still remained in service and had been re-armed with Snipes camouflaged in their wartime livery. These were Nos 37 and 78 Sqns (based at Biggin Hill until July 1919), No 112 Sqn (based at Throwley until June 1919) and No 143 Sqn (based at Detling until October 1919).

It was immediately following this period, when the years of financial stringency and retrenchment were dominant in the aftermath of the war, that the RAF's strength reached a nadir. By the close of 1919 it had been reduced to nine squadrons abroad and two at home, and of these only a single squadron (No 80 in Egypt, shortly to be re-numbered No 56) was then flying Snipes. In September 1922, the Snipes of No 56 were sent to Turkey and were presently joined by No 25 Sqn Snipes out from England. Together they operated in what became known as the Chanak crisis arising from Turkish aggression in the Dardanelles zone. They were based at San Stephano and undertook demonstration 'deterrent' flights over Constantinople.

DEFENDING THE EMPIRE

Operations overseas also engaged two other Snipe squadrons during the early 1920s. The famous No 1 Sqn (which had been flying S.E.5As in France when the war ended) was re-established at Risalpur in India in 1920, before moving to Hinaidi in Iraq in 1922, where it fought against Sheikh Mahmud's Kurdish rebel tribesmen chiefly in ground strafing sorties until disbanded in November 1926. No 1's Snipes were supplemented by three Nieuport Nighthawks which did not last long due to sand ingestion in their stationary radial engines.

Many names destined to become famous in RAF annals flew Snipes with No 1 Sqn during their Iraq operations. One of them was Flg Off Dermot Boyle (later Marshal of the RAF Sir Dermot Boyle, Chief of the Air Staff) and another was Flt Lt Oswald Gayford who later achieved a place in history as the pilot of the Fairey Long Range Monoplane, which captured the world long distance record with a non-stop flight of 5309 miles from Cranwell to Walvis Bay (South West Africa) in February 1933.

Strongly marked individuality (not to say eccentricity) was a characteristic of inter-war RAF fighter pilots and a certain Flt Lt Francis Luxmoore of No 1 Sqn adapted the hatch behind his Snipe's cockpit to carry his dog Raggis on all his flights in Iraq! Raggis is reported to have barked furiously whenever his master's twin guns were fired.

In June 1920 a second Snipe squadron (No 3) was based in India where it served at Bangalore and Ambala before disbanding in September 1921.

Left No 56 Sqn Snipes at Aboukir, Egypt, where the unit was based in 1920/22. The squadron flew Snipes from January 1920 until November 1924

Meanwhile, back in the United Kingdom, fighter defences had reached their lowest ebb and were in fact down to a single squadron of Snipes (No 25) based at Hawkinge between April 1920 and September 1922. Shortly after No 25 Sqn's posting to Turkey it was replaced by No 56's Snipes newly back from overseas, and it was not until April 1923 that the modest beginnings of a future home defence fighter force began to emerge with the formation of four new Snipe squadrons, initially with only one or two flights. These were Nos 19 and 29, both at Duxford, No 32 at Kenley

Above Flattening out the grass with his prop wash, a student pilot carefully runs his mount's Bentley B.R.2 engine up to full revs prior to taxying out for take-off

and No 41 at Northolt. In October 1923, the Snipes of No 25 Sqn returned from Turkey to their old home at Hawkinge, those of No 56 having moved in the meantime to Biggin Hill.

Thus, by the close of 1923 there were six Snipe squadrons defending the United Kingdom from aerodromes (as they were then called) at Duxford, Hawkinge, Kenley, Northolt and the recently re-opened Biggin Hill. It is interesting to note that in those far-off days the potential enemy was seen as France (which maintained a large bomber force) and with the absence of any long-range warning devices the only resource was to deploy fighters behind a 50-mile deep coastal belt.

The year 1924 saw the Snipe at the peak of its career as a Home Defence fighter, with nine squadrons deployed. In April 1924, Snipes formed the equipment of No 3 at Upavon, No 17 at Hawkinge, No 19 at

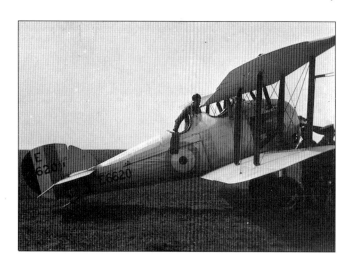

Left Two-seat Snipe E6620. Although used mainly at FTSs, one or two of these dual-control trainers were issued to most of the Snipe fighter squadrons. This simple conversion was carried out at Sopwith's Kingston-upon-Thames factory

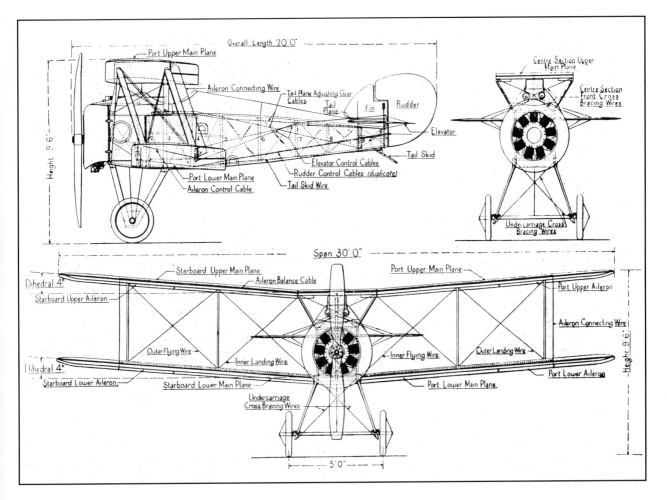

Duxford, No 25 at Hawkinge, No 29 at Duxford, No 32 at Kenley, No 41 at Northolt, No 56 at Biggin Hill and No 111 at Duxford. The new additions were No 3 Sqn, which had formed at Manston in April but quickly moved to Upavon, No 17 which formed at Hawkinge and No 111 which, curiously enough, had formed at Duxford with a flight of Gloster Grebes in October 1923 *before* Snipes were added to its strength in April 1924.

By July 1925, five Snipe squadrons had seen their aeroplanes superseded by the new Gloster Grebes and two others had converted to Armstrong Whitworth Siskins. Of the four Snipe squadrons remaining, No 3 at Upavon was to receive Hawker Woodcocks within a month, whereas Nos 23 and 43 at Henlow had only just been formed with Snipes, being the last to do so. The Henlow Snipes were also destined to become the last first-line examples of their kind with the RAF when they finally gave way to Gloster Gamecocks in April and May of 1926.

As already mentioned, many famous names of the RAF were associated with Snipes during their eight years as first-line fighters. The legendary Lt A W Beauchamp Proctor, VC (who flew S.E.5As with No 84 Sqn on the Western Front and shot down 54 enemy aircraft) finally met his death during peacetime, flying Snipe E8220 with the Central Flying School aerobatic team. He spun in off a loop whilst practising for the forthcoming RAF Pageant and crashed at Enford in Wiltshire on 21 June 1921.

COLLISHAW COMMANDS

Ray Collishaw, the famed leader of 'Naval Ten' Sopwith Triplanes and No 203 Sqn Camels, commanded No 23 Sqn when they had Snipes at Henlow and later No 41 Snipes at Northolt.

Names associated with the worlds of civil aviation and test flying can also be linked with the carefree Snipe days of the 1920s. 'Bill' Pegg (the Bristol test pilot) and 'Tommy' Rose (record-breaker and Miles test pilot) both served on Snipes when with No 43 Sqn at Henlow. Yet another name from sporting flying, C W A Scott, who with Campbell-Black flew the original Comet to victory in the 1934 England-Australia Air Race, joined No 32 Sqn at Kenley and

Left Snipe E7561 at Stag Lane aerodrome in 1925. Powered by a 230 hp Bentley B.R.2 rotary engine, the Snipe had a top speed of 121 mph at 10,000 ft. A close examination of the natural metal cowling reveals that the rivetted engine fairing has experienced a couple of knocks since it was fitted to the fighter at the Ruston Proctor factory

succeeded in writing off his Snipe during over-exuberant flying on his very first day with the unit! At No 5 Flying Training School (FTS) at Sealand, Snipe E6837 was flown by none other than that celebrated RAF character Air Chief Marshal the Earl of Bandon (always known in the Service with great affection as 'the abandoned Earl') when still a young flying officer.

One aspect of the Snipe's RAF career which is often given less than its fair share of attention is its important contribution in the field of flying training during the formative years of the peacetime Service. Almost any book of memoirs by pilots who trained during the 1920s will make reference, usually with pleasure, to their experiences on the Snipe, both as a single-seater and as a two-seater during their FTS days. Allen Wheeler's delightful book *Flying Between the Wars* (G T Foulis & Co Ltd 1972), describes very graphically the days he spent flying it at No 2 FTS at Digby in Lincolnshire in 1925.

The particular skills required to master the handling of the rotary engine were made slightly less daunting by previous experience on the Avro 504Ks that were then still standard equipment at the FTS (the radial-engined Lynx Avro 504N did not enter service until 1927), but the 230 hp Bentley presented a challenge just the same. Snipes remained a feature of FTS life well into 1927. They were first introduced at No 1 FTS at Netheravon in December 1919, the RAF

Cadet College at Cranwell in February 1920 and No 2 FTS Duxford in April 1920. Two further schools (No 3 FTS at Scopwick and No 5 FTS at Shotwick) also received Snipes in April 1920, and due to the predictable confusion arising from their names were subsequently re-christened Digby and Sealand respectively. Snipes were also delivered to the short-lived No 6 FTS which formed at Manston in April 1921 and disbanded a year later. At the Central Flying School, based at Upavon, Snipes were on the strength from March 1920 and, as already mentioned were to make a memorable appearance at the RAF Pageant at Hendon in 1921.

The concept of the Snipe as an instructional aircraft with a second cockpit was first conceived at Sopwith in February 1919 and most of the fighter squadrons in the early 1920s received one or two examples in addition to those issued to the FTS. Two-seat conversions were still being built by the HG Hawker Engineering Company (which had succeeded the old Sopwith firm in 1920) at their Kingston-on-Thames factory as late as 1922.

Mention has been made of Snipe production totals and it seems appropriate here to summarise the batches in which aircraft were completed and delivered, excluding all the cancellations, before going on to a survey of markings, paint schemes and squadron regalia generally.

The airframe serial numbers of Snipes actually constructed were:

Snipe Production for the RAF

Serials	Manufacturer	Quantity
B9962 to 9967	Sopwith	6
E6137 to 6536	Boulton Paul	400
E6537 to 6686	Coventry Ordnance	150
E6787 to 6936	Napier	150
E6937 to 7036	Nieuport & General	100
E7337 to 7836	Ruston & Proctor	500
E7987 to 8286	Sopwith	300
E8307 to 8406	Portholm	100
F2333 to 2352	Sopwith	200
H351 to 418	Ruston/Portholm	68
H4865 to 4902	Sopwith	38
H8663 to 8707	Portholm	45
J451 to 475	Boulton Paul	25
J681 to 690	March, Jones & Cribb	10
J6493 to 6522	Kingsbury	30
	Total	2122

The discrepancy to be seen here between the total reached on this analysis and that more commonly accepted (1567 already quoted) may be accounted for by the possibility that certain airframes delivered without engines direct to storage were not included in production records, but this is no more than speculation. Certainly, some airframes were returned for reconditioning at Hawkers and thereafter given new serials, examples being H7149 to 7154 and H7227.

Snipe markings remain an endlessly fascinating study for the historian of such matters, bridging as they do the typical warpaint of the 1918 scout and the transition to the colourful inter-war fighter squadron heraldry which may be said to have been pioneered by the Snipe. In the immediate post-war period all Snipes retained their wartime P.C.10 khaki-brown finish, with the areas round the cowling and forward fuselage in a pale grey. Those serving with the Occupation Forces in Germany retained their white squadron bars (eg No 70 Sqn, with three vertical bars encircling the rear fuselage, and No 208 Sqn, with two inwards-sloping bars behind the roundel). In Egypt at Aboukir No 56 Sqn, which had only been re-formed in February 1920 by re-numbering No 80 Sqn, invented a wartime style of marking consisting of a single white bar behind the roundel. Snipes in India and Iraq with Nos 1 and 3 Sqns also retained wartime finishes initially, but did not use squadron insignia as such.

From 1923 all this changed with the switch to Cellon heat-reflecting aluminium dope which produced the silvery finish so characteristic of most inter-

Below Snipe E8358 Bonzo at the RAF Pageant at Hendon on Saturday 30 June 1923. Flown by Flt Lt C A Stevens in the race for the Duke of York's Cup (in which each team entered an Avro, a Brisfit and a Snipe), Bonzo and the Halton team were victorious

war RAF biplanes. This was applied to Snipes in Iraq and soon standardised on the home fighter squadrons which, as early as 1922, began to devise individual unit markings of the kind which made all inter-war RAF fighter biplanes so instantly recognizable and aesthetically pleasing. Some of the earliest examples of this tradition were displayed by No 17 Sqn at Hawkinge, No 25 at Hawkinge, No 32 at Kenley and No 56 at Hawkinge. No 32's Snipes operated for a period with red and white 'night fighter' roundels which looked rather singular against the silver dope.

OFFICIAL MARKINGS

Such squadron insignia was initially the result of the local initiative, and officialdom only came to recognise the practice *post ad hoc*. Such documentary evidence as exists suggests that the first official Air Ministry Order on the subject of fighter markings was dated 18 December 1924. Existing squadron markings were recognised retrospectively and authority was given for flight colours to wheel discs, namely red for A flight, yellow for B flight and blue for C flight.

Thereafter, it became accepted that the addition of squadron colours not only enlivened the scene but encouraged a healthy spirit of rivalry between the units leading to enhanced operational efficiency. The practice continued to flourish until finally killed off by the introduction of drab camouflage and code letters at the time of the Munich Crisis in September 1938.

So far as is known, no photographs have ever been published of Snipes wearing the markings of Nos 19, 23, 29, 41 or 43 Sqns, although plenty of evidence for the remaining squadrons is available. If any reader has in his possession any of the proverbial 'pictures in the attic' the writer would be delighted to see them for future publication in any later edition of this book.

In 1928 the Snipe was finally declared obsolete by the Air Ministry. Only two genuine Snipes are known to survive today worldwide and none in this country. E6938 is maintained by the Canadian National Aeronautical Collection and was briefly exhibited here when on loan to the Science Museum in Kensington in 1971. It is portrayed in the markings of No 208 Sqn in 1918. The second survivor, originally marked as E8100 and later E8105, wears the insignia of No 70 Sqn in 1919 and is now with the National Air and Space Museum in Washington DC after spending many years airworthy at the famous Old Rhinebeck Aerodrome in New York State. A third Snipe (a replica) is portrayed with the serial E6837 in the Champlin Fighter Museum in Arizona.

It seems the greatest of pities that no Snipe was ever acquired for the RAF Museum at Hendon, but then one might say the same about the Hawker Fury recently allowed to disappear to Belgium!

Snipe Units in the RAF

Between 1920 and 1926, 11 squadrons flew the Snipe on Home Defence duties, as detailed below:

No 3 Squadron *Manston and Upavon, April 1924 to August 1925*

Markings: Green band along fuselage

Serials: E6342, 6343, 6475, 6531, 6648, 6837, 6942
F2387, 2350, 2476
H4880, 4883

No 17 Squadron *Hawkinge, April 1924 to March 1926*

Markings: Parallel black zig-zags along fuselage

Serials: E6490, 6544, 6804, 6826, 7432
F2484
Two-seaters: E6622, 6862

No 19 Squadron *Duxford, April 1923 to December 1924*

Markings: Blue and white checks on fuselage

Serials: E6235, 6316, 6336, 6338, 6530, 6625, 6838, 6955, 6965, 7599, 8148, 8245
F2430, 2444, 2446

No 23 Squadron *Henlow, July 1925 to April 1926*

Markings: Blue and red squares on fuselage

Serials: E6311, 6340, 6615, 6616, 7713, 7716
F2408, 2419

No 25 Squadron *Hawkinge, April 1920 to September 1922 and October 1923 to October 1924*

Markings: Two parallel black bars along fuselage

Serials: E6156, 6243, 6266, 6339, 6439, 6600, 6623, 6632, 6651, 6944, 6961, 6970, 6977, 7401, 7429, 7439, 7456, 7501, 7504, 7509, 7528, 7543, 7558, 7560, 7563, 7565, 7598, 7601, 7665, 7758, 8237, 8239
F2398, 2425, 2426, 2437, 2463, 2464, 2485

No 29 Squadron *Duxford, April 1923 to January 1925*

Markings: Red XXX pattern between parallel red bars on fuselage

Serials: E6595, 6838

No 32 Squadron *Kenley, April 1923 to December 1924*

Markings: Blue bar along fuselage with white diagonal intersections

Serials: E6268, 6308, 6629, 6646, 6651, 6792, 6794, 6834, 6839, 6974, 7550, 7556
F2426, 2433, 2434, 2442, 2456

No 41 Sqn *Northolt, April 1923 to May 1924*

Markings: Red bar along fuselage

Serials: E6316, 6618, 6646, 6825, 6965, 7599, 8245

No 43 Squadron *Henlow, July 1925 to May 1926*

Markings: Black and white checks on fuselage

Above *Built in 1918, Snipe E6938 was sold to Hollywood film star Reginald Denny in 1926. It was later restored by Jack Canary and in 1964 was sold to the Canadian National Aviation Museum. It carries the markings of No 208 Sqn*

Serials: E6530, 6612, 6622, 6644, 6836, 7432, 7538, 7565, 7724, 8165
F2340, 2387, 2435

No 56 Squadron *Hawkinge, November 1922 to May 1923 and Biggin Hill, May 1923 to September 1924*

Markings: Red and white checks along fuselage

Serials: E6964, 6969, 6309, 6335, 6481, 6484, 6525, 6601, 6616, 6791, 6819, 6841, 6941, 6951, 6964, 6969, 7467, 7510, 7511, 7512, 7513, 7518, 7520, 7521, 7522, 7523, 7525, 7526, 7528, 7530, 7539, 7559, 7594, 7604, 7638, 7639, 7647, 7829, 7989, 8105, 8243, 8245, 8247
F2425, 2439, 2465, 2472

No 111 Squadron *Duxford, April 1924 to January 1925*

Markings: Black bar along fuselage

Serials: E6617, 6643
F2441, 2527
H8704

Snipes serving overseas *1920–1926*

No 1 Squadron *India and Iraq*

Serials: E6939, 7771, 8249
F2457
H4867, 4885

No 3 Squadron *India*

Serials: E6342
F2387
H4883

No 56 Squadron *Egypt*

Serials: E6969, 7522, 7639, 7647

Sopwith 7F.1 Snipe data

Engine: Bentley B.R.2, rated 200 hp, 230 hp at 1300 rpm; maximum 234 hp at 1350 rpm

Dimensions

Span	31 ft 1 in (balanced ailerons)
Length	19 ft 10 in
Height	9 ft 6 in
Wing Area	271 ft^2

Weights

Loaded	2015 lbs
Empty	1305 lbs

Performance

Maximum speed	121 mph at 10,000 ft
	113 mph at 15,000 ft
Initial Climb	1380 ft/min
Time to 10,000 ft	9 min 25 sec
to 15,000 ft	18 min 50 sec
Service Ceiling	19,500 ft
Endurance at 15,000 ft (including climb)	3 hrs

Armament: Two fixed 0.303 in Vickers Mk 1 synchronized machine guns, using Constantinesco interrupter gear type C, four 20 lb Cooper bombs

THE GLOSTER GREBE

THE ARRIVAL IN RAF service of the Gloster Grebe single-seat fighter in 1923 was the culmination of eight years' progressive development work by one of Britain's greatest and most respected aeronautical engineers, H P (Harry) Folland. Under his design leadership (until he left to form his own company in 1937) the Gloster Aircraft Company became one of the great individual names in the British aircraft industry, until merged with Sir W G Armstrong Whitworth Aircraft Ltd in October, 1961. The Gloster Aircraft

Company had originated in 1917 as the Gloucestershire Aircraft Co and, from June of that year, with a factory near Cheltenham, established a name for itself building, under sub-contract, high-quality timber-framed aeroplanes for the RFC and RAF. With the end of the Great War in November 1918, the aircraft

Below *Gloster Grebes of No 25 Sqn taking off in formation. Note that the squadron markings, two parallel black bars, extend forward onto the exhaust collector rings*

Above J6969, the prototype Grebe. It made its first flight in time to appear at the RAFs Hendon Pageant in June 1923. The upper-wing fuel tanks are very prominent in this view

industry, which had blossomed explosively during the period of hostilities, collapsed even quicker with the rapid cancellation of contracts for very large numbers of constructors. One such casualty was the Nieuport and General Aircraft Company of Cricklewood, North London, which closed down at the end of 1920.

Consequently, the Gloucestershire Aircraft Co, which was building the Nieuport Nighthawk under licence, acquired the design rights, the designer himself being H P Folland. He had started his work in aeronautics in 1912 at the Balloon Factory and, subsequently, build up a reputation for very advanced ideas in aerodynamics, which he was to maintain throughout his professional life. Folland was a man with an eye for a pretty design when it came to creating a fighter, the best-known example of his early work being the S.E.5 series, which he began at the Royal Aircraft Factory at Farnborough in 1915. In 1917, Folland had left Farnborough and joined the Nieuport Company, where he designed the Nighthawk which bore a marked family resemblance to the S.E.5 and was intended to fulful the requirements of the Type 1 Specification for a single-seater, issued in 1918 by the RAF. Its initial success was greatly inhibited by the disastrously unsuccessful ABC Dragonfly engine.

Being determined to remain in the forefront of high-speed design, despite industrial setbacks, the Gloucestershire Company's board appointed Folland, in 1921, consultant designer and, subsequently, chief engineer and designer of the Gloucestershire Aircraft Co, (not renamed 'Gloster' until 11 December 1926). He naturally put the large stock of Nighthawk components remaining at the Cheltenham works to good use by devising a series of refinements and improvements

to the basic aeroplanes. He incorporated modifications to improve their performance, installed alternative engines and introduced new names – at first Mars (in several versions), then Sparrowhawk and others. Folland's experience in designing high-speed aircraft also led to several racing aircraft, both on wheels (notably the very successful little racer, the Mars I or 'Bamel' of 1921) and on floats, including several Schneider Trophy contestants. The advent of the Bristol Jupiter and Armstrong Siddeley Jaguar radial engines (roughly comparable in power) enabled Folland to further develop the Nighthawk, but retain the Mars name.

The Mars VI Nighthawk, with either a Jupiter III or a Jaguar II or III engine, and the Mars X Nightjar, with a Bentley B.R.2 rotary, were ordered in small quantities. Folland's preoccupation with this multitude of sub-designs of the Nighthawk gave him the opportunity to develop his idea of combining high lift with the highest possible speed, and thus most efficient interceptor fighter design. His High Lift Biplane (HLB) concept had the merit of combining a relatively thick, high-lift upper wing section (HLB 1) with a thin, low-drag (HLB 2) lower section. The resulting wing layout was judged to combine the efficiency and low-drag of a monoplane at high speeds and a biplane's high-lift for take-off and landing. This made possible a short span and a reduced centre of pressure travel which, with a short fuselage, resulted in a very nimble aeroplane indeed. The idea was tried out in 1923 in a B.R.2-engined Grouse (a modified Mars III).

If the industry had suffered drastic cutbacks in the aftermath of the Great War, the squadrons of the RAF fared no better, units being disbanded at a precipitate rate. Re-equipping the decimated air defence and bombing squadrons was therefore a matter for protracted discussion and haggling between industry and the Air Ministry with, at first, little official sense of urgency. A monolithic political stalemate in defence procurement resulted in numerous prototypes and projects but few orders. Following the emergence of yet another development of the Nighthawk, a single-seater based on the two-seat Grouse trainer, three prototypes were ordered by the Air Ministry in 1923. The first to emerge was called, unpoetically, the 'Nighthawk (Thick-winged)'. Clearly bearing the Folland imprint, the first of these (J6969) became the prototype Gloucestershire Grebe of 1923. It was a wood-structured 'sesquiplane' (unequal-span), with fabric covering, powered by a 14-cylinder Armstrong

Below Grebe prototype J6969 at the RAF Pageant at Hendon on Saturday, 30 June 1923. It was No 14 in the parade of new types, sharing the limelight with the Siskin and Flycatcher. The Avro 504s in the background were taking part in a special Challenge Cup race

Siddeley Jaguar III radial engine, developing 325 hp at full-throttle.

Thus began the very successful series of fighters produced for the RAF by the company that was to become world-famous as the Gloster Aircraft Co Ltd.

FLIGHT TRIALS

Following an appearance in the RAF Air Pageant at Hendon in 1923, the Grebe made the customary visit for trials at the Aeroplane and Armament Experimental Establishment at Martlesham Heath, Suffolk. It impressed all pilots who flew it and, with a speed of 152 mph at sea-level, it was 25 per cent faster than its predecessor, the Sopwith Snipe. So great an advance was it that the Air Ministry ordered it into production for the RAF. The Grebe's service history was not untroubled, however. Following its initial testing at Martlesham, the aeroplane required modifications. It was given a more powerful Jaguar IV engine, developing 400 hp, an oleo-type undercarriage, as well as a steerable tail skid, plus twin Vickers .303 inch machine guns, mounted ahead of the pilot and firing through the propeller arc via a CC interrupter gear. In this form, the aeroplane entered service as the Grebe II, the first being flown in August 1923 as J7283.

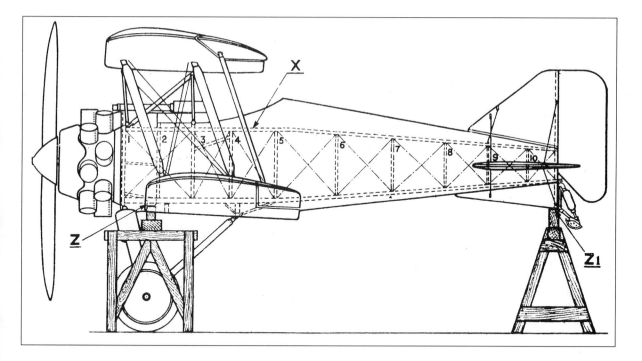

The Grebe was a very small, compact aeroplane, a mere 20 ft 3 in long. Its heavy engine and short fuselage together resulted in an exaggeratedly close-coupled and snub-nosed effect. Construction was principally of spruce, except where loads were concentrated, and there ash or plywood were used. Its fuselage was of straight forward construction, exemplifying the cabinet-maker's craft, and comprised four spindled ash longerons with glued and screwed vertical and cross-members of wire-braced spruce, with bolted steel fittings. The steel tube engine-bearers were attached to a thick plywood bulkhead, which was strengthened to take the 786 lb overhung load of the Jaguar engine. Behind this was what was euphemistically called a fireproof bulkhead, aft of which was the cockpit area, the stressed portions of which (such as the seat and ammunition boxes) were stoutly reinforced with heavy ply.

At the highly-stressed tail end of the fuselage, which had top and bottom fins, the internal struts were of ash. The tailplane was adjustable for trimming, the front spar being connected to each side of the fuselage frame by a pair of coarse-threaded screw-jacks, operated by a cable from the cockpit control level. Support for the rear spar was unusual. It was not attached directly to the wooden structure but was mounted via a cross-tube on two wire-braced star-plates, located on either side between longerons and supporting struts, so as to pivot as tailplane incidence was varied. The cruciform tail-assembly was wire-

Above A rigging illustration from A.P.1168, the RAF's manual on the Grebe, published in November 1927. The aircraft was of conventional wooden construction throughout

braced, mainly of spruce and fabric covered. To give a slightly streamlined shape aft of the cockpit, elliptical plywood formers were attached outside the basic box-shaped structure with light stringers attached and the whole fuselage was covered with fabric, except the engine cowling and cockpit decking where aluminium and ply sheet were used.

The upper and lower wings (mainplanes, to use the

Below View of J7283, the first production Grebe II, powered by a Jaguar IV engine of 400 hp. First flown in August 1923, J7283 spent most of its career at the A&AEE on flight test duties. It also spent some time with Nos 25 and 56 Sqns on Service trials in September 1924

Above J7381 was one of three Grebes sold to New Zealand. Renumbered NZ501, the ex-No 29 Sqn machine was first test-flown there on 2 March 1928, and remained in service for more than 10 years

proper Service term) were different in size, shape and span, as well as section and incidence. About the only thing in common was a 4° dihedral. The lower planes were attached beneath the lower longerons with steel plate fittings. The spars were of spruce strip, the assembly being internally wire-braced. The upper wings were joined at their inner ends, there being no separate centre section. The wire-braced wing assembly was mounted on an inverted vee of streamline steel tubes connecting the front spar to the upper longerons behind the engine, while a pyramid of steel tube similarly connected the fuselage to the rear spar ahead of the cockpit. Two 26-gal fuel tanks were installed in the upper wings. One pair of hollow spruce interplane struts were fitted on each side, with incidence-bracing wires and an acorn where they crossed. The upper wings were fabric-covered, as were the lower ones, except where local strengthening by one-eighth in plywood was required. There were ailerons on all four wings, mounted on false spars and each pair was connected by a solid-spruce inter-aileron strut. As with the tail surfaces, the aileron controls were wire operated.

UNDERCARRIAGE

The Grebe's undercarriage was of the wire-braced, cross axle type, mounted on steel tube vee struts and with energy-absorbing rubber washers and oleo shock-absorbers on the front struts. The axle was of steel tube and there were no brakes, the wheels being of the wire type, with fabric disc coverings, usually painted in flight colours. The tail skid was steerable and

rubber sprung. The Grebe was a noisy little aeroplane and, in the early stages of its service, its 14-cylinder air-cooled Jaguar radial engine had stub exhausts, making a staccato chatter. This noise was subsequently reduced somewhat when an exhaust collector ring was fitted in the front of the engine, leading to two long pipes along the fuselage sides. The engine was started either by means of a Hucks Starter (a Ford Model T chassis on which was mounted an engine-driven shaft which was made to engage, via a dog connection, on the propeller hub). The practical alternative (and it could be hand-swung if the worst came to the worst) was a Bristol gas starter, for which the Grebe was fitted. The principle used in this equipment was the introduction of petrol-air mixture into the cylinders and igniting the charge in the cylinder under compression.

The lower curved surface of each petrol tank projected below the wing surfaces, with a small sump combining a fuel contents gauge and an on/off tap easily visible and reached by the pilot. Supply pipes led fuel by gravity feed directly to the carburettor. A main fuel cock was also mounted in the cockpit, labelled 'Petrol and oil'. The purpose of this was to cut off both at once when the engine had stopped. For draining the carburettor prior to switching off ignition, the wing tank taps had to be turned off first, otherwise the engine would be drained of oil while the

Above A formation of No 29 Sqn Grebes taking off from Duxford to begin a bombing-contest rehearsal for the forthcoming RAF Pageant at Hendon, in May 1926. Parked beneath them in front of the hangars are No 56 Sqn Grebes

fuel lines drained and could be damaged or even seize. The Jaguar engine had fixed ignition timing, throttle and altitude controls, the latter of course being a mixture adjustment for weakening in compensation for an increase in altitude.

The standard armament were twin Vickers machine guns, fitted with the standard CC interrupter gear for firing through the propeller disc. They were fired by triggers within the ring at the top of the control column, and each gun was provided with 600 rounds of .303 in Mk VII ammunition, the empty cases and links of which were discharged overboard through separate chutes. The usual combination of Aldis and ring and bead gun sights was provided, normally with the Aldis set to starboard and the other on the centre line, although they were interchangeable – if the latter fit was adopted, the windscreen was

exchanged for one which allowed the Aldis sight to project through a hole cut in the glass. A light-type bomb carrier could be mounted beneath the fuselage, operated by a cable.

Two wind-driven 12 volt 250 watt electrical generators were mounted below the port and starboard main planes, within the slipstream of the propeller. One of these could provide ignition, lighting, heating (for clothing) and ignition for Holt wing-tip landing flares, while the other provided power for the radio, which was a quite effective HF T.25 transmitter and a R.31 receiver. Tuning was remotely controlled by a lever, and a 'Send, Off and Receive' switch operated the equipment. The aerial extended from the top of the rear interplane struts to the top of the rudderpost. From near the mid-point on either side, a lead-in was connected to a terminal on the top of the fuselage. In addition, two 500 litre oxygen bottles were mounted (like the radio) behind the pilot, with a control, pressure gauge and altitude device in the cockpit. Oxygen was led through a bayonet union up a 9 ft rubber tube to the pilot's mask. The pilot's instruments, mounted on a tidy panel, included an air speed indicator, altimeter, RPM counter, oil temperature and pressure gauges, an inclinometer (a lateral bubble level device) and a compass. A Pyrene-type fire extinguisher was also provided.

The Grebe made the first of three visits to Martlesham for performance trials two months later. With a top speed at sea-level of 162 mph, the Grebe II soon established itself as a very agile fighter indeed, and therein lay the principal cause for concern for its pilots. Apart from an engine whose reliability was at times only just acceptable (it was liable to catch fire in the air and was somewhat over-weight for its power), the Grebe had a persistent tendency to wing-flutter. The upper wing, which had an overhang of nearly three feet, permitted too great an elasticity. The controls were also very light and sensitive, and an

Below A splendid line-up of No 25 Sqn Grebe Mk IIs at Gloster's Hucclecote aerodrome. J7363 spent most of its Service career with this squadron except for a brief period at the Home Aircraft Depot in February 1927

unwary pilot who allowed flutter to develop could lose a wing through ham-handedness, which one or two did to their cost. Curiously, initial Martlesham reports on the Grebe do not seem to have drawn attention to the incipient problem. In addition, the very short fuselage accentuated a reluctance to come out of a spin, which would flatten if allowed to do so. After one or two accidents attributed to wing failure, the Air Ministry instituted tests to ascertain possible remedial action.

At Martlesham it was established that, with sensible handling, the Grebe was a very satisfactory aircraft, delightful in aerobatics. Nevertheless, as a result of experiments, some aircraft were fitted with a pair of V-struts attached to the lower front spar, connecting to the two upper spars, just beyond the mid point of the aileron, providing satisfactory stiffening to the outer panel at the expense of drag and appearance. The question has often been asked – why were not all Grebes thus fitted, if it worked? The answer has been elusive but the writer came across, by chance, two disconnected paragraphs in an *Air Publi-*

Above *This Grebe is pictured at RAF Northolt on the occasion of a race for fighter squadron aircraft held on 26 May 1927. This No 25 Sqn machine was flown by Flg Off L E Maynard*

Right *Grebe J7588 in the markings of No 32 Sqn, based at RAF Kenley. This Mk II aircraft later passed to No 25 Sqn*

cation relating to the Grebe and issued in November 1927 towards the end of the type's squadron service.

Air Ministry publications were usually quite pedantic in their exactitude when describing technical features of aircraft. This extract, however, is a curious exception which may give the answer without actually saying so! A paragraph in one chapter states that the 'top planes have a wash-out from the interplane struts to the tip', referring to 'Rib No 12 (first wash-out rib)' and to 'Rib No 15 (end wash-out rib)'. In the lower plane, Rib No 11 (wash-out rib) is mentioned, without a specific mention of wash-out in the text. The contours of these 'wash-out' ribs differed in their

ordinates from standard ribs, 'the thickness of the mainplane at this point is decreased'. It is apparent, therefore, that the slight but obviously significant wash-out was achieved by a small alteration in the aerofoil profile, rather than by making a rigging adjustment.

A further reference is also made to wash-out in the *Rigging Notes*, which contains the following: 'The angle of incidence of the top main planes is 3 degrees and that of the bottom main planes is 2 degrees. The bottom main planes also have a wash-out of 1 degree from the aileron strut to the tip'. No mention is made in this paragraph of the top planes, in spite of evidence

Right An unidentifiable No 25 Sqn Grebe about to be started with the aid of a Hucks Starter

to the contrary elsewhere, a rare inconsistency in Air Ministry documentation. This may seem a lengthy explanation for a one-degree twist in all the outer wings. It is important if, as seems probable, the divergent oscillation or flutter was effectively cured by such a simple device through an internal modification and the ugly extra struts were no longer needed, thus restoring the original attractive outline. The rigging diagrams of November 1927 show no sign of them.

It seems fair to conclude, therefore, that a simple but clever aerodynamic fix put the matter right, at least for the Gloster Grebe and almost certainly for its successor, the Gamecock. As if to prove the point and to establish the Grebe's real strength, as well as the stability of the wing structure, one was subjected to the first full-throttle terminal velocity dive at Martlesham and recorded 240 mph. Though somewhat over-stressed, the Grebe remained intact. It is noteworthy that, at that time, test pilots were still not usually provided with parachutes, but that on this occasion the pilot wore an Irvin-type parachute.

SQUADRON SERVICE

In many ways the Grebe was the very epitome of the 1920s RAF fighter at a period when a relatively carefree atmosphere was the vogue, and high spirited young men indulged freely in demonstrating their prowess in aerobatics and formation flying. Grebes were never called upon to fire their guns in anger, but the type encapsulated the spirit of the times and even its name was redolent of the English country house shooting party, as indeed were those of its immediate predecessors (Snipe and Nighthawk) and successors (Gamecock, Woodcock and Bulldog).

It was October 1923 when the first Grebes entered service with the RAF, at Duxford in Cambridgeshire. They equipped a single flight of the newly re-formed No 111 Sqn, and it was to be October 1924 before No 25 Sqn at Hawkinge in Kent became the first unit to be *fully* equipped with Grebes, although No 56 Sqn at Biggin Hill had already received J7290 for trials as early as March 1924. The arrival of the Grebes at Duxford had great historical significance in RAF history since they were the first fighters to be designed and built after World War 1 to join the service. The Siskin sometimes claims this distinction but it did not, in fact, enter squadron service until May 1924.

Although the Grebe was a product of the 1920s, it

was but a short step from the 1918 concept of a fighter and, due to its design lineage, still exhibited many characteristics of the S.E.5A and Nieuport Night-hawk. The S.E.5A inheritance was especially notice-able in the lines of the tail assembly, and all-wooden construction was retained in the main airframe. Arma-ment of two .303 Vickers machine-guns mounted above the fuselage directly ahead of the pilot followed familiar 1918 practice as well, but when it came to performance there was a marked advance on such

types as the Snipe, both in speed and rate of climb. This was bestowed by the 14 cylinder twin-row Armstrong-Siddeley Jaguar radial engine.

In June 1923 the RAF's new fighter made its first public appearance at the annual RAF Pageant at Hendon. This was the prototype J6969, resplendent in its new silver finish, which had by then replaced the wartime drab P.C.10 paint schemes. After extensive trials at Martlesham the Grebe was ordered into production as a Snipe replacement and, following two

more development aircraft (J6970 and J6971), contracts were issued by the Air Ministry for an eventual total of 130 Grebes, of which 20 were dual-control advanced trainers. Production batches were J7283–7294, J7357–7402, J7406–7417, J7519–7538, J7568–7603 and J7784–7786, the last contract being issued in 1924.

Six first-line fighter squadrons were equipped with the Grebe and they were familiar sights to local residents around the airfields at Duxford, Hawkinge,

Left Grebe J7520, with Flt Lt Richard Atcherley as pilot and Flt Lt G H Stainforth as navigator, taking off from Heston at the start of the two-day King's Cup Air Race, held on 5–6 July 1929. This combination won the race with an average speed of 150 mph for the 1160-mile course

Kenley and Biggin Hill during the 1920s. They could also be seen at Martlesham where they served with No 22 Sqn (not a first-line fighter squadron) on experimental and development work.

The two-seat dual-control Grebe emerged quite early in the type's RAF career. Whereas the single-seat fighters were officially designated Mk II, the trainers received the designation Mk IIIDC and the prototype (J7519) first flew in July 1924, proceeding to No 22 Sqn at Martlesham for performance trials in May 1925. Together with the second Grebe IIIDC (J7520), it shared the unusual distinction of competing in the predominantly civil event of the King's Cup Air Race, won handsomely by J7520 in July 1929. Both Grebes were flown by pilots who were to enjoy distinguished RAF careers – J7520 by Flt Lt R L R Atcherley and J7519 by Flg Off E H Fielden. Flying with Atcherley in the winning aircraft was yet another name destined to be famous, Flt Lt G H Stainforth. The victorious Grebe averaged 150.3 mph over a 1160 mile course. In later years, Atcherley became a disguished air marshal, Fielden the Captain of the King's Flight and Stainforth a prominent Schneider Trophy pilot.

Dual Grebes were issued to all the single-seat fighter squadrons using the type and also to such training establishments as the Central Flying School at Upavon, the Training Base at Leuchars, the Armament and Gunnery School at Eastchurch and No 5 FTS at Sealand. Single-seater examples were also issued to these schools as well as to No 2 FTS at Digby, No 3 FTS at Grantham and No 4 FTS in Egypt.

The Grebe with No 4 FTS did tropical trials on brief attachment to Nos 14 and 216 Sqns, but the type was never adopted for overseas squadron service.

Together with the Bristol Bullfinch and Hawker

Woodcock, a Grebe made its second appearance in the New Types Park at the annual RAF Display at Hendon in 1924. Thereafter, in full squadron service it became a star performer at every Hendon Display from 1925 until 1931 with the single exception of 1928. The year 1925 became memorable for two Grebe events. A pair of Grebes (J7600 and J7599) gave a magnificent aerobatic display, piloted by Flt Lt H A Hammersley and Flg Off J N Boothman, who later became famous as a member of the RAF High Speed Flight flying Supermarine seaplanes in the Schneider Trophy. Even more noteworthy, however, was the second Grebe event, mounted by No 25 Sqn from Hawkinge, which was led by Sqn Ldr A H Peck DSO, MC. No 25 Sqn's Grebes not only performed some immaculate squadron drill but did it under the directions of ground control using radio telephony, a startling innovation for those days. As if this were not remarkable enough, part of the display was conducted on the radio instructions of HM King George V. Part of the radio transmissions were also broadcast to the public by the medium of the BBC's pioneering 2LO wireless station.

HENDON PAGEANT

In 1926 no less than five squadrons of Grebes participated at Hendon. They were Nos 19, 25, 29, 32 and 56. In 1927 the Grebes of Nos 19, 29 and 25 Sqns took part, alongside Gamecocks of Nos 23 and 32 Sqns and Siskins of Nos 41, 56 and 111 Sqns. By 1929, Grebes had disappeared from the first-line fighter squadrons but they nevertheless continued to maintain a presence at Hendon Displays because the type was still serving with the experimental and trials unit, No 22 Sqn, at Martlesham Heath. Grebes from Martlesham were

Above *This two-seat Grebe, NZ203, was delivered to the New Zealand Permanent Air Force and assembled in 1928. The aircraft remained in NZPAF service until written off during an aerobatic display at Hornsby on 8 August 1932*

Right *Grebe II J7413 in No 56 Sqn markings. This squadron received its first Grebes, at RAF Biggin Hill, in September 1924. They were replaced with Siskin IIIAs exactly three years later*

displayed by Flt Lts Bradbury and Guest in 1929 and again in 1930 and 1931 by Flt Lts Fleming, Wincott and Addams. The Martlesham Grebes employed coloured smoke trails to add drama to their display, and this device became a familiar feature of many subsequent aerobatic teams. In addition they had distinctive markings; the upper wings, top of fuselage, fins and top of tailplanes were painted a stunning shade of bright red.

Despite its renown as an aerobatic aeroplane and its popularity with squadron pilots, the Grebe was not without its shortcomings, most significantly its tendency to wing flutter during its earlier period of service. This caused the loss of No 56 Sqn's J7411 on 27 October 1924 and No 25 Sqn's J7410 on 6 January 1925, and there were numerous other accidents. This unpleasant characteristic was later eliminated by the use of additional strut bracing at the wing tips. The same problem was later encountered (and rectified in the same way) when the Gamecock entered service.

The well-known aviation writer and former experimental test pilot, the late Oliver Stewart, was high in his praise of the Grebe's perfectly balanced controls, and such handling qualities doubtless tempted some pilots to indulge in reckless behaviour, with catastrophic results. A typical example, perhaps, is that of Plt Off 'Scruffy' Purvis who, when approaching to land, was prone to doing a series of rolls or stalled turns. He was killed at RAF Hawkinge performing just such a manoeuvre and a fine aerobatic pilot was lost to the Service.

Yet another instance of an over-exuberant Grebe pilot being lost to the RAF is cited in Graham Wallace's book *RAF Biggin Hill* (Putnam, 1957):

'The Grebe was the perfect aeroplane for aerobatics. It was strictly forbidden, but the irrepressible pilots of No 56 Sqn continued to loop-the-loop after taking off, without climbing to gain altitude. One day Flying Officer Duxmore, thinking the CO safely away, set out to beat the squadron record for consecutive loops. He made a quick climbing take-off in his Grebe and went straight into a tight loop over the airfield. As he dived to pick up speed for his second loop, the CO walked onto the grass. Luxmore ignored the Véry signals ordering him to land at once, finished the loop and zoomed up a third time. For an eternity the little Grebe seemed to hang suspended by the spinning propeller, then it flipped over, dived into the ground and burst into flames. In all, the squadron lost six pilots in flying accidents at Biggin Hill.'

So far as speed was concerned, the Grebe was more than a match for the lumbering bombers of the day such as the Vimy, Virginia, Fawn and D.H.9A. Great interest was aroused in 1925 when a new twin-engined

day bomber, the Boulton Paul Bugle, was attached to No 58 Sqn at Worthy Down for evaluation. Famed, like its successors the Sidestrand and Overstrand, for its remarkable manoeuvrability despite its size, the Bugle put up a spirited defence in a series of mock dogfights with Grebes of the CFS from Upavon, later the basis of an exciting exhibition of flying at the RAF Hendon Display.

As already mentioned, many RAF pilots later to become renowned in aviation history were associated with the Grebe, and to this list must be added the name of C W A Scott, who became a world-famous record-breaking sporting pilot in the 1930s, and who shared with Campbell-Black the triumph of winning the Mildenhall to Australia Air Race in 1934 in the Comet racer. Scott served with No 32 Sqn at Kenley in 1925–26 and records in his memoirs some vivid recollections of 'Battle Flights' in Grebes:

Below A view of eight No 25 Sqn Grebes taken at Gloster's Hucclecote aerodrome shortly after manufacture and prior to service delivery

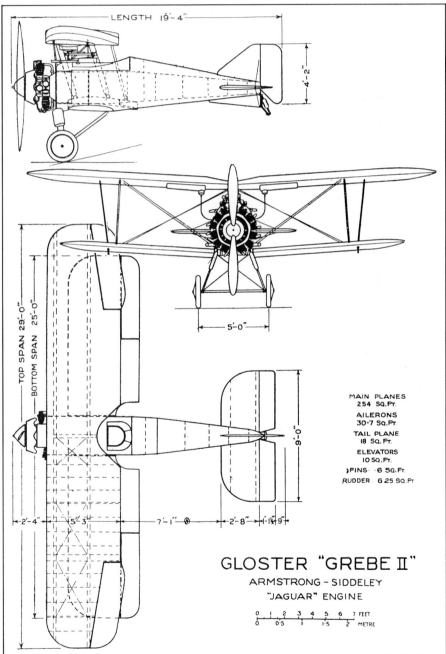

LENGTH 19'-4"

4'-2"

TOP SPAN 29'-0"
BOTTOM SPAN 25'-0"

5'-0"

9'-0"

MAIN PLANES
254 SQ.FT.
AILERONS
30·7 SQ.FT.
TAIL PLANE
18 SQ.FT.
ELEVATORS
10 SQ.FT.
FINS · 6 SQ.FT.
RUDDER 6.25 SQ.FT.

2'-4"   5½'-3"   7'-1"   2'-8"   1'-9"

GLOSTER "GREBE II"
ARMSTRONG - SIDDELEY
"JAGUAR" ENGINE

0 1 2 3 4 5 6 7 FEET
0   0·5   1   1·5   2 METRE

Above A view of Grebe J7400 taken at Pulham, Norfolk, during airship launching trials with the R33 during the final months of 1926. J7400 and J7385 were used for a series of trial launchings from R33. Quick-release attachments were fitted to the upper wings and the engines were started by means of flexible piping connected to a gas starter inside the airship. The phasing out of the dirigible from the RAF signalled the end of these trials

'Round about this period each squadron in a fighting area had to have a 'Battle Flight' each week. This Flight was on duty for the whole week and would start off on Monday mornings by putting 250 rounds through each of its front guns at the butts. They might be called at a moment's notice. We had to do three flights of at least one hour's endurance, at 20,000 ft, each week. How glad we were that we had Grebes and not Snipes, for the Grebe would get up to 20,000 in about half the time the old Snipe would take and would still be a nice machine to fly at that height, where the Snipe had had such a poor performance. But it was desperately cold at that altitude and the electrically heated clothing that we had in those days was far from being efficient, for the glove on one hand would be warm, while that on the other would be absolutely frozen. Sometimes the complete equipment would pack up and at the end of one hour one was cold enough to be at the point of frostbite. Neither had we any oxygen, but this was issued to us later.' Scott goes on to mention that it was at about this time that parachutes were first coming into use in fighter squadrons.

Some equally evocative descriptions of Grebe activities in its heyday can be found in a wonderful book by Roy S Humphreys, *Hawkinge 1912–1961* (Meresborough Books, 1981) in which he writes about the impact of No 25 Sqn's aeroplanes on the Folkestone countryside:

'The tranquillity of meadow and country lane was often shattered by snarling radial engines. Fowl and cattle leaped this way and that as screaming Grebes shot between cow shed and barn.'

More seriously, a Grebe flown by Plt Off Montgomery of No 32 Sqn, flying from Kenley, accidentally released a small practice bomb when taking off over Caterham. It struck a baker's shop in the High Street causing considerable damage but luckily there was no loss of life. The incident naturally caused a great

Above The standard engine for the Grebe was the Armstrong Siddeley Jaguar IV of 400 hp. The uncowled fitment of the powerplant to the airframe did little for the aircraft's aerodynamics, but was much appreciated by squadron mechanics

Right Grebe II J7408 was serving with No 56 Sqn when it overturned at Biggin Hill in 1925. On 21 September the following year it went to Pulham Airship Station for trials

furore in the national press and great embarrassment at the Air Ministry.

On Christmas Day in 1926 came the most spectacular of Grebe misdemeanours when Plt Off Holden (also from No 32 Sqn at Kenley) flew a dual Grebe under Tower Bridge, followed by a roll off the top of a loop and, on the way back to base, did a low-level beat-up of Swan and Edgar's at Piccadilly Circus! History was to repeat itself on 4 April 1968 when Flt Lt Alan Pollock of No 1 Sqn flew his Hunter at low-level along the Thames past the Houses of Parliament and then roared below the top span of Tower Bridge.

In addition to giving good service with the front-line fighter squadrons, the Grebe took part in many advanced flight test programmes, mostly at Martlesham. It was during one of these tests that a Grebe (possibly J7283) became the first fighter in aviation history to survive a 240 mph terminal velocity dive at full power. It is interesting to compare this with the 270 mph which the Bristol Bulldog later achieved under similar conditions.

In 1926, two Grebes (J7385 and J7400) were used in a series of trials to launch single-seat fighter aircraft from the large dirigible airship, the R.33. Quick release attachments were fitted to the upper wings and the engines were started by flexible piping connected

Above Photographed between flights at Biggin Hill in mid-1925, this Grebe wears the unmistakable chequerboard scheme of No 56 Sqn

to a gas starter inside the airship. Two pilots from the RAE, Flg Offs R L Ragg and C Mackenzie-Richards, flew the Grebes to successful landings at Pulham and Cardington respectively. Although the idea of carrying fighters below dirigibles had been found to be practicable, no further development of the scheme took place as, in fact, there was no further use foreseen for the military airship. Two other Grebes (J7408 and J7587) were also involved in airship trials.

The last Grebes in service with a first-line fighter unit in the RAF were those of No 25 Sqn at Hawkinge, which gave them up in July 1929 when they converted to Siskins. Grebes with No 22 Sqn at the A&AEE lingered on until 1931 when the type finally disap-

peared from the RAF scene, but three examples of the breed continued in service with the Royal New Zealand Air Force until as late as 1938.

Grebe Units in the RAF

Between 1923 and 1929, six first-line fighter squadrons flew the Grebe on Home Defence duties, as detailed below:

No 19 Squadron *Duxford, December 1924 to April 1928*

Markings: Blue and White checks on fuselage and between roundels on upper wings

Serials: J7284, 7294, 7357, 7358, 7368, 7372, 7373, 7374, 7375, 7376, 7377, 7378, 7386, 7387, 7389, 7390, 7391, 7407, 7408, 7417, 7524, 7526, 7528, 7530, 7531, 7532, 7568, 7569, 7572, 7574, 7577, 7578, 7579, 7580, 7583, 7585, 7587, 7592, 7594, 7600, 7601
There was also a Grebe two-seater, J7585

No 25 Squadron *Hawkinge, October 1924 to July 1929*

Markings: Black parallel bars along fuselage from engine to roundel

Left Gloster's second prototype Grebe was J6970, which, like J6969, boasted fairings for the type's twin .303in machine guns. These covers were later dispensed with prior to the aircraft entering squadron service

Right The sole civil-registered Grebe flew as a demonstrator during 1923. It was rebuilt in 1926 and fitted with a 425 hp Bristol Jupiter IV engine and Gloster Hele-Shaw Beacham experimental variable-pitch propeller. Note the Gamecock-type undercarriage

Above left The Grebe's short fuselage and stiffly sprung undercarriage often conspired with the less than flat grass aerodromes of the day to catch less experienced pilots out upon completion of a flight

(sometimes extended ahead of airscrew on cowling ring) and between roundels on top wing

Serials: J7283, 7284, 7285, 7286, 7287, 7288, 7289, 7290, 7291, 7292, 7293, 7294, 7358, 7360, 7361, 7363, 7368, 7370, 7272, 7374, 7384, 7385, 7392, 7400, 7402, 7407, 7409, 7410, 7411, 7412, 7417, 7569, 7572, 7576, 7578, 7579, 7580, 7581, 7583, 7586, 7587, 7588, 7589, 7591, 7602, 7603, 7786
There were also seven Grebe two-seaters, J7413, 7520, 7530, 7532, 7534, 7536, 7538

No 29 Squadron *Duxford, January 1925 to March 1928*

Markings: Red 'XXXX' pattern on fuselage between parallel red bars, ahead of roundel. Same markings repeated between roundels on top wing. Later, the pattern was reduced to 'XXX'

Serials: J7292, 7293, 7362, 7369, 7380, 7381, 7382, 7385, 7390, 7393, 7394, 7395, 7396, 7397, 7520, 7521, 7532, 7570, 7571, 7583, 7591, 7592, 7593, 7597, 7598, 7784, 7785, 7786
There were also six Grebe two-seaters, J7521, 7527, 7528, 7533, 7538, 7585

No 32 Squadron *Kenley, November 1924 to February 1927.*

Markings: Wide blue bar with diagonal gaps, from engine to tailplane, on fuselage. Pattern repeated above the top wings

Serials: J7361, 7399, 7571, 7599, 7360, 7361, 7365, 7369, 7371, 7399, 7586, 7588, 7599, 7601
There was also a Grebe two-seater, J7526

No 56 Squadron *Biggin Hill, September 1924 to September 1927*

Markings: Red and white checks ahead of roundel on fuselage and between roundels on upper wing. Initially, this marking was a long narrow strip of small squares (as earlier seen on No 56 Snipes) but later changed to larger and fewer red and white squares

Serials: J7283, 7289, 7290, 7537, 7358, 7359, 7385, 7393, 7401, 7406, 7408, 7409, 7410, 7411, 7412, 7413, 7414, 7415, 7416, 7417, 7582, 7583, 7584, 7585
There were also two Grebe two-seaters, J7522, 7535

No 111 Squadron *Duxford, October 1923 to June 1924.*

One flight only was equipped with Grebes, later joined by one flight of Snipes and one flight of Siskins

Markings: Black bar along the fuselage and possibly (but not definitely confirmed) across the upper wings between the roundels

Serials: No records of initial issue, but clearly they were from the first production batch starting with J7283 which left the factory in August 1923. Later, after No 111 Sqn had fully converted to Siskins, a Grebe two-seater J7524 was on strength

Gloucestershire Grebe II data

Engine: Armstrong Siddeley Jaguar IV, 14-cylinder direct drive, unsupercharged; 385 hp at normal 1700 rpm; 420 hp at maximum 1870 rpm

Dimensions

Span	29 ft 4 in
Length	20 ft 3 in
Height	9 ft 3 in
Wing Area	254 ft^2

Weights

Loaded	2600 lbs
Empty	1720 lbs

Performance

Maximum Speed	162 mph at sea level
Stalling Speed	53 mph
Time to 20,000 ft	24 min
Service Ceiling	23,500 ft

Endurance
at 20,000 ft (including climb)   3 hr

Armament: Two fixed 0.303 in Vickers synchronized machine guns, using Constantinesco interrupter gear, four 20 lb Cooper bombs

THE ARMSTRONG WHITWORTH SISKIN

THE ARMSTRONG WHITWORTH SISKIN of the 1920s was as striking in appearance, which was angular, as was its impact on the ear, which could be raucous. The ungeared 14-cylinder Armstrong Siddeley Jaguar engine, bristling with cylinders and exhaust stubs, made a noisy crackle, little diminished by the fitting to most squadron Siskins of long tail-pipes at each side. The big overhang of the upper wing lent itself admirably to the largest roundels ever sported by an RAF fighter, like great eyes, evocative of the Peacock butterfly. A sesquiplane with diminutive lower wings, the roundels above and below the upper wing surfaces overlapped the ailerons – those being the days before the painting of control surfaces was banned, principally for balance purposes.

Any further resemblance of the aeroplane to the Peacock, or to the shy and discreet little bird after which it was named, was purely co-incidental. The Siskin, angular and noisy creature though it was, has a very definite place in the developing history of the fighters of the RAF, not least for its becoming the Service's first all-metal fighter. Sadly, only a wing of the Siskin survives today, thanks to the RAF Museum at Hendon, simply as an example of its type of construction. The striking difference in size between upper and lower wings, and their v-shaped interplane struts so characteristic of the aeroplane, did not in fact appear until the Mk III version.

Over the years, there has been much discussion about the origins of the Siskin. Because of the intimate association between the companies manufacturing its

Below View of the Siddeley-Deasy S.R.2, later known as the Siskin. Following a period of inactivity, S.R.2 C4541 reappeared in March 1921 fitted with the new Armstrong Siddeley Jaguar radial engine

airframe and engine, neither can be considered without the other. At the conclusion of the Great War in 1918, the fledgling RAF had well over 22,000 aircraft on its strength. Within a year, the Service had been decimated in numbers of aircraft, squadrons and personnel. Hopes for a rapid growth in civil aviation were not fulfilled for some years and, in the interim, the outlook for the aircraft industry, particularly in the military sector, was bleak in the extreme.

During 1917, following the Burbidge Report into alleged shortcomings on the part of the Royal Aircraft Factory at Farnborough, its substantial design and construction capability was dismantled, its function changing to one principally of research, as the Royal Aircraft Establishment. This change led to some very experienced senior designers leaving and joining other aircraft constructors, among them Maj F M Green, who had been in charge of design, John Lloyd, head of the Stress Department and S D Heron, the engine designer. At Farnborough, Green and Heron had been responsible for what would otherwise have emerged as the 300 hp, R.A.F.8 14-cylinder air-cooled radial engine. The Siddeley-Deasy Motor Car Co at Coventry, headed by John Siddeley, was determined to remain in the aircraft and engine industry and in 1917 provided the opportunity for this team to continue their development work, particularly on the new engine. A condition was that, first, the Siddeley Puma had to be developed into the satisfactory power-plant which it was eventually to become. Following a dispute with Siddeley, Heron left for the USA and was replaced by F R Smith. There was accordingly some delay to the development of the new radial engine.

Lloyd was, meanwhile, setting up an aeroplane design department, resulting in the Siddeley R.T.1, a

Above J9198, *first flown in July 1928, served with Nos 54, 111 and 25 Sqns before being relegated to training duties with No 5 FTS at Sealand, where it joined dozens of other weary Siskins in September 1933*

modified R.E.8. Significantly, this was followed by the S.R.2 fighter, soon to be named 'Siskin'. Owing to the hold-up in progressing with work on the original R.A.F.8 design and creating the new engine, an ABC Dragonfly was substituted on the prototype Siskin. Even with this unsatisfactory engine, when first flown in July 1919 it had better handling and performance than its similarly-powered competitors, achieving 145 mph at 6500 ft and reaching 10,000 ft in under eight minutes. Six were ordered, but owing to late delivery of Dragonfly engines, only three were delivered – C4541, C4542 and C4543.

The debacle concerning the Dragonfly's reliability resulted initially in the virtual disappearance of the Siskin. However, in March 1921, C4541 re-emerged painted, first, as the 'Siddeley Siskin No 1' and, following a change of name by the manufacturer, it

Right *Siskin II G-EBJQ competed in the 1922 King's Cup air race and was flown by Frank Courtney, but had to retire when a centre-section fitting broke shortly after leaving Glasgow. The outsized external fuel tanks grafted on to the upper wing may have had something to do with the strut failure!*

then became known as the Armstrong Whitworth Siskin I. It was powered by the Jaguar, as the 14-cylinder engine had been named, its manufacturer now known as Armstrong Siddeley Motors Ltd. It had an all-wood structure and parallel interplane struts. It also bore a striking resemblance to previous designs which had emerged from Farnborough under the supervision of Green and Lloyd, although suggestions that the design had originated as a possible S.E.7 were denied by both.

The Siskin's qualities, now suitably powered, were impressive enough to prompt the Air Ministry to encourage Armstrong Whitworth to develop the design, with the caveat that future orders would, as a matter of policy, only be issued for aircraft with all-metal structures. The Siskin was described by Oliver Stewart, the distinguished test pilot, writer and commentator, as

extremely easy to fly, gentle and calm, though ' . . . a great uncouth brute of a thing, but with a heart of gold', by comparison with previously introduced single-seater fighters, which he described as '. . . quick, snappy, short-tempered and sometimes vicious'. The company proceeded cautiously, building next (in 1922) the two-seat Siskin Mk II, with a steel-tube fuselage but retaining the wood-framed wings. Registered G-EBEU, it was entered in the King's Cup Air Race in 1922 but had to retire following damage to a centre-section fitting. Converted to a single-seater, G-EBEU won the race the following year, averaging 148.7 mph over a course of 809 miles. This and a second Siskin II, G-EBHY, were used on extensive overseas sales tours which unfortunately failed to secure any substantial orders for the Armstrong Whitworth fighter.

The next and most important development was the Siskin III, which boasted a truly all-metal structure. It was also the first version to have the striking appearance which was to become familiar from 1924 onwards. The all-metal Siskin prototype, J6583 (a modified Mk II rather than a true Mk III), was flown for the first time by F T Courtney on 7 May 1923, and was powered by a 325 hp Jaguar III engine.

The Air Ministry initially ordered three Siskin IIIs, the first being J6981. The major difference from the earlier version was the narrow-chord lower wing with a single spar, necessitating a v-shaped pair of interplane struts connecting to the big upper wing. The angular, leggy undercarriage did little to improve the grace of the Siskin, and nothing to improve its performance. It was, nevertheless, a strong and very manoeuvrable

Above Siskin III G-EBJS also took part in the 1924 King's Cup. Piloted by Frank Courtney, it suffered a broken spinner and had to retire from the race at Brough

Right The second Siskin II, G-EBHY, gained its C of A on 25 June 1924. It eventually went to Sweden, where it flew with an experimental ski undercarriage

Above Siskin Mk III J7000 was delivered to the A&AEE and the RAE during the latter part of 1924. It was converted into a dual trainer and subsequently flew with Nos 22 and 1 Sqns

fighter, with an engine which was adequately powerful and reliable.

The first of these, J6981, flew on 24 March 1924. Two of the earliest Siskin IIIs were civil-registered as G-EBJQ and G-EBJS, both competing in the 1924 King's Cup race, the former finishing fourth out of five, at 126 mph over 950 miles. A significant detail of the design was that like the prototype, it had a substantial under-fin, although the fuselage itself was rather deeper at the tail. The large balanced rudder projected to the base of the fin and was cutaway to clear the tail skid. The pilot sat high with his eyes in line with the upper wing, giving him an excellent view in most directions. The design philosophy was unusual. It was claimed that, thanks to its strong metal construction with alternative load paths, if a bracing wire should break or even a strut shot away, the wing

structure was designed not to collapse. The complicated levered and wire-braced undercarriage had shock-absorber cords of rubber, damped by oil dash-pots working on the main telescopic struts.

In all, about 485 Siskins were built, many of them by sub-contractors including Blackburn, Bristol, Gloster and Vickers. The most important production version was the Mk IIIA, the first of which, J7001, was a conversion from a Mk III and was flown on 21 October 1925 by Frank Courtney. The new model differed in several ways from the earlier version, including a rather tidier aft end featuring a deepened rear fuselage with the tailplane mounted somewhat higher than on earlier versions. This was due to the abolition of the under-fin, and the design also boasted a neater arrangement of centre-section struts. The dihedral of the top wing was reduced from $3\frac{1}{2}°$, to $1°$, although the lower wing remained at the original figure. There was a standard provision for a super-charged Jaguar engine.

The Siskin's fuselage was built as two frames, front and rear, joined behind the pilot's seat and was

Left Siskin Mk III J6982 was deliverd to the A&AEE in November 1923 and the RAE in March the following year. In July 1924 the Siskin was registered G-EBJS for participation in that year's King's Cup race and returned to RAF service in November

constructed of steel tubing with four longerons, braced throughout by swaged tie-rods. The engine bearer plate was supported by triangulated assemblies, based on the longerons, and a fire bulkhead was mounted behind it. The bottom wing (or mainplane, as it was then named) was attached to a strong steel tube centre-plane spar, built integral with the fuselage as a cross-member. This was stiffened between the longerons and braced to withstand the loads imposed by inverted flight, and also to support the front struts of the rigid part of the main undercarriage assembly. The undercarriage itself had helically-sprung telescopic legs with oleo shock-absorbers. The fuselage front frame had detachable aluminium covers at the top, fabric-covered sides and aluminium sheet along the bottom. The upper area around the cockpit comprised a wooden framework, covered with plywood. Ahead of it, there were mountings for the two Vickers .303 in machine guns, mounted ahead of the pilot, with access panels and apertures on either side for link and case chutes.

The fabric-covered rear fuselage frame was swept quite sharply upwards. This feature was not apparent externally because of the upper decking, which resulted in an exceptionally deep cockpit region. The tail structure allowed for varying the incidence of the tailplane by means of a screw jack. A pivoting tail skid was connected to the rudder and had a helical spring shock-absorber, the shoe being of cast aluminium with a renewable steel rubbing block. The wire-braced tailplane and fin assembly were constructed of rolled steel strip and tube and also braced internally with swaged tie-rods. The elevators, on a common spar, and rudder were similarly constructed, the whole tail assembly being fabric-covered.

WING CONSTRUCTION

Both wings were also fabric-covered, their construction being similar to that of the tail, made of drawn or rolled steel strip, internally braced with the tie rods. The upper wing was of conventional two-spar construction, built in two halves, there being no separate centre section. The wing was attached to the top longerons by four splayed-out faired tubular struts linked to the spars, and the struts were wire-braced at the sides and rear but not at the front. This arrangement was unlike that on the Mk III, which had three additional struts on either side, the front four of which, in pyramid layout, joined the upper longerons to the front spar, together with the rear pair which connected the longerons to the rear spar, also on the wing centre-line. Ailerons were mounted on the upper wings only, hinged to three wing ribs which were

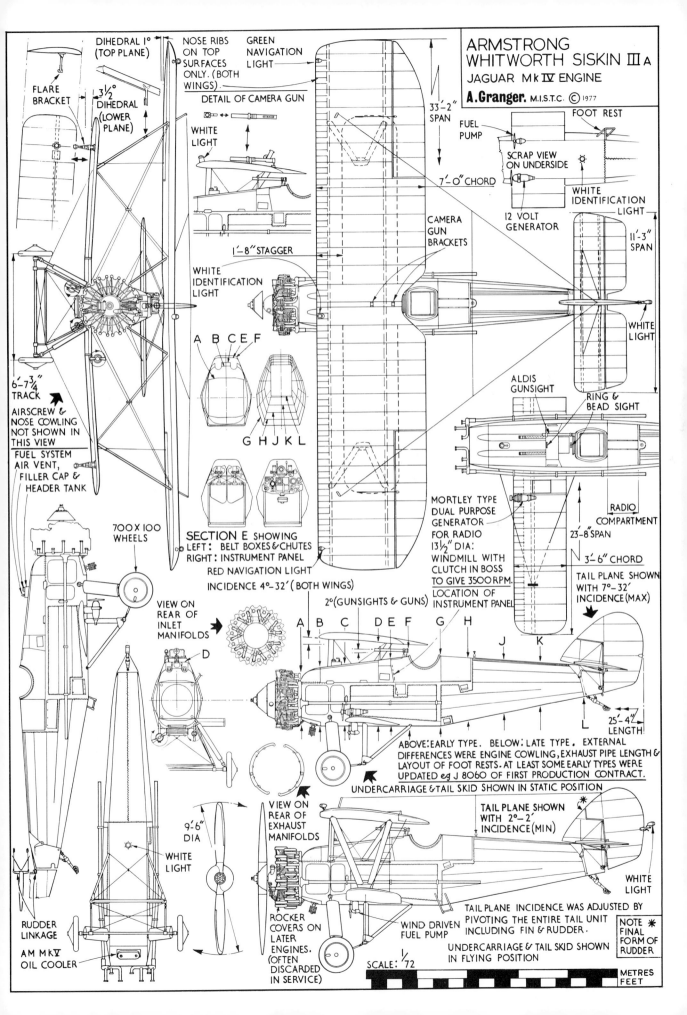

ARMSTRONG WHITWORTH SISKIN IIIA
JAGUAR Mk IV ENGINE
A. Granger. M.I.S.T.C. © 1977

DIHEDRAL 1° (TOP PLANE)
NOSE RIBS ON TOP SURFACES ONLY. (BOTH WINGS).
GREEN NAVIGATION LIGHT
FLARE BRACKET
3½° DIHEDRAL (LOWER PLANE)
DETAIL OF CAMERA GUN
WHITE LIGHT
33'-2" SPAN
7'-0" CHORD
FUEL PUMP
FOOT REST
SCRAP VIEW ON UNDERSIDE
12 VOLT GENERATOR
WHITE IDENTIFICATION LIGHT

1'-8" STAGGER
WHITE IDENTIFICATION LIGHT
CAMERA GUN BRACKETS
11'-3" SPAN
WHITE LIGHT

A B C E F
G H J K L
SECTION E SHOWING
LEFT: BELT BOXES & CHUTES
RIGHT: INSTRUMENT PANEL
RED NAVIGATION LIGHT
INCIDENCE 4°-32' (BOTH WINGS)

ALDIS GUNSIGHT
RING & BEAD SIGHT

6'-7¾" TRACK
AIRSCREW & NOSE COWLING NOT SHOWN IN THIS VIEW
FUEL SYSTEM AIR VENT, FILLER CAP & HEADER TANK

700 X 100 WHEELS

MORTLEY TYPE DUAL PURPOSE GENERATOR FOR RADIO 13½" DIA. WINDMILL WITH CLUTCH IN BOSS TO GIVE 3500 R.P.M.
LOCATION OF INSTRUMENT PANEL
RADIO COMPARTMENT
23'-8" SPAN
3'-6" CHORD
TAIL PLANE SHOWN WITH 7°-32' INCIDENCE (MAX)

2° (GUNSIGHTS & GUNS)

VIEW ON REAR OF INLET MANIFOLDS
D

A B C   D E F   G H
J   K
L
25'-4" LENGTH

ABOVE: EARLY TYPE. BELOW: LATE TYPE. EXTERNAL DIFFERENCES WERE ENGINE COWLING, EXHAUST PIPE LENGTH & LAYOUT OF FOOT RESTS. AT LEAST SOME EARLY TYPES WERE UPDATED eg J 8060 OF FIRST PRODUCTION CONTRACT.
UNDERCARRIAGE & TAIL SKID SHOWN IN STATIC POSITION

9'-6" DIA
WHITE LIGHT
VIEW ON REAR OF EXHAUST MANIFOLDS

TAIL PLANE SHOWN WITH 2°-2' INCIDENCE (MIN)
WHITE LIGHT

RUDDER LINKAGE
AM MkV OIL COOLER
ROCKER COVERS ON LATER ENGINES. (OFTEN DISCARDED IN SERVICE)
WIND DRIVEN FUEL PUMP

TAIL PLANE INCIDENCE WAS ADJUSTED BY PIVOTING THE ENTIRE TAIL UNIT INCLUDING FIN & RUDDER.
UNDERCARRIAGE & TAIL SKID SHOWN IN FLYING POSITION

NOTE ✱ FINAL FORM OF RUDDER

SCALE: 1/72
METRES
FEET

Right Flg Off H T
Andrews competing in the
Sir Philip Sassoon Cup at
RAF Northolt on 26 May
1927 in No 41 Sqn Siskin
IIIA J8386. He was
placed fourth in the race,
averaging 142 mph for the
100-mile course, which
started at Northolt and
returned there via Duxford
and Halton

Below Sqn Ldr E O
Grenfell of No 1 Sqn, in
Siskin IIIA J8834, taking
part in the Sassoon Cup
race at Northolt on 28
May 1929

connected by a short false spar. The single-sparred lower wing, carrying the splayed-out vee-struts, was also braced externally both to the centre-section struts and to the undercarriage, the struts being jig-assembled to ensure accurate rigging.

According to some published reports, the Siskin III could be powered by either the 325 hp Jaguar III or the 385 hp Mk IV version, both unsupercharged. Similarly, the Siskin IIIAs are often quoted as being distinguished from the previous model because of having the supercharged Jaguar IV, as distinct from the unblown Jaguar III referred to above. A perusal of a relevant *Air Publication* (official manual) concerning the Mk IIIA avoids any such distinction, if the reader concludes that the Air Ministry knew what was promulgated in its name (a reasonable assumption, thus avoiding the risk of consignment to the Tower of London). 'The (Siskin IIIA) aircraft may be fitted with a Jaguar Mk IV supercharged or the ordinary Jaguar Mk IV engine', states the *AP*. A slight amplifi-

Above J7161 was first flown in June 1924 and was later fitted with a Jaguar IVS engine. Later it was converted to dual control and ended its days with Nos 3 and 5 FTSs

cation is added in the introduction by the statement that the supercharged version is ground-throttled ('gated'), which of course it would need to be to prevent damage, for example, following take-off. A 'gated' throttle ensures that it cannot inadvertently be opened beyond the gate at low altitude, but can be progressively opened up through the gate as conditions allow, maintaining maximum permissible boost up to the rated altitude, at which the throttle is wide open. These were days before automatic boost control, and the boost gauge was still a novelty.

Two fuel tanks were mounted in front of the pilot, the main holding 25 gal and the service tank 22 gal. Fuel was fed to the carburettor by gravity from the service tank and by a wing-mounted, wind-driven pump from the main tank. A hand-pump was provided to transfer the feed to the service tank, should the mechanical pump fail. With a supercharged engine fitted, an oil-cooler was fitted and both types of engine had provision for a gas starter as well as the traditional

Hucks-type dog on the propeller shaft. Service equipment in the Siskin IIIA comprised armament, high-pressure oxygen and a short-wave R/T transmitter and receiver. The radio installation was mounted immediately behind the pilot, the Siskin leading the way in the earliest installations of short-wave radio-telephony in RAF squadrons. The fixed aerial ran from short posts on the upper surface of the wing to another on top of the rudder, with leads from the mid-points to an insulator on the top of the fuselage above the wireless set. Aldis and ring-and-bead sights were provided and twin CC interrupter gear was fitted as standard. A Type G.III camera gun could be mounted on the top plane and a light-type bomb carrier could be mounted beneath the fuselage.

MODIFIED SISKINS

The rugged strength of the Siskin's structure and its generally satisfactory service as a fighter, despite a certain lack of aesthetic elegance, encouraged experiments to improve various aspects of its performance. In 1930, a modified and stronger lower wing was fitted but was found to be in need of still further strengthening. The upper wing tips also required stiffening and an improved tail-operating jack was provided. Three years earlier, Farnborough had undertaken a series of spinning tests at the request of the Aeronautical

Above J8428 fitted with heater muff on the engine exhaust. First flown in October 1925, this Siskin spent much of its life to-ing and fro-ing between the RAE and its makers

Right J7155 first flew in June 1924 and was delivered to No 111 Sqn. It later passed to No 41 Sqn and on 6 May 1926 was damaged following engine failure while taking off from Northolt

Research Committee with Siskin IIIA J8428. Prolonged spins, of up to 13 turns were made by three RAE pilots. When trimmed fully forward, it was difficult to persuade the Siskin to spin at all. Having established the aircraft in a spin, it became rather slow and jerky. Started at about 14,000 ft, seven turns incurred a loss of about 3000 ft. At all cg positions, even fully aft, a spin in either direction stopped quickly when the controls were centred.

In 1929 the RAE, in a programme of basic research, conducted further experiments using J8850 to investigate stalling characteristics and the effect on lateral control, which was always positive, if somewhat heavy. These tests involved the fitting of slots and spoilers and the effect of interlinking them with the ailerons. The results showed that the Siskin was even more difficult or impossible to spin with the slots fitted, but no modifications to the basic aircraft ensued. In attempts to improve the performance of the Siskin, experiments were made to reduce cooling drag. In January 1925 a Mk III, J7148, was fitted with a Jaguar II and a tightly-fitting cowling, with circular holes ahead of the cylinders. Needless to say, cooling problems ensued, and although an extra 5 mph was achieved, this was at the expense of extra weight and almost total inaccessibility of the engine, which could

only be reached after completely dismantling the cowling – it did not find favour.

Another Mk IIIA, J8627, was fitted with a geared and supercharged Jaguar VIII with a Townend ring cowling in January 1929. Higher crankshaft rpm, together with the supercharger, enabled the engine to maintain its power up to 15,000 ft and, at this height, the Siskin IIIB was 20 mph faster than the IIIA at 164 mph. Its rate of climb was improved as well, reaching this altitude in just over 11 minutes, some two minutes less than the IIIA. The prototype was J8627, but it did not go into production.

The general layout of the two-seat fuselage of the Siskin II led to a two-seat trainer version of the Mk III, known as the IIIDC (Dual Control). Almost 80 were built, powered by Jaguar IIIs, and some of this number were converted single-seaters. These were used by civilian flying schools as well as by RAF training units. Mention must also be made of the Siskin IV and V, which reverted in outline to the single-seat Mk II, except for the lower fin, and also went back to mixed construction with wooden wings and parallel struts. The Mk V was unsuccessful, although in 1925 export orders were initially obtained for a substantial number. Deliveries were at first

Above This Siskin IIIDC spent much of its service life with the RAF College at Cranwell, until it nosed over following a forced landing in June 1933

Below Siskin III J7002 was delivered to No 41 Sqn in January 1924 and subsequently saw service with Nos 19 and 111 Sqns before relegation to Nos 3 and 5 FTSs. It was finally taken off RAF charge in April 1933

Right No 43 Sqn Siskin IIIAs up from RAF Tangmere in August 1930 flying in echelon starboard, stepped up. Leading the formation in Siskin J8959 is the squadron's highly decorated CO, Sqn Ldr C N Lowe, MC, DFC, of tied aerobatic fame

frustrated by accidents, and finally cancelled. The single Mk IV was a clipped-wing racing variant of the Mk V. Early Armstrong Siddeley engines, to the disillusionment of historical researchers, had ill-defined mark numbers, resulting in a thoroughly confusing situation. Many could be supplied either supercharged or unsupercharged. To ensure even inlet distribution, they were always fanned (plain fan – PF, or geared fan – which gave a slight supercharge), with direct or geared propeller drive, any permutation being permissible and probable. The fan was driven directly by the crankshaft to ensure even mixture distribution to the induction pipes of all cylinders. Specific mark numbers, from which the particular version could unquestionably be identified, came a little after the early Jaguar engines but even then not always with certainty.

PROLIFIC FIGHTER

With its angular lines, singularly cumbersome-looking stalky undercarriage and sesquiplane wing structure, the Siskin was arguably the least aesthetically appealing of all the RAF's inter-war biplane fighter family. Notwithstanding this, it was the most prolific until the emergence of the Gladiator era, with no less than 450 examples (including two-seat trainer variants) being delivered to the RAF between 1924 and 1930.

As with its predecessor, the Gloster Grebe, the Siskin's design origins could be traced to World War 1 when the Siddeley Deasy Company (predecessor of Armstrong Whitworth) created the Siddeley S.R.2, envisaged as a 14-cylinder two-row radial-engined fighter, but in the event making its much delayed appearance with the unsatisfactory ABC Dragonfly. It was in this form that the father of all RAF Siskins, the Siddeley Siskin C4541, appeared at the RAF Pageant at Hendon in June 1920. In March 1921 it was re-fitted with the Armstrong Siddeley Jaguar radial engine, which then became standardised in all subsequent Siskins, including the first with an all-metal airframe (J6583), which flew on 7 May 1923 and subsequently appeared, in the RAF's new silver doped finish, at the Hendon Air Show in June 1923.

Siskin J6583 still retained the parallel interplane struts and wide chord lower wing of the original S.R.2

design, and it was not until the three Siskins J6981, J6982 and J6983 were supplied to Air Ministry contract in 1923 that the classic sesquiplane layout made its appearance, with a very narrow chord lower wing and the vee interplane struts reminiscent of the Nieuport Scout of the 1916–18 period. The all-metal structure followed new Air Ministry orthodoxy of the period and enabled the Siskin to go down in history as the 'RAF's first all-metal fighter'.

In May 1924 what was to become an eight-year span of service with RAF fighter squadrons began at Northolt where No 41 Sqn started to replace its Snipes with the new Siskin III. The following month, a flight of Siskins was added to the Snipes and Grebes of No 111 Sqn at Duxford, which became fully equipped in January 1925. These were the only two first-line fighter squadrons to fly the original production version, the Siskin III, before going on to the defini-

Above Siskins appeared at all the 1927–1931 RAF Pageants at Hendon. In 1930, No 43 Sqn gave a display of tied-together formation aerobatics

Left Chequers were very popular with RAF fighter units in the 1920s and 30s, no less than three Siskin squadrons decorating their aircraft with a proliferation of squares. Parked amongst the hangars at Duxford in mid-1929, Siskin IIIA J9901 wears the pale blue and white markings of No 19 Sqn

tive Siskin IIIA in March 1927 and September 1926 respectively.

Siskin IIIs (distinguishable, of course, from the later IIIA by the deeper rudder and the auxiliary fin below the rear fuselage, as well as having noticeably greater dihedral on the top wing) made their first appearance before the public at the RAF Hendon Air Display in June 1925 when No 41 Sqn, sporting their new red bar squadron insignia, joined Grebes of Nos 25 and 32 Sqns in an exhibition of low-level bombing on an Army tank placed in the middle of the airfield. Three of No 41's pilots (Flt Lt H W Jones MC and Flg Offs R C Brading DFC and S Trower) then proceeded

to demonstrate the latest fighter tactics against a 'hostile formation'. The Siskin III had about a 20 mph speed advantage over the Fairey Fawn day bombers then in service.

In June 1926 the Siskins of No 41 Sqn were joined by those of No 111 Sqn at the RAF Hendon Display, and the public enjoyed some spectacular aerobatics by Flg Off A Rhind and Plt Off J D Armour of the latter squadron. This was the last occasion when the public saw Siskin IIIs at Hendon – at the 1927 show they had been superseded by Siskin IIIAs. No 111 Squadron's redoubtable Flg Off Rhind was featured once again, this time in a climb-to-height competition with one of

No 56 Sqn's Siskins. Unfortunately, the result of the fly-off has passed unrecorded.

Although by March 1927 the Siskin III was withdrawn as a first-line fighter, over 30 examples continued in service after being converted into two-seat dual control trainers, designated Siskin IIIDCs. The prototype (J7000), had first flown on 31 October 1924, and by 1926/27 the two-seaters were being issued both to Siskin IIIA fighter squadrons (each of which held a few DCs on strength) and to the FTSs and Cranwell College. The converted aircraft were supplemented by a production run of 47 new-build Siskin IIIDCs in 1928/29. First off the line was J9190, which flew on 7 June 1928 and the last to be delivered was J9236 in

Below Photograph of Siskin III J7148, showing the experimental cowlings enclosing the Jaguar II radial engine, which offered little speed improvement

Left Totally devoid of unit markings a factory-fresh Siskin IIIA returns from a pre-delivery test flight. This aeroplane was built as part of the 52-strong batch constructed at Vickers

June 1929. Thus it came about that the Siskin's period of service with the RAF was extended for some years after the last single-seat fighter had left the squadrons, and as late as the autumn of 1933, some were still to be seen flying with No 5 FTS at Sealand, and observed by the author (as a schoolboy spotter!) cavorting over the Cheshire countryside.

'OLD GENTLEMAN'S AEROPLANE'

John Nesbitt-Dufort DSO in his captivating book *Open Cockpit* (Speed and Sports Publications, 1970) provided some interesting comments about the Siskin IIIDC, describing it as 'an old gentleman's aeroplane to fly', fully aerobatic and with no vices, though the instructor's (ie rear) cockpit was the draughtiest he could ever remember. Possibly because of the extended tailskid, it was easier to make a three-point landing which, on the Siskin IIIA, was many a pilot's undoing, resulting in countless nose-over crashes and embarrassing photographs.

The Siskin IIIA's arrival in service with No 111 Sqn at Duxford in September 1926 opened a new phase in which the type was to become the predominant fighter of the RAF, equipping, at its zenith in the summer of 1929, no less than ten squadrons. By the summer of 1932 they had all been replaced by Bulldogs and Furies, with the exception of No 56 Sqn at North Weald, which retained Siskins until October 1932.

During its long career with the fighter squadrons the Siskin was flown by some remarkable personalities. Air Commodore Sir Frank Whittle, the world-famous jet engine pioneer, was reported disqualified, when a young pilot officer at Cranwell, from winning

the top flying prize (which he would have added to his Abdy Gerrard Fellowes Memorial Prize for Aeronautical Sciences) by including in his spirited aerobatic display a bunt (outside loop) then considered unsafe in a Siskin. Lord Douglas of Kirtleside (who during his distinguished RAF career became AOC Fighter Command and Chief of the Air Staff), as a young wing commander and station commander at North Weald, led a brilliant wing formation drill by Siskins of No 56 Sqn (North Weald) and Nos 19 and 29 Sqns (Duxford)

Right A Cranfield instructor's worst nightmare! No, just Nos 1, 25 and 43 Sqns performing a 'follow my leader' routine at Hendon in June 1929. No less than 27 Siskins participated in this little free for all!

Below Wonderful period photograph of the extremely delicate looking Siddeley-Deasy S.R.2 Siskin

at the 1929 Hendon Air Display. This item was known as 'Threading the Needle' and entailed No 56's Siskins and their leader diving through a circle of tail-chasing Siskins of Nos 29 and 19 Sqns.

During that same June of 1929, spectators were treated to the sight of 27 Siskins of No 3 Wing taking off in formation. They belonged to Nos 1, 25 and 43 Sqns, later in the 1930s to become the elite Fury interceptor units. The previous year, in 1928, No 1 Sqn's Siskins had joined No 111's, and Grebes from No 32, in a scramble interception of D.H.9As from the Auxiliary No 605 Sqn. At this period No 1 Sqn was commanded by the well-remembered Sqn Ldr Eustace Grenfell who flew J8834.

In the 1920s it was considered modish for senior RAF officers to have their personal aircraft vividly painted in some non-standard scheme, and this certainly added a theatrical touch to their tours of inspection. One such case was that of Air Commodore C R Samson (earlier of RNAS fame), who as AOC No 6 Group used all-white Siskin J7171 to visit fighter stations at Biggin Hill, Northolt, Hawkinge and Kenley. Another great character was Sqn Ldr H M 'Daddy' Probyn DSO who, when commanding No 25 Sqn at Hawkinge, was known to take photographs of his Siskins whilst flying his private Westland Widgeon light monoplane.

However, for outstanding work by a Siskin squadron commander, honours must go to Sqn Ldr C N Lowe, MC, DFC. He inspired No 43 Sqn to become the world's first tied-together aerobatic team. Headed by Lowe in his famous and much-photographed J8959, the nine Siskins flew as three flights of three aircraft tied together by cotton cords. They performed formation loops with ease, keeping tight and accurate even in bumpy air conditions, and usually climaxed the show with a 'Prince of Wales feathers' which finally broke the cords. They were the undoubted stars at the 1930 RAF Hendon Display, and the precursors of the long line of RAF formation teams culminating in today's world-renowned Red Arrows.

The Hendon Display programme for 1931 registered the Siskin's final appearance, represented by Nos 41 and 56 Sqns. The limelight had shifted to the new Bulldogs, which by then had four squadrons to display and, of course, the glamorous new Hawker Furies of No 43 Sqn.

Although first and foremost a home defence fighter, the Siskin saw some service abroad in small numbers. Tropical trials were conducted in India and J7157 (converted to IIIA) went to Nos 5 and 20 Sqns, the former also using the converted IIIA J7176. These

Below Siskin III J7148 was first flown in May 1924 and, following tests with the A&AEE fitted with enclosed cowlings, was later converted into a dual-control trainer. It was subsequently written off in January 1928

trials took place at Kohat, Risalpur and Lahore during 1927–28 and the Siskins were eventually returned to England for normal service. There were also tropical trials in Egypt at No 4 FTS with Siskins J7178 and J7179, both Mk IIIs converted to Mk IIIAs.

PARACHUTES

Coincidental with the Siskin's period of service with the fighter squadrons was the standardisation of parachutes, which came in 1927, the search for higher operating altitudes which resulted in supercharged engines replacing the normally aspirated Jaguars, and the necessity of providing new (and rather unreliable) heating flying suits for the pilots. No 111 Sqn had all its Siskins re-engined with supercharged Jaguar IV engines (in place of Jaguar IIIs) in 1926 and subsequently became the first officially designated high altitude squadron in the RAF. It was also the first of the Siskin squadrons to indulge in night-flying, which was a rather hit or miss operation in those days with

the use of primitive flares. The heated flying suits were notable for their erratic functioning and, in one case at least, believed to have been the cause of a fatal accident. This resulted in the death of Sgt Pearce whose Siskin of No 25 Sqn unexpectedly fell away from a battle climb formation out of Hawkinge and crashed in a sports ground near Folkestone. The Court of Enquiry concluded that there had been a leak of carbon monoxide fumes from the Siskin's cockpit heating system.

Equipped for high altitude flying, the Siskin was well adapted for service with the Meteorological Flight at Duxford where it served for many years, using J8048, 8392, 8365, 8872, 8882 and 9895. In later years the work was taken over first by Gauntlets and later by Gladiators.

Naturally enough, Siskin squadrons made copious use of camera guns to record results during mock

Below A line-up of No 19 Sqn Siskin IIIAs – an Avro 504N may be seen in the background

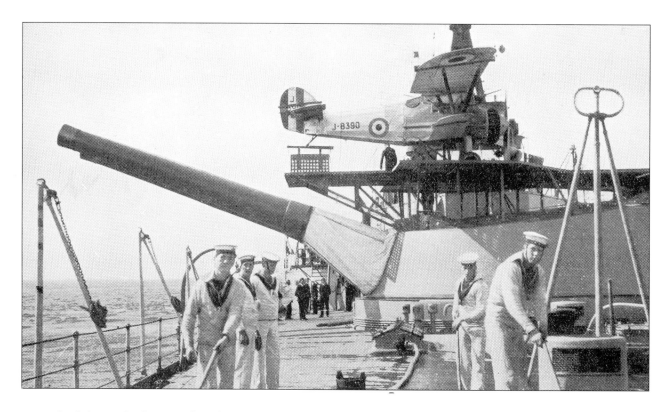

Above Siskin IIIA *J8390 pictured aboard the battle cruiser* HMS Repulse *during weathering tests in 1929. Built by Armstrong Whitworth themselves, this Siskin spent most of its life undertaking trials work*

dogfights and other exercises, but more unconventional uses were known! A possibly apocryphal story records that Siskins from No 25 Sqn made regular low-level sorties from Hawkinge to visit (and photograph) a private swimming pool just inland from Southampton Water which was liberally sprinkled with naked bathing beauties. The magic lantern shows which followed back at the base were no doubt well attended.

It cannot be denied that the Siskin, despite its long and widespread service as a front-line fighter and its popularity as an aerobatic mount, was notorious also for its propensity to accidents, particularly when landing and taxying. Mention has already been made of its habit of tipping over on its nose (especially the IIIA) when pilots were trying to execute three-point landings. The unfortunate victims of such all too frequent mishaps were readily identified afterwards by what became known as 'the Siskin nose', facial brusings inflicted by the projecting covers of the twin machine-guns which extended back into the cockpit above the instrument panel. This had its comic side, to be sure, but more serious was the tendency to 'put a wing in' when landing, especially in a cross-wind. This caused many fatalities and resulted in small protective skids being fitted beneath the lower wing tips. Ground collisions were, in all probability, caused by the poor view forward when taxying due to the long nose and large radial engine.

Endeavours to improve the performance of the Siskin during service, mainly by supercharging the Jaguar as previously mentioned, resulted in the Siskin IIIB (J8627), which in its final form, with a 480 hp Jaguar VIII made its first flight on 25 October 1928. From January to May of 1929 it was given extensive tests with No 22 Sqn by the A&AEE at Mantlesham Heath. Fitted with a Townend ring (a narrow-chord cowling over the engine), it had a distinctly 'new look' and made its appearance as No 4 in the New Types Park at the Hendon Air Display in June 1930. Despite having a 20 mph speed advantage over the standard Siskin IIIA, and a much better rate of climb, it did not find favour with the Martlesham pilots and any hopes entertained by its makers that further production orders might result were rapidly dissipated with the successful introduction of the new Bristol Bulldog.

With a production total for the RAF of 450, the Siskin finally ceased manufacture in 1930. In 1931 there were still 179 on the RAF inventory (142 IIIA and 37 IIIDC), but by the autumn of 1932 they finally left first-line service and only the DC trainers remained until at last disappearing with the standardisation of the Hart Trainer at FTSs.

Manufacture of the Siskin had been widely dispersed throughout the aircraft industry, and production details are tabled below:

Siskin Production for the RAF

Siskin III (64)	J6981–6983
	J6998–7003
	J7145–7181
	J7549–7554
	J7758–7764
	J7820–7822
Siskin IIIDC (47)	J9190–9236
Siskin IIIA (340)	
A.W.-built (88)	J8048–8060
	J8381–8404
	J8428
	J8623–8672
Blackburn-built (42)	J8864–8905
Bristol-built (85)	J8822–8863
	J9304–9330
	J9897–9911
Gloster-built (74)	J8933–8974
	J9331–9352
	J9912–9921
Vickers-built (52)	J9353–9379
	J9872–9896

So far as is known, not a single Siskin survives in the world today, though it is believed that the RAF Museum may have two upper mainplanes in storage. The only other country to use the type was the Royal Canadian Air Force, which received 12, some of which survived until 1939 but none, unfortunately, were preserved for museum purposes.

Above *Two-seater on strength with No 4 FTS in Egypt*

Below *An anonymous Siskin IIIA two-seater*

Siskin Units in the RAF

Between 1924 and 1932, 10 first-line fighter squadrons flew the Siskin on Home Defence duties, plus one squadron which used dual-Siskins only as interim equipment whilst awaiting re-equipment with Bulldogs. Details are as follows:

No 1 Squadron *Tangmere, February 1927 to February 1932*

Markings: Two red bars, parallel ahead of the roundels on the fuselage and tapering aft. Parallel red bars between the roundels on the upper mainplane

Serials: J8054, 8058, 8059, 8635, 8637, 8638, 8639, 8640, 8630, 8632, 8634, 8626, 8629, 8659, 8660, 8667, 8826, 8829, 8834, 8859, 8861, 8936, 8939, 8943, 8947, 8959, 8961, 9341, 9887, 9892, 9909, 9920
Also used dual-control Siskins J7000, 9292

No 17 Squadron *Upavon, September 1928 to October 1929*

Markings: Parallel black zig-zag bars ahead of roundel on fuselage and between roundels on upper mainplanes

Serials: J8056, 8656, 8876, 8880, 9355, 9358, 9359
Also used dual-control Siskins J9197, 9200, 9232

No 19 Squadron *Duxford, March 1928 to September 1931*

Markings: Blue and white checks ahead of the roundel on the fuselage and between the roundels on the upper mainplanes

Serials: J8056, 8382, 8392, 8825, 8828, 8846, 8847, 8851, 8852, 8857, 8858, 8870, 8874, 8886, 8887, 8888, 8889, 8890, 8891, 8901, 9892, 9901, 9913
Also used dual-control Siskins J9193, 9197

These two illustrations are from Air Publication 1317, *the official RAF manual on the Siskin IIIA, issued in February 1928.* **Right** *The fuselage primary structure – note the unswept aft end.* **Right below** *The instrument panel, with cutouts at the top for the twin machine-guns*

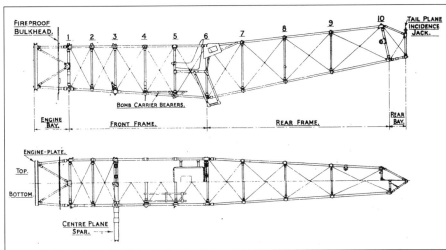

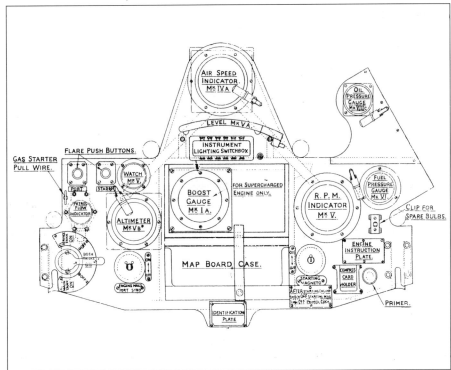

Left *The Siskin IIIB prototype. This improved version was not particularly liked by Martlesham Heath pilots and the variant was not put into production*

No 25 Squadron *Hawkinge, May 1929 to March 1932*

Markings: Two parallel black bars ahead of the roundel on the fuselage and between the roundels on the upper mainplanes

Serials: J8629, 8852, 8878, 8885, 8889, 8958, 9305, 9306, 9307, 9308, 9311, 9312, 9313, 9325, 9326, 9327, 9328, 9329, 9346, 9348, 9349, 9350, 9352, 9874
Also used dual-control Siskins J9192, 9218

No 29 Squadron *Duxford, March 1928 to June 1932*

Markings: Two parallel red bars with three red 'XXX' between, on fuselage ahead of roundels and also on the top mainplanes between the roundels with six red 'XXXXXX' between the bars

Serials: J8052, 8056, 8058, 8060, 8625, 8637, 8641, 8643, 8646, 8651, 8659, 8662, 8662, 8663, 8664, 8665, 8666, 8667, 8668, 8670, 8835, 8933, 8938, 8945, 8950, 8957, 8962, 8964, 9878, 9912, 9918, 9919, 9920
Also used dual-control Siskins J7554, 9194

No 32 Squadron *Kenley, April 1928 to January 1931*

Markings: Blue bar with three white diagonal inter-sections ahead of roundel and solid blue bar behind roundel, on fuselage. On upper mainplanes, a blue bar between the roundels with three white diagonal inter-sections

Serials: J8060, 8660, 8830, 8843, 8844, 8850, 8852, 8853, 8854, 8855, 8856, 8861, 8862, 8864, 8873, 8874, 8882, 8892, 8893, 8894, 8946, 8959, 8960, 8961, 8964, 8969, 9316, 9317, 9323, 9338, 9339, 9342, 9370, 9376, 9377
Also used dual-control Siskins J9190, 9193, 9210

No 41 Squadron *Northolt, Siskin III from May 1924 to March 1927 and Siskin IIIA from March 1927 to November 1931*

Markings: Broad red bar ahead of roundel only on early aircraft. On later aircraft the red bar was continued along the fuselage to the leading edge of the tailplane. Broad red band between the roundels on the upper mainplanes

Serials: (Siskin III) J6998, 6999, 7001, 7002, 7003, 7146, 7147, 7149, 7151, 7152, 7153, 7155, 7159, 7162, 7163, 7165, 7166, 7167, 7171, 7172, 7173, 7177, 7180, 7820, 7821, 7822

(Siskin IIIA) J7178, 7179, 8049, 8053, 8056, 8381, 8382, 8383, 8384, 8385, 8386, 8387, 8388, 8389, 8391, 8392, 8398, 8402, 8645, 8652, 8653, 8654, 8655, 8829, 8830, 8831, 8838, 8839, 8849, 8877, 8935, 8936, 8939, 8849, 8935, 8936, 8939, 8947, 8948, 8954, 8963, 8969, 9873, 9877, 9883, 9884, 9893, 9900, 9905, 9910
Also used dual-control Siskins J7148, 7149, 7180, 7549, 7552, 7554, 9203, 9232

No 43 Squadron *Tangmere, June 1928 to May 1931*

Markings: Black and white checks ahead of roundel on fuselage and between roundels on upper mainplanes

Serials: J8381, 8383, 8386, 8394, 8632, 8631, 8642, 8644, 8648, 8651, 8653, 8666, 8670, 8822, 8826, 8827, 8828, 8836, 8837, 8842, 8844, 8846, 8866, 8875, 8878, 8879, 8890, 8893, 8898, 8849, 8853, 8859, 8860, 8863, 8905, 8941, 8944, 8948, 8951, 8958, 8959, 8963, 8953, 8957, 8966, 8969, 9304, 9318, 9321, 9326, 9340, 9341, 9362, 9365, 9369, 9358, 9359, 9375
Also used dual-control Siskins J7169, 7173, 7820, 7821, 9201, 9211

No 54 Squadron *Hornchurch, January 1930 to October 1930*

Markings: This newly re-formed squadron was scheduled to receive Bulldogs but owing to a delay made temporary use of Siskin IIIDC aircraft. There is no evidence that they employed the yellow bar insignia later used by Bulldogs

Serials: (Siskin IIIDC) J7145, 7146, 7156, 9197, 9198, 9201, 9229

Left Pilot of a No 56 Sqn Siskin IIIA looks down at his instruments to check that the fuel pressure and boost gauges are working prior to taxying out for take-off

No 56 Squadron *North Weald, September 1927 to October 1932*

Markings: Red and white checks ahead of roundel on fuselage and across the upper mainplanes between the roundels

Serials: J8382, 8392, 8393, 8400, 8401, 8623, 8624, 8627, 8628, 8633, 8647, 8648, 8649, 8661, 8641, 8832, 8833, 8836, 8933, 8937, 8944, 8948, 8949, 8952, 8965, 8971, 8973, 9310, 9312, 9875, 9878, 9879, 9890, 9891, 9895, 9921
Also used dual-control Siskins J7169, 7170, 9192, 9197

No 111 Squadron *Duxford, Siskin III from June 1924 to November 1926 and Siskin IIIA from September 1926 to February 1931*

Markings: On the initial batch of Siskin IIIs a broad black bar appeared ahead of the roundel only on the fuselage, but on later Siskin IIIs this was changed to a narrower black bar which ran the entire length of the fuselage to the stern-post. Also black bar between the roundels on upper mainplane. On Siskin IIIAs the fuselage bar was noticeably wider than on the earlier Siskin IIIs

Serials: (Siskin III) J6998, 7001, 7002, 7146, 7152, 7153, 7154, 7155, 7156, 7157, 7158, 7161, 7164, 7168, 7181
(Siskin IIIA) J8048, 8049, 8050, 8051, 8052, 8053, 8054, 8055, 8056, 8057, 8058, 8059, 8060, 8397, 8398, 8626, 8636, 8651, 8663, 8861, 8862, 8867, 8893, 8896, 9322, 9872, 9917
Also used dual-control Siskins J7150, 7180, 7549, 7552, 7553, 9193, 9198, 9229

Flying Training
The dual control Siskin IIIDC, in addition to being used by first-line fighter squadrons, saw widespread service with the RAF's flying training units where they were supplemented by single-seat Siskins (IIIs and IIIAs) as detailed below:

RAF College, Cranwell
(Siskin IIIDC) J7149, 7153, 7154, 7156, 7549, 7550, 7763, 9191, 9194, 9195, 9203, 9209, 9214, 9215, 9216, 9218, 9219
(Siskin III) J7174, 7175
(Siskin IIIA) J7176, 8434, 8628, 8842, 8845, 8848, 8883, 9305, 9314, 9316, 9323, 9364, 9365, 9366, 9367, 9371

Central Flying School, Wittering
(Siskin IIIDC) J7150, 7170, 7171, 9193, 9236
(Siskin IIIA) J8392, 8855, 8837, 8869, 8886, 8905, 8955, 8965, 9320, 9322, 9332, 9355, 9357, 9360, 9361, 9365, 9378, 9379

No 1 FTS Netheravon
(Siskin (IIIDC) J7158

No 2 FTS Digby
(Siskin IIIDC) J9236
(Siskin IIIA) J8383, 8898, 8942, 9343, 9379

No 3 FTS Spittlegate
(Siskin IIIDC) J7002, 7146, 7149, 7161, 7170, 7762, 7764, 9190, 9201, 9212, 9219, 9224, 9225, 9226, 9228, 9229, 9232, 9235
(Siskin IIIA) J8649, 8867, 8884, 8894, 8898, 8838, 8839, 8858, 8935, 8942, 8964, 9304, 9310, 9312, 9313, 9321, 9324, 9326, 9327, 9329, 9332, 9335, 9336, 9339, 9370, 9378, 9379, 9882

No 4 FTS Egypt
(Siskin IIIA) JR8659, J7178, 7179

No 5 FTS Sealand
(Siskin IIIDC) J7002, 7003, 7149, 7156, 7157, 7158, 7161, 7162, 7173, 7551, 7552, 7762, 7764, 9198, 9207, 9213, 9216, 9217, 9220, 9221, 9222, 9223, 9225, 9228, 9231, 9233, 9234
(Siskin III) J7162
(Siskin IIIA) J7177, 7178, 8051, 8386, 8629, 8823, 8824, 8825, 8842, 8845, 8847, 8853, 8856, 8858, 8859, 8959, 9339, 9340, 9356, 9368, 9373, 9374, 9920

Armament and Gunnery School
J7148, 8381, 8871, 9370

Training Base Leuchars
J7821, 9198

Armstrong Whitworth Siskin IIIA data

Engine: Armstrong Siddeley Jaguar IV, 14-cylinder direct drive, supercharged; 385 hp at normal 1700 rpm; 420 hp at maximum 1870 rpm

Dimensions

Span	33 ft 2 in
Length	25 ft 4 in
Wing Area	293 ft²

Weights

Loaded	3012 lbs
Empty	2061 lbs

Performance

Maximum speed	143 mph at sea level
	153 mph at 10,000 ft
Time to 20,000 ft	17 min
Service Ceiling	27,100 ft
Endurance	1.2 hr full throttle

Armament: Two fixed 0.303 in Vickers Mk II synchronized machine guns, using Constantinesco interrupter gear, with 600 rounds per gun, four 20 lb Cooper bombs

THE HAWKER WOODCOCK

THE ARMISTICE OF 11 November 1918 at the end of the Great War left Britain and the Allies in a state of shock. The subsequent drastic reduction of the RAF and curtailment of its capacity for both attack and defence, fortunately did not last for very long. The wholesale disposal and destruction of a large number (22,640) of redundant and largely outdated wartime aircraft in fact came as something of a blessing in disguise, making way for a new generation of aircraft and engines. A reappraisal of Britain's defence requirements was needed to clarify the situation and it took nearly two years for the initial results to appear. In the meantime, the RAF had to make do with the best of the few remaining aircraft at their disposal. A

series of requirements had been made known to industry by the Government at the end of the war for new types of aircraft appropriate to particular operational tasks.

The Directorate of Requirements of the Air Ministry issued a list of over 20 basic categories of military aircraft. These were mostly very brief and sketchy but, in the desperate competition for the scant orders forthcoming, it became necessary to specify the requirements much more narrowly and in far greater depth. The subsequent official Air Ministry Specifications began to be issued, starting in 1920, numbered and classified, according to the year of issue and often prefixed by a letter indicating the category and

Left Up on a trestle outside the squadron hangar at Upavon in Wiltshire, this pugnacious looking Woodcock wears the distinctive black zig-zags of No 17 Sqn on its ample fuselage

Above A Flight *photograph of Hawker Woodcock Mk II J7962 being demonstrated for the Press at Brooklands on 26 March 1926. This aircraft later served with No 2 Sqn and was based at RAF Kenley*

purpose of the specification. Needless to say, the aircraft submitted for Air Ministry approval under the specifications were direct successors to the mostly tried and trusted types of aircraft with which the RAF had found itself equipped upon its formation on 1 April 1918, and did not differ in any marked degree from their predecessors.

Wood, being cheap and plentiful, was the principal material used in their construction. Engines were, however, in an increasingly competitive phase of their development. The air-cooled rotary had just about reached its zenith in terms of power output, and the

noisy radial was about to make its presence heard and felt. The battle to the death between Armstrong Siddeley and Bristol was engaged. Sopwith, the great aircraft building company in Kingston-on-Thames, was fatally hit by a combination of the recession and the lack of a credible government policy towards aviation, and went into receivership in 1920. Thanks to careful and efficient management, the Treasury and creditors were paid in full and, later in the same year, what had been the Sopwith Aviation Company re-emerged from the foreseen impending calamity as the HG Hawker Engineering Company.

An even worse but quite unforeseeable calamity occurred on 12 July 1921 when Harry Hawker, the chief pilot and a director in whose name the new company was formed, was killed in a crash while practising for that year's Aerial Derby in the Nieuport Goshawk. His name, embodied for decades in the title of the great line of aircraft with which the RAF and many other fighting services throughout the world were to be equipped, was to be his memorial. As suggested above, the fledgling post-war aircraft industry was issued with pathetically small crumbs in the form of Air Ministry orders for military prototypes. The H G Hawker Engineering Company appointed Capt Bertram Thomson as chief designer in 1922. In the same year, the Air Ministry issued Specification 25/22 for a single-seater night-fighting aeroplane. For obvious reasons, such a machine needed to have good climbing ability as an interceptor and, above all, good handling qualities.

Hawker's entry (its first fighter design) was called 'Woodcock'. It was a somewhat clumsy, two-bay biplane, powered by a 358 hp Armstrong Siddeley Jaguar II 14-cylinder radial, its name seeming a little inappropriate by comparison with the nimble flight of the bird, although its speed and rate of climb was an advance on that of the wartime fighters preceding it. Although the design had fairly small ailerons, these were integrated with drooping full-span Fairey-like trailing edges for use as landing flaps. Three Wood-cocks were laid down initially, J6987–9. The first, J6987, was flown by F P Raynham late in 1923, the actual date (probably in July) seems to have been unrecorded.

SPINNING PROBLEMS

The Woodcock arrived at the Aeroplane and Armament Experimental Establishment at Martlesham Heath on 14 August and was immediately declared unfit for spinning because of its completely ineffective rudder. An inadvertent spin, especially at night, was naturally to be avoided. Further, it had a strong tendency to wing flutter at high speeds and the aileron control was excessively heavy. Nevertheless, it was easy to maintain and the pilot's view was excellent. It was returned to the makers for major modifications the following month. The situation resulted in Capt Thomson resigning from the company, to be replaced as chief designer by George Carter, formerly chief draughtsman with Sopwith (later, to become the chief designer of the Gloster Aircraft Company after H P

Folland left to form his own firm). Carter's first job then, was the redesigning of the Woodcock, following which it was to emerge with single-bay wings of greater chord but shorter span, narrow-chord ailerons, the elimination of the connected flaps, and a revised vertical tail (the first of three such alterations) and a 380 hp nine-cylinder Bristol Jupiter IV. Thus modified, it went to the RAE at Farnborough in November 1924, prior to entering squadron service.

Two other Woodcock prototypes, J6988 and J6989, were ordered under separate contracts. The latter was (as a private venture) an all-metal variant and, in the

Above A photograph of the first prototype Hawker Woodcock J6987, fitted with its third fin and rudder. Note too the addition of tailplane struts – the elevator controls were now within the fuselage

event, emerged in a greatly different form and was clearly no longer a Woodcock. In outline, it cast a shadow forward to the Fury, except that it was powered by a 455 hp Bristol Jupiter VI, and in 1925 it was officially renamed the Heron. The second Woodcock, J6988, with a Jupiter IV, was the definitive version. It was built as a Mk II, the precursor of an

Right Hawker Woodcock prototype J6987 with its original fin and second, enlarged, rudder. It was re-engined with a Jupiter IV, and later rebuilt to production standard and issued to No 3 Sqn

Left The second prototype Hawker Woodcock, J6988, with the number '2' painted on the fuselage for the 1924 RAF Hendon display. Note the machine-gun located below the cockpit – another was installed on the port side

initial contract for ten to revised Spec 3/24. First flown in August 1923, it remained at Hawker's factory at Brooklands for six months undergoing testing, during which time problems with the engine were tackled. Icing of the valve gear was encountered and an attempt to cure this was made by encasing the cylinders individually with 'helmets', each having an outlet through which the temperature could be controlled. After appearing in the new types park at the RAF Pageant at Hendon in June 1924 as 'No 2', it went to Martlesham for night fighter trials.

The problems regarding the fin and rudder and lack of directional control persisted and the flutter problem was not entirely eliminated, this being echoed in subsequent service when there were cases of wing spar failures. The Woodcock was back at Martlesham in November for armament trials. Meanwhile, icing problems were overcome partly by the introduction of the Bristol exhaust collector ring which was soon to become so familiar on the Jupiter, resulting in the helmets being removed. The Woodcock was finally accepted for service as a night-fighter and, as such, was a well-liked aeroplane for night flying, having the remarkably slow stalling speed of 48 mph. The Woodcock was constructed of wood, with metal fittings and steel bracing. The fuselage was built in three portions and was in the classic form established since before the Great War.

The engine and its mounting was attached directly to the front fuselage. This was a parallel-sided, square-section structure of ash longerons and spruce struts, and contained the fuel and oil tanks. It also contained the pilot's cockpit, which had a special bucket-type seat (adjustable to four positions) for an Irving-type parachute, one of the first to be so provided in the RAF. The lower longerons were slightly bowed downward to accommodate the lower wing root-ends. The rear fuselage was bolted to the front portion and

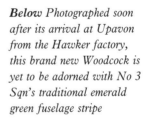

Right A *classic* Flight *photograph taken of the prototype Woodcock Mk II at Brooklands on 26 March 1926*

Below Photographed soon *after its arrival at Upavon from the Hawker factory, this brand new Woodcock is yet to be adorned with No 3 Sqn's traditional emerald green fuselage stripe*

tapered straight to the vertical stern post, the whole structure being braced with swaged steel rods, which were sometimes referred to as 'wires'. The fuselage was faired into an elliptical section, but with a flat bottom, by means of light ply formers and stringers, the whole being covered with fabric, except at each end, where detachable metal panels gave access to internal fittings.

The wood-framed and one-piece tailplane, of symmetrical section, was mounted on the upper longerons by means of two pivoting brackets attached to the front spars. The tailplane's rear spar was attached to a screw jack, providing variable incidence of $+/-3°$ and, thereby, longitudinal trim by means of a cockpit control. The fin, which was braced to the tailplane was of similar construction and fabric covered, as were the

Above A trio of Hawker Woodcocks from No 3 Sqn take off from Upavon. The squadron flew Woodcock IIs from July 1925 until September 1928, when they were superseded by Gloster Gamecocks

rudder and elevators. Pivoted just ahead of the stern-post, the steel-shod pivoting tail skid was sprung by rubber shock cord.

The big Jupiter radial engine was mounted in the normal manner on a triangulated steel-tube structure, which was in turn bolted to the front wooden portion of the fuselage and incorporated a fire-proof bulkhead. The complete engine mounting was attached to the front fuselage, via special ball and socket joints, to each of the four longerons. The 55 gal fuel and 6 gal oil tanks were mounted immediately aft of the engine. An oil cooler was located below the fuselage. From the port exhaust pipe, a branch led through the fuselage to the carburettor, warming the air intake (thus reducing the risk of icing) and discharging on the starboard side. In an open cockpit, carbon monoxide poisoning seems to have been an acceptable risk.

The wire-braced centre-section of four struts was mounted on the upper longerons. The upper wings, or mainplanes as they were then known, were of wood construction and fabric covered. The bracing was normal and incorporated duplicated lift wires. Unlike the Woodcock I, the Woodcock II had a single pair of inter-plane struts and the usual wire-bracing between the wings. Both the upper and lower wings had a

Above The cowled Bristol Jupiter Mk IV radial engine of the second Woodcock prototype, J6988

dihedral of 2° 30', with 2° of incidence. With a 2° parallel sweepback and dihedral, a stagger of 4 in was maintained throughout. Each pair of ailerons was differentially operated by cranks and linked by a single strut, the upward-moving unit travelling slightly farther than the downward-moving pair. The lower wings, of similar construction, were attached to short stubs which projected a few inches outboard from the fuselage sides. The stubs were extensions of the first and third lower cross-members of the front fuselage, to which were attached the main wing spars.

The outer ends of the front spar stubs also served as attachment points for the undercarriage compression legs, residual loads being transferred, via short adjustable steel struts inclined inwards, to the middle of the first vertical frame of the fuselage structure. Wire cross-braced radius rods were attached to fuselage frame 3 at the longerons and connected with the axle ends. As every part of the undercarriage was subjected to movement, all components were pin-jointed together and, of course, greased. This cross-axle oleo

Left J7974 spent most of its life alternating between Hawker, the RAE, the A&AEE and No 3 Sqn – its career ended in 1928 after spar failure. Here, the Woodcock was fitted with slats, and judging by its overall finish had seen little service up to this point in its brief history

undercarriage absorbed landing shocks through rubber buffers and oil dampers, and is an example of how even the simplest-looking structure can, upon examination, be quite involved.

In those days, it was common to find that the most vertical, shock-absorbing leg of an undercarriage was somewhat thicker than the other struts. In the case of the Hawker Woodcock, within this thickened external fairing was a pair of stacks of rubber washers, $4\frac{5}{8}$ in deep, each washer being separated from the next by a duralumin disc. Between these two stacks was a telescopic pair of tubes, partly filled with oil and connected through valves by an oil channel. The sudden load applied on taxying or landing to the telescopic struts on both sides of the aeroplane compressed the rubber buffers. The vertical movement of the strut opened the internal valves, forcing oil to travel from one chamber to the other. After the load

Below An unmarked Woodcock sits quietly between flights. The unusual siting by Hawker's of the aircraft's twin .303s is clearly apparent in this view

had reached its maximum intensity and started to decrease (a maximum travel of 10 in being allowed for), the potential energy built up within the rubber buffers began to extend the leg to its normal length. The valve sequence was then reversed, the oil returning to its original chamber. The restricted passage between the chambers meant that this was relatively slow after the shock-absorbing effect of the buffers, so preventing a violent rebound.

ARMAMENT

Like other RAF fighters of the inter-war period, the Woodcock mounted two forward-firing Vickers rifle-calibre machine guns, synchronized to fire through the propeller disc. Unlike most such installations, however, these were mounted outside the fuselage, unfaired and unprotected from the airflow, although the drag effect was then relatively unimportant and the cocking levers were easily reached by the pilot from his seat.

Before the days of corporate conglomerates and

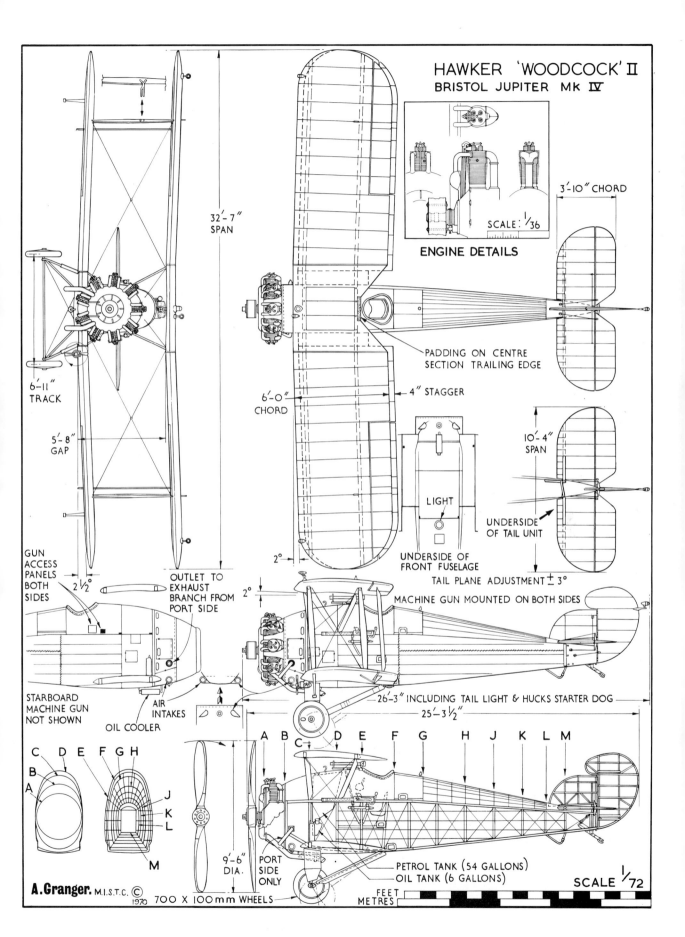

HAWKER 'WOODCOCK' II
BRISTOL JUPITER Mk IV

ENGINE DETAILS

SCALE 1/36

3'-10" CHORD

32'-7" SPAN

6'-11" TRACK

5'-8" GAP

6'-0" CHORD

4" STAGGER

PADDING ON CENTRE SECTION TRAILING EDGE

10'-4" SPAN

UNDERSIDE OF TAIL UNIT

LIGHT

2°

UNDERSIDE OF FRONT FUSELAGE

TAIL PLANE ADJUSTMENT ± 3°

GUN ACCESS PANELS BOTH SIDES

2½°

OUTLET TO EXHAUST BRANCH FROM PORT SIDE

2°

MACHINE GUN MOUNTED ON BOTH SIDES

STARBOARD MACHINE GUN NOT SHOWN

AIR INTAKES

OIL COOLER

26'-3" INCLUDING TAIL LIGHT & HUCKS STARTER DOG

25'-3½"

C D E F G H
B
A
J
K
L
M

A B C D E F G H J K L M

9'-6" DIA.

PORT SIDE ONLY

PETROL TANK (54 GALLONS)
OIL TANK (6 GALLONS)

A. Granger. M.I.S.T.C. ©
1970 700 X 100mm WHEELS

SCALE 1/72

FEET
METRES

Left A view of Woodcocks from No 17 Sqn flying at the Bristol Air Pageant at Filton on 22 June 1927. Nearest the camera is J8297; Flg Off Thorn is leading in J8300. Five days later J8300 caught fire on the ground at its Upavon base

the first in the RAF's history to identify the requirement from the design stage onwards. Full night flying equipment to the amended Specification 25/22 was installed, resulting in Woodcocks being the only RAF fighters specifically tasked for night fighting from 1925 to 1928, and the first to enter squadron service in such a role. Curiously enough, for the next ten years night fighting was merely a secondary role for day fighters such as the Siskin, Bulldog and Gauntlet, and specialised night fighter squadrons, with converted Blenheims, did not emerge until 1938.

June 1924 saw the first public appearance of a Woodcock at the RAF Display at Hendon when the second prototype (J6988) was exhibited as 'No 2' in the New Types Park. The other new fighters accompanying it were the prototype Bristol Bullfinch and Gloster Grebe. Woodcock J6988 was a very different aeroplane from the original prototype (J6987) which had first flown in 1923 and was characterized by two-bay wing struts like its family ancestor the Snipe. F P Raynham, a famous test pilot from the Sopwith days, had made the maiden flight when the powerplant was an Armstrong Siddeley Jaguar II; this was later exchanged for a 380 hp Bristol Jupiter IV, which thereafter became the standard installation. Designated Mk I, J6987 was later re-built as a standard Mk II and issued to No 3 Sqn early in 1927.

multi-nationals, the names and identities of British aircraft companies were usually associated with a single field of endeavour. That of the Hawker Company was long identified with high performance and glamorous fighter aircraft and it seems singular, therefore, that its first product in this category to enter regular service with the RAF should have been such a ponderous and oddly characterless aeroplane as the Woodcock.

There is an old saying in aviation circles that if an aeroplane looks right, then it is right. It will come as little surprise, therefore, to learn that the Woodcock was never renowned for its aerobatic prowess, and the type's poor manoeuvrability was criticised from the outset of its career – the prototype was even banned from spinning. Yet on the credit side it offered a good field of view from the cockpit, was easy to maintain and its solid, wide-track undercarriage made it easy to land. Some of these features no doubt emanated from the fact that it had been designed to a Specification of 1922 calling for a fighter suitable for night operations,

WOODCOCK MK II

The 1924 prototype (J6988), as seen at RAF Hendon, was designated Mk II and indeed was, in all essentials, similar to the production Woodcocks which were to enter squadron service the following year. The notable difference from the original design was the introduction of single bay wings. However, due to cooling troubles with the Jupiter engine, cylinder helmets were fitted but these had been discarded by the time Woodcocks entered service.

In August 1924, Woodcock J6988 was sent to

Left Maj P W S 'George' Bulman taking off in pouring rain from Croydon on 3 July 1925 on the first leg of the King's Cup race. Bulman was forced to land at Luton because of the bad weather and the aircraft was damaged on landing. This demonstration aircraft was previously J7515

Above Woodcock *J8299 before it was delivered to No 17 Sqn in April 1928*

Martlesham to undergo night fighter trials, and following their success the Air Ministry placed a production contract with Hawker's Kingston factory. The first production Woodcock II (J7512) flew on 21 April 1925 and an eventual total of 63 aircraft entered service with the RAF.

Four contracts were issued between August 1924 and September 1926 for Woodcock IIs serialled J7512–7517, J7592–7595, J7725–7737, J7783, J7960–7977 and J8292–8312. Because the serials J7592–7595 were issued in error and compromised airframe numbers already allocated to Gloster Grebes, these aircraft were re-serialled with the numbers J8313–8316. One Woodcock (J7515) was temporarily diverted to civil use with the registration G-EBMA, and in this guise competed in the annual King's Cup Air Race on 3 July 1925. It was damaged when it hit a tree during a forced landing in fog near Luton in Bedfordshire, but was later repaired, converted back to Service livery and delivered to No 3 Sqn on 28 July 1925.

Woodcocks first entered service with the RAF in May 1925 when they began to replace the veteran rotary-engined Sopwith Snipes of No 3 Sqn at Upavon

in Wiltshire. Nearly a year later, in March 1926, a second squadron (No 17) based at Hawkinge in Kent also relinquished its Snipes for Woodcocks. On 14 October 1926, No 17 Sqn moved to Upavon to join No 3. The purpose of this re-deployment was to concentrate night fighter defences where they could protect the industrial towns of the Midlands against bomber attacks, which the Air Ministry planners of the day imagined could only be mounted under the cover of darkness because of the long ranges involved. It has to be remembered that, in the 1920s, the only conceivable threat from an 'enemy' air force was from France.

Both the Woodcock squadrons were commanded by officers with distinguished records as fighter pilots in World War 1. Sqn Ldr J M Robb DFC, who commanded No 3 Sqn, had flown D.H.2s with No 32 Sqn and S.E.5As with No 92 Sqn over the Western Front and claimed seven victories. Later he went on to become the commander of the Air Defence of Great Britain (ADGB) in 1944 and retired in 1951 as Air Chief Marshal Sir James Robb KBE GCB DSO DFC.

Left No 17 Sqn trio perform another precision fly by at Filton during the Bristol Air Pageant. Appropriately, the lead Woodcock streams a flight commander's pennant from its rudder

In May 1926 Robb led a formation of Woodcocks on a night fly-past at the Birmingham Torchlight Tattoo. By all accounts, this was a spectacular occasion, as each of the Woodcocks was illuminated by about 80 light bulbs fitted to the mainplanes.

The other wartime ace associated with the Woodcock's history was Sqn Ldr John Leacroft MC, who commanded No 17 Sqn. John Leacroft, who claimed 22 victories, had served over France with No 19 Sqn flying Spads. He went on to serve as a group captain in World War 2.

NO AEROBATICS

Unlike its contemporaries the Grebe and the Siskin, the Woodcock was no aerobatic aeroplane and, indeed, had suffered its share of main spar failures; it is perhaps for this reason that its squadrons exhibited only once at the renowned annual RAF Display at Hendon. This took place in 1928 and it was whilst practising for this event on 5 June that two Woodcocks were lost in an air collision. During a combined attack on a Hawker Horsley day bomber of No 11 Squadron from Netheravon, J7728 of No 3 Sqn was hit by J8316 from the same unit. This was the second time that Woodcocks had suffered such an accident since No 17 Sqn lost J7967 by fire when it collided with J7976 at Northolt in July 1927 during ADGB exercises.

Throughout its life the Woodcock had suffered from various structural shortcomings and its history contains many incidents involving such maladies as wing flutter, mainspar weakness and undercarriage collapse on rough surfaces, especially in the Hawkinge days. Sad to relate, therefore, that on 21 August 1928 all Woodcocks were grounded. They had already

disappeared from No 17 Sqn, where they had been superseded by Gloster Gamecocks in the previous January. The grounding instruction followed a series of accidents, the last one leading to the death of Flt Lt L H Browning of No 3 Sqn when wing failure occurred during gun firing over Holbeach Range whilst operating from the Armament Practice Camp at Sutton Bridge. By August 1928, No 3 Sqn was already scheduled to receive the new Bristol Bulldog, but owing to delays in production they received Gamecocks instead, these aircraft having been passed on by No 23 Sqn at Henlow and No 43 Sqn at Tangmere. By early September 1928 all the Woodcocks had gone.

Not many newsworthy incidents can be connected with the Woodcock but one story is worthy of note. On 2 June 1927, Woodcock J8295 of No 17 Squadron was loaned to the famous American airman, Col Charles Lindbergh, so that he could return to Paris from London by air shortly after his epic non-stop transatlantic flight in the Ryan monoplane *Spirit of St Louis*. Lindbergh's comments on his experience are not, so far as is known, recorded.

Apart from its equipment of Nos 3 and 17 Sqns, other Service use of the Woodcock included the issue of J8313 and J8314 to the station flight at RAF Duxford, J8308 and J8300 to the Home Aircraft Depot and J7733 to No 22 Sqn, the trials unit at Martlesham. One aircraft (J8312) was also sent overseas to Aboukir in Egypt for tropical trials. Also at Martlesham were J6988 for night fighter trials in August 1924, J7594 for similar experiments in August 1925 and the batch J7512 to 7517 inclusive. Woodcock J7517 and J7974 conducted tests with slotted wings but these were not adopted for regular service. From March to June 1926 a solitary Woodcock (J7727) was in service with No 4 Sqn, an Army Co-operation unit with Bristol Fighters based at Farnborough.

Despite the fact that the Woodcock was the least glamorous of all the RAF's inter-war fighters, and was little mourned when it passed from the scene, it shared in the colourful heraldry of its time and details of the squadron markings appear below.

Woodcock Units in the RAF

During the period May 1925 to August 1928, two first-line fighter squadrons were equipped with Woodcocks and details are as follows:

No 3 Squadron *Upavon, Wiltshire, from May 1925 to August 1928*

Markings: A single emerald green stripe in front of and behind the roundel on the fuselage, extending to the rudder post. Above the mainplanes, a single emerald green stripe extending from port to starboard roundel

Serials: J7512, 7513, 7514, 7515, 7517, 7725, 7726, 7727, 7728, 7729, 7730, 7731, 7732, 7733, 7734, 7735, 7736, 7737, 7783, 7962, 7963, 7974, 7974, 8292, 8293, 8294, 8298, 8302, 8303, 8304, 8305, 8316

No 17 Squadron *Hawkinge, Kent, from March 1926 to October 1926 and then Upavon, Wiltshire until January 1928*

Markings: Black parallel zig-zags along the fuselage sides, in front of and behind the roundel. These were repeated across the upper mainplane between the roundels

Serials: J7512, 7514, 7516, 7592, 7593, 7595, 7724, 7729, 7732, 7735, 7960, 7961, 6964, 7967, 7968, 7969, 7971, 7972, 7975, 7976, 7977, 8292, 8295, 8296, 8297, 8299, 8300, 8305, 8306, 8307, 8311

Hawker Woodcock II data

Engine: Bristol Jupiter IV, nine-cylinder, direct drive, unsupercharged, 380 hp

Dimensions

Span	32 ft 7.5 in
Length	25 ft 3.5 in
Height	10 ft 3 in
Wing Area	346 ft²

Weights

Loaded	3040 lbs
Empty	2080 lbs

Performance

Maximum Speed	143 mph at sea level
	138 mph at 10,000 ft
Time to 20,000 ft	28 min
Service Ceiling	21,500 ft
Endurance	3.5 hr

Armament: Two fixed 0.303 in Vickers Mk II synchronized machine guns, using Constantinesco interrupter gear, with 750 rounds per gun

Below *A line-up of No 17 Sqn Woodcocks. The zig-zag squadron markings were black; engine cowlings were dark grey*

THE GLOSTER GAMECOCK

THE GLOUCESTERSHIRE GAMECOCK prototype, J7497, first flew in February 1925, an obvious successor to the Grebe which had entered RAF service the previous year. It was designed by H P Folland, and was a logical continuation of the line of small, nimble single-seater fighters from that great designer's drawing board; the company was not renamed 'Gloster' until 11 December 1926. Folland had a reputation for very

advanced ideas in aerodynamics, the best-known example of his early work being the S.E.5 series, which he began at the Royal Aircraft Factory at Farnborough in 1915.

The early 1920s and the advent of the Bristol Jupiter and Armstrong Siddeley Jaguar radial engines, roughly comparable in power though not yet reliable, enabled Folland to develop further his ideas for fighter

Above The first prototype Gamecock, J7497, after
installation of a horn-balanced rudder

aircraft. Folland believed in combining high lift with
the highest possible speed as the most efficient interceptor fighter design.

Developed from the Grouse trainer, three single-
seat prototypes were ordered by the Air Ministry in
1923, the first being called, unpoetically, the 'Nighthawk (Thick-winged)'. Clearly bearing the Folland
imprint, the first of these became the prototype
Gloucestershire Grebe of 1923. Thus began the very
successful series of fighter biplanes for the RAF by the
Gloster Aircraft Co Ltd, a company which, under
Folland's design leadership (until he left to form his
own company in 1937), was to become one of the great
names in the British aircraft industry, and finally
merged with Sir W G Armstrong Whitworth Aircraft
Ltd in October 1961.

The Jaguar engine was not then a satisfactory
power unit and a more powerful Jaguar IV engine,
developing 400 hp, was substituted in August 1923.
The Jaguar, a two-row 14-cylinder engine, was both

Left Classic Flight *photograph of Flg Off Howard Saint
DSC, Gloster's chief test pilot, demonstrating Gloster
Gamecock II J7910 in February 1928*

heavy and complicated to maintain, and the early
versions were unreliable. The contemporary Bristol
Jupiter nine-cylinder engine was showing considerable
promise and, although somewhat greater in diameter
being a single-row engine, was simpler to service and
lighter. At the beginning of 1924, the Jupiter IV was
about to become available and the Air Ministry issued
Specification 37/23 for a fighter, initially to be called
the Grebe Mk II but, subsequently and more appropriately, the Gamecock. Three prototypes were
ordered, the first two having the 398 hp Jupiter IV and
the third, J7757, being powered by the 435 hp Jupiter
VI to Spec 18/25. This latter aircraft was to become the
prototype for the production Gamecock I.

While at Martlesham, the first prototype, J7497,
was tested with an experimental Jupiter IV with
variable valve timing which, with experiments involving propellers of various pitch and intake heating,
eventually gave a remarkable 500 hp at 1825 rpm.
Tests on controllability and manoeuvrability were
both good, with a 'uniformity of feel of lateral and
longitudinal controls'. Tested against a Siskin IIIA
and an ADC Martinsyde (both powered by Jaguars),
the Gamecock had a slightly greater radius of turn
than the Siskin, but compensated by a superior climb
on vertical turns. Changing from right to left vertical
turns was about the same as the Siskin. Flattening out

Left The same aircraft in its original form, with S.E.5a/Grebe-type rudder

from a steep dive required considerable pull and the machine sank bodily in the process. The elevator control was probably sufficiently powerful to break the machine if used too heavily. Modified elevators might improve the turning circle, provided that the quality of the existing controls was not upset.

The speed range was most satisfactory and good control was maintained at the lowest speed. Against the Martinsyde, the Gamecock proved superior in radius of turn, climb and ease of manoeuvre. Like its immediate antecedent, the Gamecock was a very small and compact aeroplane, its overall length being even shorter at 19 ft 8 in. The bulky Jupiter engine and short fuselage gave it a barrel-like appearance, resulting in a similar close-coupled and snub-nosed appearance to that of the Grebe. The prototype Gamecock, J7497, had a Grebe-type tail unit, with a straight-edged fin and unbalanced rudder.

SERVICE TRIALS

It made its first visit to Martlesham Heath on 20 February 1925 for performance trials. It was as prone to the same tail instability as the Grebe and was returned to Gloster at Hucclecote for modifications. Two months later, on 8 April, it was back at Martlesham. After visits back to Gloster and Bristol, it went to the RAE at Farnborough on 8 August. Although its

top speed of 150 mph at sea level when powered by a Jupiter IV hardly equalled that of the Grebe II, the Gamecock soon established itself, like its predecessor, as a very agile little fighter indeed. Its very agility became the cause for concern among squadron pilots because of a persistent tendency to wing-flutter. As on the Grebe, the upper wing, which had an overhang of nearly three feet, permitted too great an elasticity. The controls were also very light and sensitive and an unwary pilot who allowed flutter to develop could lose a wing. Another unwelcome similarity was its ferocious spin, which was timed at 50 rpm (300° per second) and could become stabilized and flat. The very short fuselage could blanket the tail, and engine torque tended to accentuate the reluctance to come out of a spin. The rudder of the production aeroplane was distinguished from the prototypes by its horn-balance, and the upper fin by its low aspect-ratio curved shape.

Following accidents attributed to wing failure, the Air Ministry instituted tests to ascertain possible remedial action. At Martlesham it was established that, with sensible handling, both the Grebe and Gamecock were very satisfactory aircraft and delightful in aerobatics. The Gamecock's aileron control was remarkable, and a 'falling-leaf' manoeuvre was frequently to be seen when a Gamecock pilot was at play. As a result of experiments, some aircraft were fitted with a pair of V-struts attached to the lower front spar, connecting to the two upper spars just beyond the mid-point of the aileron, thus providing stiffening to the outer panel at the expense of drag and appearance.

Right J7757 was the third prototype Gamecock and was powered by a 425 HP Juiter VI. It was last flown in December 1927

Left A standard Gamecock I was given the civil registration G-EBNT, registered to the Gloucestershire Aircraft Company and used as a demonstrator during 1926

Above Gamecock J7910 was used for dive and anti-flutter trials by the A&AEE during 1927 and was later converted to Mk II standard. It was powered by a 425 hp Jupiter VI radial

Right Flg Off Howard Saint DFC wrung the little Gamecock out for the benefit of Flight *during their photo session in the bleak winter of 1928*

Not all Grebe and Gamecock aircraft were thus fitted. The reason has been elusive but the answer seems to be the same as that found in the *Air Publication* relating to the Grebe and issued towards the end of its squadron service in November 1927. An *AP* published only four months later relating to the production Gamecock is not so specific, but there is no reason to suppose that the deduction would vary, since both structures were so nearly identical.

This 1° washout in all the outer wings which afflicted both the Gloster fighters is important if, as seems possible, the divergent oscillation or flutter was effectively cured by such a simple device and the ugly extra struts were no longer needed, thus restoring the original attractive outline. Neither the rigging diagrams of November 1927 nor March 1928 show any sign of them. It seems fair to conclude, therefore, that a simple but clever aerodynamic fix contributed to putting the matter right for both the Gloster Grebe and its successor, the Gamecock. In addition, there were anti-flutter experiments with parallel-chord upper ailerons which seem to have been inconclusive. At all events, to establish the Gamecock's strength, as well as the stability of the wing structure, Gloster's test

pilot, Howard Saint, made a full-throttle terminal velocity dive, recording 275 mph.

Though somewhat over-stressed, with stretched flying wires, the Gamecock and its intrepid pilot survived. The pilot's position in the Gamecock seemed so upright and exposed that he appeared to be standing up in the cockpit – this was characteristic of Service aeroplanes at the time – little protection seeming to be considered necessary, resulting in many contemporary pictures of pilots and gunners hunched against the cold and relying, hopefully, on electrically-heated suits. Despite this apparent defect, the A&AEE report on the Gamecock stated that the cockpit was comfortable and not draughty. Apart from the engine, the armament arrangements and of course

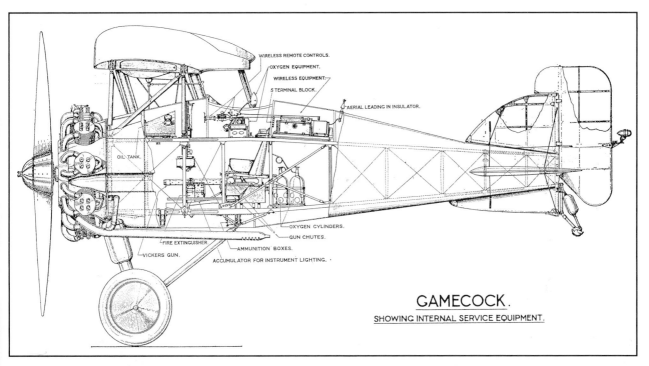

WIRELESS REMOTE CONTROLS.
OXYGEN EQUIPMENT.
WIRELESS EQUIPMENT.
5 TERMINAL BLOCK.
AERIAL LEADING IN INSULATOR.

OIL TANK.

OXYGEN CYLINDERS.
GUN CHUTES.
FIRE EXTINGUISHER.
AMMUNITION BOXES.
VICKERS GUN.
ACCUMULATOR FOR INSTRUMENT LIGHTING.

GAMECOCK.
SHOWING INTERNAL SERVICE EQUIPMENT.

the vertical tail, there were very few obvious external differences between the Grebe and Gamecock.

The construction was principally of spruce, except where loads were concentrated, and there ash or plywood were used. Its fuselage was a straightforward example of the cabinet-maker's craft. Four ash longerons were in one piece or made in two portions with an 18 in spliced joint. At the front, the longerons fitted into sockets in the engine bearer bulkhead. The front bulkhead comprised an outer, rectangular framework of angled mild steel plate surrounding a circular steel frame, which contained the nine holes to take the engine mounting bolts by which the steel tube engine-bearers were attached. The bottom corners of the outer frame had attachment points for the front lift

wires for the top main planes. Immediately aft of this frame was a fire-proof bulkhead of aluminium-faced asbestos, and behind this there was the 'Instrument Board' bulkhead. This comprised a frame, the upper part of which was of thick ply and carried the flying and engine instruments. Behind this was the multi-plywood frame which constituted the rear of the cockpit and carried the pilot's seat and harness.

The remainder of the fuselage was composed of glued and screwed vertical and cross-members of wire-braced spruce, with bolted steel fittings. To give a streamlined shape aft of the cockpit, elliptical plywood formers were built outside the basic box-shaped structure with light stringers attached. The Gamecock had its twin Vickers machine guns mounted half way down

each side of the fuselage, firing along troughs between the cylinders. They were mounted outside the fuselage frames but inside the overall contours, with only the air-cooled barrels showing. The two ammunition boxes lay end to end across the fuselage, the feed being outwards to each gun, cartridge and link chutes being provided to discharge them overboard.

TWIN FINS

At the tail end of the fuselage there were top and bottom fins. The lower fin had a spruce framework, covered with fabric and housed the two king posts which allowed the tailplane incidence to be adjusted and the sternpost, of ash, carried the tail plane rear

Right Maurice Piercey demonstrating Gamecock J7908 at Brockworth in March 1926. This aircraft was later delivered to No 43 Sqn, based at RAF Tangmere from April 1926 until June 1928

Left Duck! Doing his best North by North West *impression, the* Flight *photographer ducked and weaved as well as Cary Grant 30 years later, whilst Howard Saint buzzed around him in Gamecock II J7497. Could Hitchcock have been influenced by these amazing shots in the production phase of his 1959 thriller epic?*

spar and rudder hinges. The tailplane was adjustable for trimming and built in two portions, butt-jointed at the front spar. This was connected to the pilot's trim control which altered the incidence from $+5\frac{1}{2}°$ to $-2°$ by means of a coarse-threaded screw-jack, operated by a cable from the cockpit control lever. The rear spar was attached directly to the stern post, via a bracket, upon which it could pivot as the front spar was raised or lowered as the tailplane incidence was varied. The cruciform tail-assembly was wire-braced, mainly of spruce and fabric covered.

As the whole fuselage was covered with fabric (except the engine cowling and cockpit decking where aluminium and ply sheet were used), the method of covering the fuselage with fabric, a time-honoured skill, is worth recording. A bag was made of four strips sewn so that the seams lay approximately along the longerons. Holes were cut where there were projections and the edges were supported by soft leather. The smaller projections were marked off when the bag was fitted and the fabric attached round them. Where access to the interior was required, lacing was employed to hold these portions in position. When first fitted, certain edges were fastened by copper tacks and the fabric was stretched to lie evenly on the formers and stringers. When evenly tight, the rows of

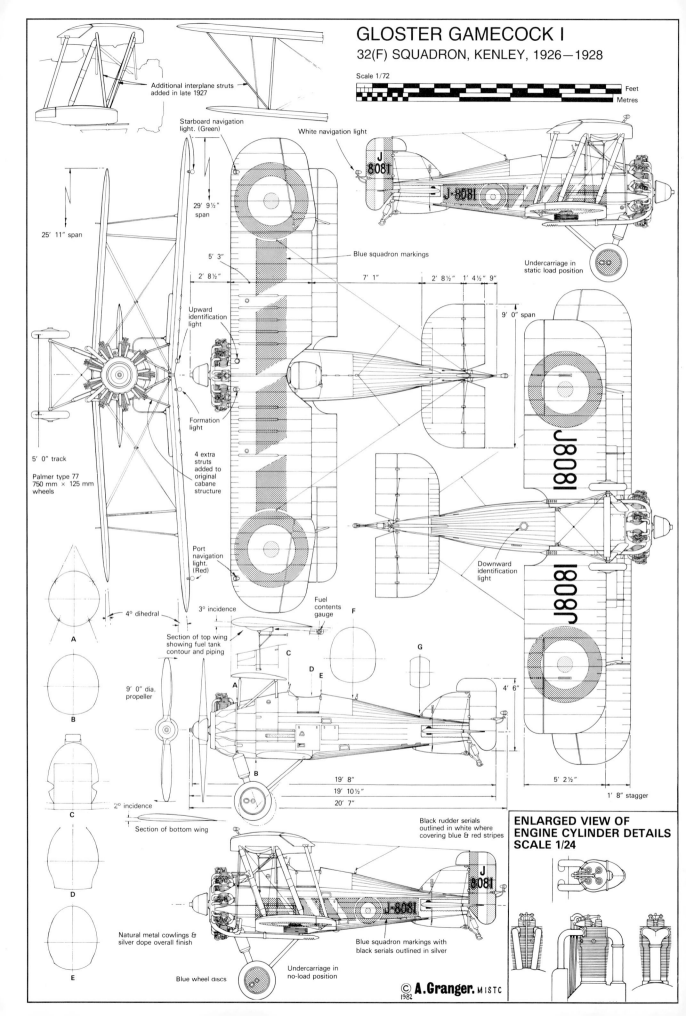

GLOSTER GAMECOCK I
32(F) SQUADRON, KENLEY, 1926—1928

Scale 1/72

Feet
Metres

Additional interplane struts added in late 1927

Starboard navigation light. (Green)

White navigation light

Blue squadron markings

J 8081

J-8081

Undercarriage in static load position

29' 9½" span

25' 11" span

5' 3"

2' 8½"

7' 1"

2' 8½" 1' 4½" 9"

9' 0" span

Upward identification light

Formation light

4 extra struts added to original cabane structure

Port navigation light. (Red)

Downward identification light

5' 0" track

Palmer type 77 750 mm × 125 mm wheels

J8081

J8081

4° dihedral

3° incidence

Fuel contents gauge

F

C

D E

G

4' 6"

9' 0" dia. propeller

Section of top wing showing fuel tank contour and piping

A

B

B

A

2° incidence

Section of bottom wing

19' 8"

19' 10½"

20' 7"

5' 2½"

1' 8" stagger

A

B

C

D

E

Natural metal cowlings & silver dope overall finish

Undercarriage in no-load position

Blue wheel discs

Black rudder serials outlined in white where covering blue & red stripes

J 8081

J-8081

Blue squadron markings with black serials outlined in silver

ENLARGED VIEW OF ENGINE CYLINDER DETAILS SCALE 1/24

© A. Granger. MISTC
1982

tacks were covered by fabric strips with frayed edges and doped in position, after which the whole covering was doped for shrinking and the fabric was also doped to the plywood decking around the cockpit.

The upper and lower wings were different in size, shape and span, as well as section and incidence, the only thing in common being a 4° dihedral. The lower planes were attached beneath the lower longerons with steel plate fittings. The spars were of spruce, spindled to I-section and the ribs were built up of spruce strip, the assembly being internally wire-braced with compression struts stabilizing each structure against the tension. The outer compression strut carried a lever for operating the aileron control. The upper wings were joined at their inner ends, there being no separate centre section. The wire-braced wing assembly was mounted on an inverted vee of streamline steel tubes connecting the front spar to the upper longerons behind the engine, while a pyramid of steel tube similarly connected the fuselage to the rear spar ahead of the cockpit. Two 30-gal fuel tanks were installed in the upper wings. One pair of hollow spruce interplane struts were fitted on each side, with incidence-bracing wires and an acorn where they crossed, and a connecting tube between the front and rear lift and anti-lift wires in each plane. All four wings were fabric-covered, except where local strengthening by $\frac{1}{8}$ in

Above Gamecock I *J8073 of No 32 Sqn, RAF Kenley, flown by Flg Off A H Montgomery in the Sir Philip Sassoon Cup at RAF Northolt on 26 May 1927*

plywood was required. There were ailerons on all four wings, mounted on false spars, and each pair was connected by a solid-spruce inter-aileron strut, the upper ailerons being operated in a push-pull manner by the lower units. As with the tail surfaces, the aileron controls were cable operated.

The Gamecock's undercarriage was of the wire-braced, cross axle type, the rear radius struts connecting to the lower wing rear spar attachments to the

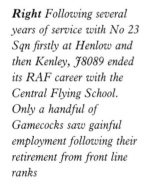

Right Following several years of service with No 23 Sqn firstly at Henlow and then Kenley, *J8089* ended its RAF career with the Central Flying School. Only a handful of Gamecocks saw gainful employment following their retirement from front line ranks

longerons. It was mounted on steel tube vee struts, with rubber energy-absorbing rubber washers and oleo shock-absorbers on the front struts, these being attached as mentioned before, to the engine. The oil damping, shock-absorbing device, as it was called, consisted of telescopic tubes and rubber buffers. The damper itself consisted of a valve and piston and the oleo leg was filled with oil. Older readers might, perhaps happily, recall *Air Ministry Technical Order No 111* of 1927 requiring it to be ' . . . oil, paraffin, 30 per cent and oil, castor, pure, 70 per cent'. The plain cross-axle was of high-tensile steel tube and there were no brakes, the wheels being of the wire type, with fabric disc coverings that were usually painted in flight colours (red for 'A' Flight, yellow for 'B' Flight and blue for 'C' Flight, with similar colours on spinners and occasionally even on elevators, until balance problems caused this custom to be stopped). The tail skid was steerable and rubber sprung.

Unlike its predecessor the Grebe, which was a noisy little aeroplane, the Gamecock had a distinctive and musical Bristol hum, with an exhaust collector ring

Above Guess who? Yes, that's right, it's Howard Saint once again! From this angle, the faired-in trough mounting for the starboard .303 Mk II Vickers is clearly exposed

fitted to the front of the engine, leading to two pipes below the lower wing.

The power output of the engine was controlled by two levers on the same pivot, one operating the throttle and the other the altitude control (in other words, varying the mixture with alteration in height). The Gamecock's Jupiter VI engine normally had fixed timing and a gated throttle, with the exception of some early engines, whose valve timing was adjustable. The standard armament was of twin Vickers machine guns, using the standard CC interrupter gear for firing through the propeller disc. They were fired by triggers within the ring at the top of the control column. The usual Aldis and ring and bead gun sights were provided, normally with the Aldis set over the centre line and the other to starboard, although they were interchangeable, in which case the windscreen was exchanged for one which allowed the Aldis sight to project through a gap in the glass. A light-series bomb carrier could be mounted beneath the fuselage, operated by a cable.

A wind-driven 12 volt 500 watt electrical generator was mounted below the starboard main plane, within the slipstream of the propeller. This could provide ignition, lighting, heating (for clothing) and ignition for the Holt wing-tip landing flares, while providing power for the radio, which was a quite effective HF T.25 transmitter and a R.31 receiver. Tuning was remotely controlled by a lever and a 'Send, Off and Receive' switch operated the equipment. The aerial extended from the top of the rear interplane struts to the top of the rudder post. From near the mid-point on either side, a lead-in was connected to a terminal on the top of the fuselage. In addition, two 500 litre oxygen bottles were mounted (like the radio) behind the pilot, with a control, pressure gauge and altitude device in the cockpit. Oxygen was led up a bayonet

Below No 43 Sqn Gamecock I J7908. Based at RAF Tangmere, this Gamecock remained with the squadron from April 1926 until June 1928

union through a 9 ft rubber tube to the pilot's mask. The pilot's instruments, mounted on a tidy panel, included an air speed indicator, altimeter, RPM counter, oil temperature and pressure gauges, an inclinometer (a lateral bubble level device) and a compass. A Pyrene-type fire extinguisher was also provided. The control column had the usual cord-bound spade grip, encircling twin gun-operating levers.

POOR ACCIDENT RATE

The tubby little Gamecock was something of a paradox among inter-war RAF fighters. Renowned for its aerobatic prowess it nevertheless had a poor accident record, killed a disproportionate number of its pilots and, in squadron service, was banned from certain manoeuvres altogether, notably the right-hand spin. Yet it remained a popular aeroplane and was undoubtedly a spectacular performer in the hands of a skilled and confident aerobatic pilot. Its snappy loops and rolls (including those in the vertical plane) were reportedly breathtaking to watch and it had a fair turn

Right The experimental Gamecock III J8047, with lengthened fuselage, enlarged fin and parallel-chord ailerons. J8047 later became G-ADIN and survived until May 1936, when it was written off at Sywell following an undercarriage collapse

Left Proudly wearing the highly coveted '1' in the New Types Park at the 1925 RAF Display at Hendon was Gamecock prototype number two J7756. In this fuzzy photograph, the aircraft is being refuelled by hand pump prior to the Gloster factory pilot performing his display

of speed as well, repeatedly defeating other contemporary fighters such as the Siskin in air racing events. There are those who claim that the performances of Gamecocks at the RAF Hendon Displays of its day were never quite equalled by its later and heavier successors.

What, then, were the accidents all about? The main problem was attributed to the dreaded wing flutter which had also plagued the Gamecock's predecessor, the Grebe, and the remedy, following the earlier days of its service, was the introduction of additional interplane struts in the form of a vee between the base of the existing forward strut and the upper mainplane below the overhang. This modification, introduced late in 1927, resulted in the pretty little Gamecock being named, rather unkindly, as 'Folland's Cock's Cradle'.

Spinning at 50 turns a minute

Originally from an RAE report comes the following alarming description of tests on flat-spinning by a Gamecock: 'To make a convincing demonstration, it was decided to use a Gamecock, a single-seater fighter, which although popular in the Royal Air Force, had a reputation for spinning fast and flat. Apart from its reputation, it had all the features which were known to lead to flat spins: a short, fat, round body . . . and a badly-shielded fin and rudder . . . It seemed necessary to establish that it really had a dangerous spin. The aeroplane was accordingly loaded to what was thought to be its safest condition and provided with a few recording instruments.

'The pilot for this flight was Flt Lt C E Maitland, and responsibility for the experiment lay mainly with S B Gates. Gates went out to the tarmac and watched Maitland climb to 15,000 ft with instruments to do a few turns of a spin and then recover. The spin started and, . . . watched from the tarmac with increasing anxiety as their number mounted, after no less than 40 turns the spin suddenly stopped. A few minutes later Maitland taxied in and gave a terse description of what must have been a most harrowing experience. After a turn or two the Gamecock had 'flicked' into a very fast and flat spin which had made him giddy and confused. He had immediately reversed the controls for recovery but this made no difference. The spin continued unabated (subsequent analysis showed a rotational speed of more than 50 rpm) and he had tried all the artifices he could think of – bursts of engine, rocking of the controls and so forth – without success. Eventually he had chanced to look down at his feet and been amazed to discover that he was holding the aeroplane INTO the spin with the rudder. He had then reversed the rudder and the aeroplane slowly stopped spinning. So beyond establishing that the Gamecock spun unpleasantly fast, the experiment proved nothing.

'Maitland at once volunteered to repeat it. After adding an instrument to record the rudder angle, spectators again repaired to the tarmac to watch another spin. This time Maitland completed 34 turns – the last 25 of them against his will. The instrument showed that there had been no mistake with the rudder this time and all were satisfied that they had a thoroughly dangerous spin to correct'.

For this courageous and useful test flight, Maitland was awarded the A.F.C.

(Report written by Prof A V Stephens FRAeS)

In addition to the flutter problems (which could lead to structural failure) and difficulties with spin recovery, the Gamecock could also be tricky to land, and altogether no less than 22 examples were crashed in the first 18 months of the fighter's Service career. None of these factors, however, detracted from the general enthusiasm which the Gamecock aroused in squadron pilots during its five-year span of service from 1926 to 1931.

Following closely on the heels of the Grebe through the Gloster factory, the Gamecock had been built to meet a requirement for what was virtually a Jupiter-engined development of its forerunner, with subtle airframe refinements.

The Grebe's Jaguar radial had given an unsatisfactory serviceability rate due to lubrication problems and the Jupiter was welcomed by fitters as posing far fewer maintenance headaches on the flight line. The lighter and more reliable Jupiter also contributed an improved rate of climb, the Gamecock reaching 20,000 ft in a battle climb in 20 instead of 23 minutes.

NEW TYPES PARK

The prototype Gamecock (J7497) first flew in February 1925 and a second prototype (J7756) appeared as 'No 1' in the New Types Park at the RAF Display at Hendon in the summer of 1925. By this time the familiar balanced rudder had replaced the original Grebe design.

Production orders for the Gamecock were placed by the Air Ministry in September 1925, essentially to supplement the Grebes already in service rather than to replace them – during the first period of the Gamecock's squadron service there were still three Grebe squadrons (Nos 25, 29 and 56) in the front line. The first Gamecocks to enter service in fact replaced long-obsolete Sopwith Snipes.

RAF Henlow, in Bedfordshire, was the station from which Gamecocks first operated with RAF fighter squadrons. These were the renowned No 43, which took its first Gamecock on charge in March 1926, and No 23 Sqn which received its first aircraft in

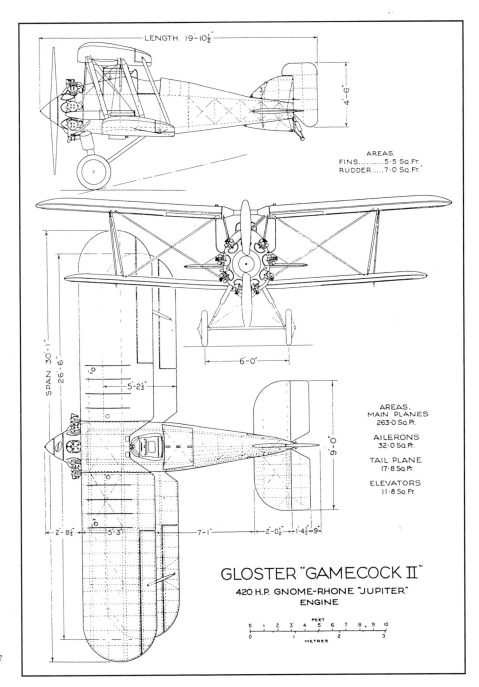

LENGTH 19´-10½´

4´-6˝

AREAS.
FINS..........5·5 SQ.FT.
RUDDER.....7·0 SQ.FT.

SPAN 30´-1˝

26´-6˝

6´-0˝

5´-2½˝

9´-0˝

AREAS.
MAIN PLANES
263·0 SQ.FT.

AILERONS
32·0 SQ.FT.

TAIL PLANE
17·8 SQ.FT.

ELEVATORS
11·8 SQ.FT.

2´-8½˝   5´-3˝   7´-1˝   2´-0½˝ 1´-4½˝ 9˝

GLOSTER "GAMECOCK II"
420 H.P. GNOME-RHONE "JUPITER" ENGINE

FEET
0 1 2 3 4 5 6 7 8 9 10
0   1   2   3
METRES

Left Flight *photograph of Gamecock I J8409, showing well the No 23 Sqn fuselage markings. At the controls is Sgt Freeman from RAF Kenley, the aircraft taking off from RAF Northolt on 28 May 1929 at the start of the Sassoon Cup race. He came fourth*

May 1926. Both squadrons had flown rotary-engined Snipes since re-forming at Henlow in July 1925, and it must have come as a welcome relief to have a modern fighter at last.

Coincidentally, with the arrival of Gamecocks on No 43, the Air Ministry was encouraging units to devise badges and mottoes and so it was that the Gamecock inspired the name, 'The Fighting Cocks', which has remained ever since with this celebrated fighter squadron. The motto, '*Gloria Finis*', was the family motto of their popular and distinguished com-

manding officer, Sqn Ldr A F 'Pongo' Brooke, an Ulsterman who was the brother of Lord Brookeborough, later Prime Minister of Northern Ireland. Sqn Ldr Brooke was originally in the 10th Hussars before serving in the RFC, and his enthusiasm for the Gamecock was such that he even ordered for his wife a diamond-studded cockerel brooch from Carringtons to commemorate the initiation of the 'Fighting Cocks'. It was also at this time that the celebrated black and white checkerboard markings were applied to No 43 Sqn's aeroplanes for the first time and subsequently maintained, in various guises, on Siskins, Furies, Spitfires, Meteors, Hunters, Phantoms and Tornados. During his period of command, Sqn Ldr Brooke flew Gamecock J7904 and had it painted with a double line of checks on the fuselage spine as well as sporting chequered pennants.

COLLISHAW'S GAMECOCKS

The rival No 23 Sqn at Henlow was commanded by an equally colourful character, namely Sqn Ldr Raymond Collishaw DSO OBE DSC DFC, who was world famous as the leader of the 'Black Flight' of No 10 Naval Squadron on the Western Front with Sopwith Triplanes. Later he flew Camels with No 13 Naval Squadron and eventually commanded No 3 Naval Squadron (later No 203) also with Camels. As OC of No 23 Sqn's Gamecocks, Collishaw's personal aeroplane was distinguished by a line of blue and red squares along the spine of the fuselage in addition to the standard squadron regalia.

Whilst at Henlow, both Gamecock squadrons worked extremely hard to attain maximum proficiency in aerial gunnery, practice interceptions, battle climbs, formation flying and aerobatic routines. No 43, in particular, made constant use of a reservoir near

Biggleswade to practise formation 'dive-bombing' attacks with light bombs and strafing with the front guns although, according to one account, it was rare for both guns to fire simultaneously! Together with their sister squadron at Henlow (No 23), No 43's Gamecocks made a memorable appearance at the 1926 RAF Display at Hendon and even succeeded in pulling off a formation landing by the entire squadron which attracted the plaudits of no less a person than Air Chief Marshal 'Boom' Trenchard himself.

Mention has already been made of the Gamecock's successes in air racing. This activity was stimulated by the presentation of a cup, open to all the fighters of the Air Defences of Great Britain, for the fastest aircraft round a 110 mile course, known as the Sassoon Cup. This was awarded annually and presented by Sir Philip Sassoon.

In 1927 it was won by Gamecock J8073 of No 32 Sqn against competition provided by two other Gamecocks, three Grebes, two Woodcocks and a Siskin. Flg Off Montgomery, in J8073, attained an average speed of 156 mph, covering the course in 43 minutes 27 seconds. The two other Gamecocks, flown by Flt Lt Collier of No 43 Sqn and Flg Off MacDonald of No 23 Sqn, came in second and third after a closely fought tussle.

Above No 43 Sqn Gamecock I J8037. Pennants were often carried by aircraft flown by squadron commanders

Left Two No 23 Sqn Gamecock Is possibly photographed at RAF Kenley. Nearer the camera is J7914, destroyed when it stalled off a steep turn after taking off from Sutton Bank, Lincs on 14 August 1929. Behind is J8406

WORLD WAR ONE ACES

With Ray Collishaw's promotion to a staff appointment, No 23 Squadron was subsequently commanded by two more World War One aces. Sqn Ldr A G Jones-Williams MC took over in January 1928, by which time the Gamecocks had been at Kenley from the previous February. Sqn Ldr Jones-Williams had served with Nos 29 and 65 Sqns over the Western Front and claimed 11 victories. Tragically, he was to lose his life piloting the Fairey Long Range Monoplane J9479 when it crashed in the Atlas Mountains in Tunisia during an attempted record flight from Cranwell to South Africa. During his time with No 23 Sqn, Jones-Williams invited his old friend Richard 'Batchy' Atcherley to join the squadron. If one can be

permitted an anachronism, one might say that Flg Off Atcherley became 'a legend in his own lunchtime' for his astonishing demonstration of Gamecock aerobatics during the midday interval at the RAF Display at Hendon on 3 July 1926.

The third of the World War One fighter aces to lead No 23 Sqn's Gamecocks was Sqn Ldr H W Woollett DSO MC, who commanded at Kenley from January 1930 until December 1931. He was consequently the last officer to command a Gamecock squadron in the RAF. Sqn Ldr Woollett was one of the most outstanding Sopwith Camel pilots on the Western Front and had scored no less than 35 victories by the end of hostilities in November 1918.

At the 1927 RAF Display at Hendon, No 23 Sqn's Gamecocks were joined by those of No 32 Sqn, which had received them in place of Grebes, the previous September. Commanded by Sqn Ldr R B 'Rex' Mansell, they were the only example of Grebes being superseded by Gamecocks in the same squadron. In April 1928 they went over to Siskins, thus joining the mass Armstrong Whitworth ranks.

Right *Colourful line-up of No 43 Sqn Gamecocks at the Birmingham Air Pageant of 1928. This was the squadron's last public display in the Gamecock, the unit transitioning onto Siskins at the Tangmere base weeks after this photograph was taken in June 1928*

TANGMERE

That classic fighter aerodrome of the interwar years, Tangmere, first housed Gamecocks from December 1926 when the 'Fighting Cocks' brought their black and white chequered aeroplanes from Henlow. The following year they were joined by the Siskins of No 1 Sqn and so began a famous rivalry, between two of the RAF's crack fighter squadrons, which was to make Tangmere the most prestigious fighter station in Great Britain, especially in the days of the Hawker Fury. The colourful Gamecocks were to remain a familiar sight to residents of nearby Chichester until they finally departed in June 1928 with the arrival of Siskins.

In common with other fighter biplanes of its era, the Gamecock occasionally indulged in night-flying activities and was equipped with pyrotechnic wing-tip flares which were employed in conjunction with four or five goosenecks laid out in a T on the ground. This was not a very popular activity with squadron pilots, which is scarcely surprising in view of the total absence of navigational or landing aids as known today. An amusing story is told of a Gamecock pilot on his first night flight who was alarmed to discover, as he thought, that his starboard wing-mounted generator was on fire. After a hasty emergency landing he found out for the first time that what he had witnessed was the normal exhaust flame of a throttled-back Jupiter engine. Another story from the night flying days

concerns Ray Collishaw who, it is alleged, once tried powerful car headlights fixed to the undercarriage of his Gamecock to avoid using the unpopular wing-tip flares which were considered to be a fire-hazard in any landing mishap. The experiment was not a success!

Although night fighting was given a somewhat low priority in the RAF of the 1920s, there were nevertheless two squadrons based at Upavon in Wiltshire which, from 1925 onwards, were tasked with night operations as a specialist role. These were Nos 3 and 17 Sqns, flying Hawker Woodcocks, and when these were withdrawn the operational requirement was handed over to Gamecocks. No 17 Sqn received Gamecocks in January 1928 and flew them for nine months before exchanging them for Siskins. Their commanding officer was Sqn Ldr A R Arnold DSO DFC who had flown Sopwith Pups and Triplanes with the famous No 8 Naval Squadron of the RNAS over the Western Front, and later commanded No 79 Sqn with Sopwith Dolphins. Between April and June 1917 he had shot down five Albatros Scouts.

No 3 Sqn, the second of the night fighter units at Upavon, was commanded by Sqn Ldr E Digby Johnson AFC and received its Gamecocks in August 1928. After a short-lived period of service which lasted until the early summer of 1929, the new Bristol Bulldogs made their delayed debut and the Gamecock's interim, and to a large extent fortuitous, career as a night fighter (caused by the grounding of the Woodcocks) came to a close.

Below A line-up of four No 23 Sqn Gamecock Is. Nearest the camera are J8408, J8041 and J8083. The squadron's eagle badge (an eagle preying on a falcon) may be seen on the fin of J8408

Above A formation of three No 23 Sqn Gamecocks led by J7903 with J7894 nearest the camera. J7903 was lost on 7 November 1929 when it collided with J8409 near Wallington, Surrey

By this time, only one squadron of Gamecocks remained in service with the RAF. No 23 Sqn was still soldiering on at Kenley and remained active until as late as September 1931, having made notable appearances at the RAF annual displays at Hendon in 1929, 1930 and 1931. The last appearance was perhaps the most historic of all, as one of the two pilots featured in the integrated dual aerobatic display was none other than Plt Off D R S Bader, who partnered Flt Lt M M Day in the other Gamecock.

Their performance, before an excited crowd of 170,000 people, was absolutely spell-binding and a memorable swan-song for the classic Gamecock. It was less than six months later – only three months after No 23 Sqn had forsaken its Gamecocks – that Douglas Bader was to lose his legs in the tragic accident which ensued when demonstrating low rolls in one of the new Bulldogs at Woodley on 14 December 1931.

Unlike its stablemate, the Grebe, the Gamecock was to see comparatively little service in the flying training role in the RAF. Whereas the Grebe had been widely used in a dual-control variant, only one Gamecock was ever seen in the two-seat configuration in regular service, and this was a converted single-seater J7900, formerly with No 43 Sqn, which went to the CFS. Apart from this, about half a dozen Gamecocks were on the strength of the CFS at various times, one was allocated to the RAF College at Cranwell and one or two made their appearance at Nos 2 and 3 FTSs at Digby and Spittlegate respectively.

MARTLESHAM GAMECOCKS

The A&AEE Martlesham Heath used seven Gamecocks between June 1925 and July 1928, including the prototypes J7756 and J7757. The first production Gamecock, J7891, did its performance tests at Martlesham in August 1926, J7910 flutter trials and aileron tests in May 1927, J8047 spinning trials in February 1928 and J8075 trials with a Mercury engine installed in July 1927.

In July 1928, a specially-built Gamecock II (J8804) was on trials with a Jupiter VI engine and both J7910 and J8075 were subsequently converted to Gamecock II standard, although this variant never entered regular squadron service with the RAF.

In August 1928 a re-built J8047 with lengthened fuselage and enlarged fin and rudder was flown but never came to anything. By this time, the RAF was fully committed to the Bristol Bulldog as its next standard fighter, and it was duly bought in large numbers.

It was during these many tests at Martlesham that the Gamecock was subjected to a series of terminal velocity dives, reaching 250 mph, and it was during one of these tests that Flg Off G V Wheatley was killed whilst flying a Gamecock with No 22 Sqn.

The high accident rate experienced with Gamecocks has already been mentioned (18 were lost in 1927 alone) and it was no doubt fortunate that by the time of its introduction into service, the parachute was finally recognised as a crucial part of the pilot's flying equipment, and had been fitted by regulation in RAF aircraft.

The first Gamecock pilot to save his life in this way was flying J8039 from No 23 Sqn at Kenley when he had to abandon his aeroplane which had got into an uncontrollable spin. The date was 22 April 1927.

With the final departure of the Gamecock from first-line service in 1931, the RAF said goodbye to its all-wooden biplane fighters, and the final link with traditional conceptions and maintenance procedures had been severed. It was the end of an era in fighter history.

Considering the high profile attained by the Gamecock, doubtless due to its sparkling exhibitions before the public at RAF Displays at Hendon on five separate occasions, it comes as a surprise to realise that only 90 examples were ever delivered to the RAF. The full production list (excluding prototypes) is as follows:

Gamecock Production for the RAF

J7891–7920 (30)	Delivered February to May 1926
J8033–8047 (15)	Delivered August to October 1926
J8069–8095 (27)	Delivered January to August 1928
J8405–8422 (18)	Delivered February to August 1928

Left The premier Gamecock outfit in terms of longevity on type was No 23 Sqn. this unit flying the Gloster fighter from May 1926 through to September 1931. This wonderful shot shows a full squadron line-up of 12 aircraft plus pilots and mechanics

Left below No 23 Sqn Gamecock I J8082 has just been started with the help of a Hucks starter, which is about to attend to the second aircraft

Right Amongst the first batch of 30 Gamecocks delivered to the RAF, J7914 served initially in the chequered colours of No 43 Sqn from March 1926 until being transfered to No 23 Sqn in June 1928

Gamecock Units in the RAF

No 3 Squadron *Upavon, August 1928 to June 1929*

Markings: Emerald green bar on fuselage, ahead of and behind roundel. Green bar across the upper mainplanes

Serials: J8034, 8044, 8071, 8074, 8083, 8407, 8408, 8410, 8411, 8412, 8417

No 17 Squadron *Upavon, January 1928 to September 1928*

Markings: Black parallel zig-zags on fuselage from behind the engine bay to tailplane leading edge. Black zig-zags repeated between the roundels on the upper mainplanes

Serials: J8405, 8408, 8414

No 23 Squadron *Henlow, May 1926 to February 1927 and then Kenley until September 1931*

Markings: Red and blue alternate squares ahead of and behind the roundel on the fuselage, repeated above the upper mainplanes between the roundels

Serials: J7892, 7893, 7894, 7895, 7896, 7897, 7898, 7899, 7901, 7902, 7903, 7904, 7905, 7907, 7910, 7912, 7913, 7914, 7915, 7916, 8034, 8036, 8039, 8040, 8041, 8044, 8045, 8071, 8073, 8075, 8076, 8077, 8078, 8080, 8082, 8083, 8084, 8085, 8089, 8091, 8093, 8094, 8095, 8096, 8406, 8408, 8409, 8410, 8412, 8415, 8420, 8421

No 32 Squadron *Kenley, September 1926 to April 1928*

Markings: Broad blue bar with diagonal intersections on fuselage, repeated above the upper mainplanes between the roundels

Serials: J7907, 8042, 8043, 8044, 8069, 8070, 8073, 8074, 8080, 8081, 8087, 8091

No 43 Squadron *Henlow, March 1926 to December 1926 and then Tangmere from December 1926 to June 1928*

Markings: Black and white checks on fuselage from engine bay to roundel, repeated above the upper mainplanes between the roundels

Serials: J7900, 7904, 7905, 7906, 7907, 7908, 7909, 7911, 7914, 7918, 7919, 7920, 8035, 8036, 8037, 8038, 8090, 8095, 8414, 8415, 8416, 8417, 8418, 8420, 8421

A&AEE
The Martlesham testing squadrons No 15 and 22 had J7756, 7757, 7891, 7910, 8047 and the Mk II J8804 on strength

CFS
Issued with J7900 (dual control), J8046, 8047, 8074, 8076, 8089, 8093

Cranwell
The RAF College had J8077 on strength

A&GS
The Armament and Gunnery School was issued with J8033, 8072, 8088

No 2 FTS
J8076 on strength

No 3 FTS
J8089 on strength

HCF
The Home Communication Flight operated J8073, 8085, 8088, 8413

No 19 Squadron

A solitary Gamecock (J8035) was issued following service with No 43 Sqn and artwork has been published depicting it in blue and white checks, but No 19 was never a regular Gamecock squadron

Gloster Gamecock I data

Engine: Bristol Jupiter VI, nine-cylinder direct drive, unsupercharged; 400 hp at normal 1700 rpm; 435 hp at maximum 1870 rpm at 5000 ft

Dimensions

Span	29 ft 9.5 in
Length	19 ft 8 in
Height (tail on trestle)	9 ft 8 in
Wing Area	254 ft^2

Weights

Loaded	2863 lbs
Empty	1930 lbs

Performance

Maximum Speed	153 mph at sea level
Gliding Speed	75 mph
Stalling Speed	50 mph
Rate of climb	
Sea Level	2000 ft/min
Time to 20,000 ft	20 min
Service Ceiling	23,000 ft

Endurance

at 20,000 ft (incl climb)	3.25 hr

Armament: Two fixed 0.303 in Vickers synchronized machine guns, using Constantinesco interrupter gear, 600 rounds Mk VII ammunition per gun, four 20 lb Cooper bombs

THE BRISTOL BULLDOG

DESPITE ITS AGGRESSIVELY warlike name and snub-nose, the Bristol Bulldog was one of the most perfectly-proportioned fighters to enter service with the RAF, and its adherents have always been fiercely loyal. 13 September 1964 was, therefore, a very sad day for them, and for all interested in historic aircraft preservation. All but the earliest visitors to the SBAC Show at Farnborough arrived to find a tangled heap of wreckage lying close to the end of the runway. This was all that remained of the one remaining Bristol Bulldog in Britain.

Originally registered G-ABBB, this was a Bulldog IIA powered by a supercharged Bristol Jupiter VIIFP nine-cylinder radial engine and had formerly been used as the manufacturer's demonstrator and engine test-bed. After storage, it had passed into the hands of the Science Museum and then to the Shuttleworth Trust. Apprentices and enthusiasts at the Filton

Below The prototype Bulldog I, construction number 7155 – it never carried an RAF serial. Powered by a Bristol Jupiter VII, it first flew on 17 May 1927

Above Bristol Bulldog IIA K1085 *was delivered to the RAF early in 1930 and served with Nos 17 and 29 Sqns, but was struck off charge in October the same year*

Works of the Bristol Aeroplane Co, where it had first been built, lovingly restored it, but while on a flight before the SBAC show itself opened, the Bulldog had suffered engine failure at low altitude, leaving the pilot in a very tight corner and without enough room to get safely back on to the runway. Luckily there was no fire and it was a miracle that the pilot was not seriously hurt. The Bulldog itself was a write-off.

The fighter's crash highlighted the need for careful handling of the engine at all times, and particularly of the aircraft at low speeds should the engine lose power near the ground. When flown by pilots experienced on the type, the handling of this little fighter was delightful. That aerobatics gave particular joy and exuberance to those who flew it was very evident. Nevertheless, it could bite hard and quickly if liberties were taken with it, as some pilots found to their cost. It has been aptly described as a very pretty little aeroplane and it had an extraordinary ability to look

variously pugnacious or attractive, according to the angle from which it was observed; the blunt, aggressive Jupiter engine belied the very trim shape of its elegant wings, particularly when seen from behind. For very different reasons, the Bulldog has always had its admirers.

FIRST FLIGHT

The Type 105 was first flown at Filton by Bristol's Chief Test Pilot, Cyril Uwins, on 17 May 1927. It was built as a private venture at the same time as its stable companion, the Bullpup Type 107, both being contenders for Air Ministry Specification 9/26, and the chief rival being the Hawker Hawfinch. The Bullpup had been designed to be powered by the new geared Bristol Mercury but, owing to delays in the engine's production, completion of the Bulldog went ahead first, powered by the tried and trusted Jupiter in its new supercharged Mk VII version.

The Bulldog was originally intended to be of equal-span but the design was altered to the now familiar outline following wind-tunnel tests. The lower wing

Above Bristol test pilot Cyril Uwins flying the prototype Bulldog at Filton in July 1927

was of Clark YH section, whereas the upper wing was of a special Bristol 1A section, devised by the company's chief designer Frank Barnwell, and his assistant Leslie G Frise (pronounced 'Freeze', not Fries!). Frise, the designer of the type of aileron aerodynamic balance which bears his name had, in 1919, devised a 'park-bench' type of aileron balance which was characterized by a very small aerofoil, mounted rigidly on horns attached to the upper surface of the aileron and projecting ahead of the hinges. By coincidence and unknown to Frise, an exactly similar device had just been patented by A V Roe & Co, a matter which was settled amicably. Frise then devised his neat and well-known solution to the ever-increasing need for aerodynamic balancing, used on the Bristol Brandon and numerous other aircraft from 1924 onwards.

The Bulldog airframe was principally of steel, covered with fabric except where quickly-detachable aluminium panels were required for easy access to internal equipment. The endless problems associated with traditional wood construction (such as shrinkage and infestation, particularly in the numerous hot climates in which the RAF then operated), had resulted in many airframes having to be re-built and a notable decision being made by the Air Ministry that future production orders for Service aircraft would be restricted to all-metal airframes. In the light of this, a system of steel construction was devised by Harry Pollard at Filton, using high-tensile steel strip rolled into varying cusped and flanged sections. Built as the primary airframe structures, this system had originally been devised by J D North at Boulton Paul Ltd in Norwich.

Pollard, who used a minimum of steel tubes for stiffening purposes, riveted the rolled-strip edges

together longitudinally, forming longerons, vertical and diagonal cross-bracing. Intersecting members were stabilized with simple steel riveted or bolted gusset-plates, rather than the expensively machined

Above *The prototype Bulldog with original fin and rudder*

Below *Bulldog IIA G-ABBB in September 1935 after it had been fitted with an Aquila I engine*

Left The Bulldog's cockpit. The rudder bar was adjustable to suit the pilot's leg length and a handwheel was turned to adjust the tailplane incidence

Below Bristol Bulldog II J9480 was modified to become the prototype IIA in 1932. As this photograph shows, the aircraft was maintained in showroom condition by the company

end-fittings normally associated with drawn tubes. The resulting structure, which was stove-enamelled for protection against corrosion, was not only lighter and stronger, but considerably easier and cheaper to build. The Bulldog prototype, which bore no serial number, performed well enough to be sent to Martlesham Heath in June and appeared at the RAF Pageant at Hendon the following month.

Initially, the spinning characteristics of the proto-type Bulldog were unsatisfactory and tended to flatten, but in an A&AEE report dated 26 October 1927 following the preliminary tests, a larger fin and rudder were fitted and the aircraft was spun with more satisfactory results. Loading, cg and power unit were all unchanged, but the tailplane and elevator, fin and rudder volume co-efficients had been increased slightly. The pilot reported that the aircraft was put into a series of spins. At first, a left-hand spin was made with the tail adjustment fully forward. The Bulldog was stalled and full left rudder applied with the control column right back and to the left. The aircraft was difficult to get into a left hand spin and the rudder had to be applied just at the correct moment. The spin was fast with a jerky motion for the first two or three turns, after which it settled down to a steady spin with the nose well down. After nine turns the rudder was centralized and the stick put forward. The aircraft came out immediately.

The next spin was made with the tail adjustment 'half back', and the stick and rudder applied as on the previous occasion. The Bulldog did eight turns, after

which the rudder was centralized, the control column put forward and the aircraft came out as before. The tail adjustment was next put in the 'right back' position and the aircraft put into a spin. With the tail adjustment set like this, the spin was a little more flat. After eight turns the rudder was centralized and the stick pushed forward. After about a three-quarter turn the aircraft came out comfortably. The first spin to the right was with the tail adjustment in the full forward position. The aircraft spun much more easily to the right and a trifle faster.

SPIN TRIALS

To start, the Bulldog was stalled, full right rudder applied with the control column hard back and to the right hand side. The first two or three turns produced a very noticeable jerk, after which the aircraft settled down to an even spin. On centralizing the controls the aircraft came out of the spin almost immediately. The aircraft was next spun with the tail adjustment in the 'half-back' position. This spin was as before and on centralizing the controls it came out after one half turn. The last spin was with the tail adjustment in the 'full back' position. This time, it was in a much flatter altitude than the others and not quite so fast. After nine turns the rudder was centralized and the control

Below During the winter of 1932/33 a batch of 17 Bulldog Trainers was delivered to the RAF, the first of which was K3170, which went to the CFS

column pushed forward. After one turn the aircraft came out in a quite normal dive. There was no uncomfortable feeling in any of the spins and the Bulldog prototype came out of each quite easily. The Martlesham pilot concluded that, with the larger fin and rudder and the CG on the aft limit, the aircraft was satisfactory in spins to left or right, recovery being easy and comfortable.

The report therefore recommended that the larger fin and rudder be standardized. However, the larger area resulted in cross-wind taxying problems and it was decided instead to lengthen the fuselage and retain the smaller rudder. This, together with other modifications, resulted in the Type 105A Bulldog II. An order for a prototype was placed in November 1927. Flown on 21 January 1928 as J9480 and bought by the Air Ministry on 21 August for extended trials at Martlesham, this aircraft became the winner of Spec F.9/26. It was ordered into production to Spec F.17/28 and the first was delivered on 8 May 1929.

Spinning problems persisted, however, there being a right and a wrong way to stop a Bulldog spinning without considerable loss of height, and these were

Left *Bristol Bulldog IIA K1085 of No 17 Sqn up from RAF Upavon in June 1930. The maintenance stencilling is clearly visible on the fin of this machine*

Right *A trio of Bulldogs on a low-level bombing exercise at RAF Eastchurch, Kent, on 11 May 1936. They were preparing for Empire Air Day, when RAF stations throughout the UK opened their gates to the public*

covered by several further A&AEE reports. In this connection it should be noted that the Bulldog II and the improved Mk IIA had a relatively heavy exhaust collector ring, whereas the Mk I did not. This and later versions of the Bulldog (some of which were also fitted with the Townend ring cowling) acquired greater vertical tail area which reduced the problems associated with spinning the aeroplane. Wheel brakes, fitted later, balanced the weathercock effect of the larger tail. Bulldog J9567 was the first production Mk II, powered as in the Mk I by a 440 hp Jupiter VII engine, and had a gross weight of 3490 lbs. The improvements to the Mk II airframe, including revisions to the ailerons and airframe, were incorporated in G-ABBB and a strengthened, wider undercarriage allowed an increase in the all-up weight to 3530 lbs. This was the basis of the well-known Mk IIA which equipped most of the RAF fighter squadrons of the period. The engine remained a Jupiter VIIF, or VIIFP, both with an automatic boost control, and later engines were provided with automatic ignition control. Two fuel tanks mounted in the upper wings carried a total of 70 gal, which was gravity-fed to the carburettor.

The tailplane incidence was adjustable by a handwheel and the rudder bar was adjustable to suit the pilot's leg-length. The modifications which resulted in the Mk IIA as a standard squadron aircraft were not

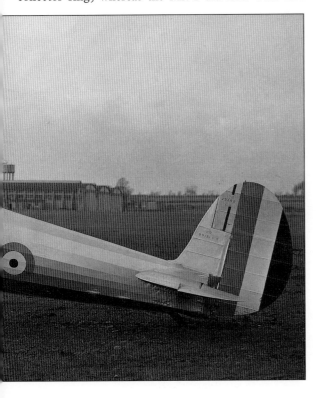

Left *The prototype Bulldog II with lengthened fuselage, engine helmets and headrest. It was first flown on 21 January 1928 by Uwins*

without penalties. The first volume of the official *Air Publication* on the Bulldog IIA contains a note which states that, owing mainly to strength considerations (and partly to design), consequent upon the greater total loaded weight of the Bulldog IIA, the interchangeability of most of the structural components of the two aeroplanes had been affected. No Bulldog II components other than the fin, rudder, elevators, ailerons, engine mounting and tail skid assembly might be fitted to any IIA aeroplane but, with the exception of the main and centre planes, all components of the IIA might be fitted without alteration to the II aeroplane.

As regards the interchangeability of the main and centre planes, a type II outer main plane must not be fitted to a type IIA aeroplane. However, type IIA main planes (top and bottom) could be fitted to type II Bulldogs, provided that suitable provision was made for the stronger landing wires and their attachments and, in the case of the bottom centre plane, provided

that the fuselage fitting which took the incidence wire was modified to the type IIA fitting. The change-over was not recommended, however, in view of the modification required to the fuselage. Early in 1933, further spinning tests were carried out in a Bulldog IIA with a partially mass-balanced rudder with results little, if at all different from the standard aircraft. Later in the year, Martlesham put K2188 through trials with mass-balanced rudder and ailerons.

These trials included spinning, diving and aerobatic handling tests, and were made in comparison with the standard rudder and ailerons. It was found that there was no perceptible change in the spinning characteristics of the Bulldog as a result of mass-balancing the rudder and ailerons. The rudder was quite satisfactory in all diving and aerobatic tests. There was, however, a sluggishness of the lateral control which became more noticeable when the ailerons were mass-balanced. Diving tests to the limiting crankshaft speed of 1980 rpm were made with engine on and off. That limitation did not allow the terminal velocity to be reached, the maximum speed

Below Ailerons were fitted to the top mainplanes

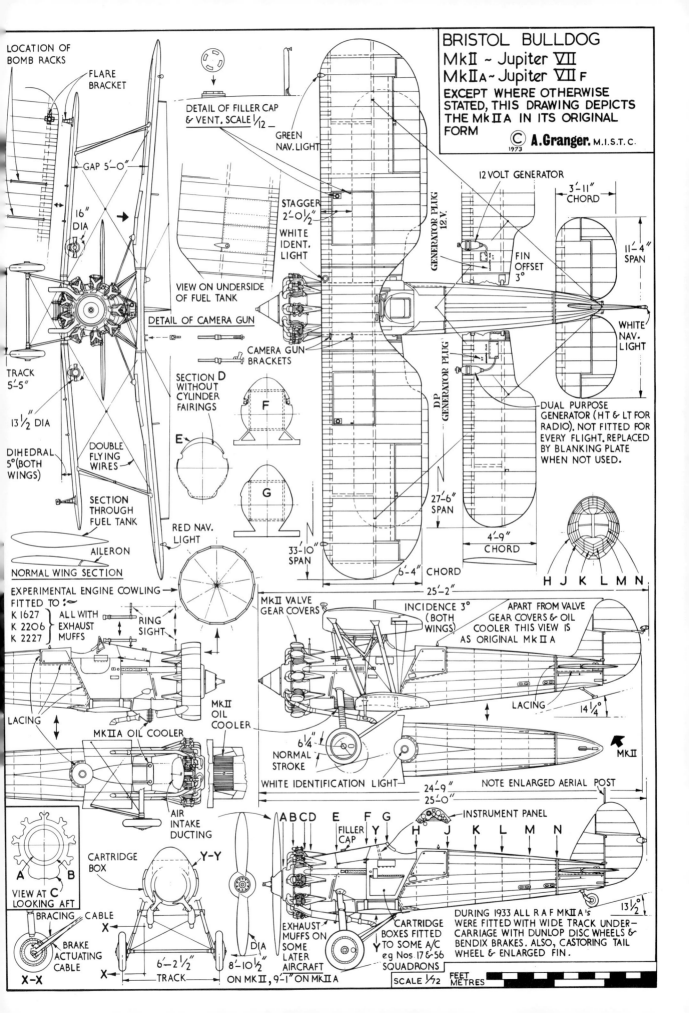

BRISTOL BULLDOG
Mk II ~ Jupiter VII
Mk IIA ~ Jupiter VII F
EXCEPT WHERE OTHERWISE STATED, THIS DRAWING DEPICTS THE Mk IIA IN ITS ORIGINAL FORM
© 1973 A. Granger. M.I.S.T.C.

LOCATION OF BOMB RACKS
FLARE BRACKET
GAP 5'-0"
16" DIA
DETAIL OF FILLER CAP & VENT. SCALE 1/12
GREEN NAV. LIGHT
STAGGER 2'-0½"
WHITE IDENT. LIGHT
VIEW ON UNDERSIDE OF FUEL TANK
DETAIL OF CAMERA GUN
CAMERA GUN BRACKETS
TRACK 5'-5"
13½" DIA
SECTION D WITHOUT CYLINDER FAIRINGS
F
E
G
DIHEDRAL 5° (BOTH WINGS)
DOUBLE FLYING WIRES
SECTION THROUGH FUEL TANK
AILERON
NORMAL WING SECTION
RED NAV. LIGHT

12 VOLT GENERATOR
GENERATOR PLUG 12 V.
FIN OFFSET 3°
3'-11" CHORD
11'-4" SPAN
WHITE NAV. LIGHT
DP GENERATOR PLUG
DUAL PURPOSE GENERATOR (HT & LT FOR RADIO). NOT FITTED FOR EVERY FLIGHT. REPLACED BY BLANKING PLATE WHEN NOT USED.
27'-6" SPAN
4'-9" CHORD
33'-10" SPAN
6'-4" CHORD
25'-2"
H J K L M N

EXPERIMENTAL ENGINE COWLING FITTED TO :—
K 1627
K 2206
K 2227
} ALL WITH EXHAUST MUFFS
RING SIGHT
LACING
MK IIA OIL COOLER
MK II OIL COOLER
AIR INTAKE DUCTING

MK II VALVE GEAR COVERS
INCIDENCE 3° (BOTH WINGS)
APART FROM VALVE GEAR COVERS & OIL COOLER THIS VIEW IS AS ORIGINAL MK IIA
LACING
14¼°
6¼" NORMAL STROKE
WHITE IDENTIFICATION LIGHT
24'-9"
25'-0"
NOTE ENLARGED AERIAL POST
MK II

A
B
VIEW AT C LOOKING AFT
BRACING CABLE
BRAKE ACTUATING CABLE
X-X
CARTRIDGE BOX
Y-Y
6'-2½" TRACK
8'-10½" DIA
ON MK II, 9'-1" ON MK IIA
X
X
DIA

A B C D E F G Y
FILLER CAP
EXHAUST MUFFS ON SOME LATER AIRCRAFT
CARTRIDGE BOXES FITTED TO SOME A/C eg Nos 17 & 56 SQUADRONS
INSTRUMENT PANEL
H J K L M N
Y
13½°
DURING 1933 ALL R A F MK IIA's WERE FITTED WITH WIDE TRACK UNDER-CARRIAGE WITH DUNLOP DISC WHEELS & BENDIX BRAKES. ALSO, CASTORING TAIL WHEEL & ENLARGED FIN.
SCALE 1/72
FEET
METRES

achievable being at full-throttle, 245 mph being reached at 10,000 ft from a dive started at 14,000 and recovery completed at 8500 ft. The Bulldog exemplified the painstaking identification and elimination of problems by the A&AEE. Even by the 1930s, the dynamics of the spin were imperfectly understood and trial and error were very much the order of the day.

BULLDOG TRIBUTE

The late and much lamented Tony Harold, whose tragic death in a Nieuport 27 in April 1991 robbed the vintage aircraft preservation world of one of its leading and most knowledgeable personalities, once wrote that the Bulldog was one of the 'few aeroplanes which can be seen as a mirror of their age'. This much-loved biplane fighter, from the same stable as the immortal

Bristol Fighter of World War 1 fame, was exactly that. Born in the 1920s, and very much a product of that era, it did not finally disappear from front-line fighter squadrons until July 1937. During its tenure of service it equipped no less than 10 fighter squadrons of what was then known as the Air Defence of Great Britain (ADGB) and was still serving with four squadrons (Nos 3, 17, 32 and 54) on the formation of the new Fighter Command in July 1936. At the apex of its career in mid-1933 Bulldogs in all their splendid heraldry were to be seen at six of the now historic fighter stations surrounding London, namely Kenley (Nos 3 and 17 Sqns), Duxford (No 19 Sqn), North Weald (Nos 29 and 56 Sqns), Biggin Hill (No 32 Sqn), Northolt (No 111 Sqn) and Hornchurch (No 54 Sqn).

With its dominant place in the history of RAF fighter evolution, it might be supposed that the

Left Bulldog IIA K2159 in the colours of No 19 Sqn. This aircraft wears the CO's pennant on its rudder

Below Bulldog IIA K1088 in No 17 Sqn markings. Delivered to the RAF early in 1930, this aircraft served with No 17 Sqn at RAF Upavon until struck off charge in February 1933

Far left No 17 Sqn Bulldog IIs up from RAF Upavon in June 1930. Not all the fighters boast the traditional zig-zags synonymous with the unit during this period

Bulldog enjoyed some superlative performance characteristics by comparison with its contemporaries, but this was not, in fact, the case. Firmly rooted in the traditional design philosophies which continued to find favour with the defence planners of the day at the Air Ministry, the Bulldog was barely 20 mph faster than the Gamecocks and Siskins which it replaced and, subsequently, some embarrassment was to be caused by reports that it was frequently outpaced by the contemporary light day bomber, the Hawker Hart, during Air Exercises. During competitive trials in 1928 with the rival Hawker Hawfinch J8776, the Bulldog II prototype J9480 found a strong contender and there was considerable division of opinion about

the merits of the two types among squadron pilots who conducted Service trials. In the end the deciding factor in favour of the Bulldog was not so much performance as ease of maintenance in the field, a potent consideration in times of financial stringency, then as now. According to some historians, the same economic considerations weighed heavily in favour of the continued production of the Bulldog at a time in the early 1930s when the clearly superior Hawker Fury came on to the scene. It is not without relevance to note that each Bulldog cost the Air Ministry a mere £3900 instead of £4800 for the Fury.

The Bulldog I prototype (no serial number) had made its first flight on 17 May 1927 and its first appearance before the public was in the New Types Park at the RAF Hendon Display of that year. The definitive Bulldog II for which the first production contract was placed in August 1928, was to Specification 17/28. This was for 25 aircraft and was the first major contract for RAF aircraft from the historic Bristol factory since their renowned Bristol Fighter had gone out of production in 1927.

During the next five years, seven more Air Ministry

contracts followed and the eventual total of Bulldog fighters to the RAF was 302, ending with K3513 delivered in November 1933.

Bulldog Fighter Production for the RAF

Quantity	Type	Serial batches
25	Mk II	J9567 to J9591
23	Mk II	K1079 to K1101
92	Mk II	K1063 to K1694
100	Mk IIa	K2135 to K2187
		K2189 to K2234
20	Mk IIa	K2476 to K2495
14	Mk IIa	K2859 to K2872
18	Mk IIa	K2946 to K2963
10	Mk IIa	K3504 to K3513

The first RAF fighter squadron to receive the new Bulldogs was No 3, stationed at Upavon in Wiltshire. It had originally been the intention for the Bulldogs to replace the Hawker Woodcocks which No 3 Sqn had flown since May 1925, but the grounding of Woodcocks in August 1928 and a delay in delivery of Bulldogs meant that an interim issue of Gloster Game-

Right Although the identity of the jolly chap in the cockpit has been lost over the decades, we do know that this Bulldog was one of 12 No 111 Sqn machines based at Hornchurch in the early 1930s

Below The massed ranks of No 17 Sqn at Upavon in the spring of 1930. Again several of these aircraft appear to lack fuselage and upper wing markings

cocks were the aeroplanes which the first Bulldogs eventually superseded, and it was not until 22 May 1929 that Flt Lt H W Taylor collected No 3's first aircraft. A full complement of 12 had been received at Upavon by the end of September 1929, and in the meantime three of No 3's Bulldogs led by Flt Lt J L Airey had displayed the new fighter in their emerald green squadron markings at the RAF Hendon Air Display on 13 July 1929.

LONGEST SERVING

No 3 Sqn, as it turned out, were to retain Bulldogs longer than any other RAF fighter squadron, only relinquishing them in the summer of 1937 with the arrival of Gloster Gladiators. They were also unique among Bulldog squadrons in having served for a period overseas. This was during the Abyssinian Crisis of 1935–36 when 18 of No 3 Sqn's Bulldogs served in the Sudan from October 1935 to August 1936. On returning to the UK (they were, of course, transported by ship in crates) they were based at Kenley for their final year's service and received slightly modified squadron markings foreshadowing those of the Gladiators which were to follow – the green bar on the fuselage sides was replaced by a green 'tear-drop' design.

No 17 Sqn, which was No 3's sister unit at Upavon, exchanged its Siskins for Bulldogs in October 1929 and by October 1932 six more Siskin squadrons had gone over to Bulldogs (Nos 19, 29, 41, 54, 56 and 111) in addition to Nos 23 and 32, which had been flying Gamecocks. With the exception of the three Fury squadrons on the south coast, the Bulldog reigned supreme by 1932, although in No 23 Sqn there were

already signs of changes to come with the incorporation of one flight of Hart two-seat fighters which led on to the Demon. Although based on a flawed tactical concept, these two-seaters were actually faster than the Bulldog and eventually displaced them not only in No 23 but also in Nos 29 and 41 Sqns.

By older members of the general public, the Bulldog is best remembered for its spectacular displays of formation aerobatics, especially with coloured smoke trails, at the annual RAF Displays at Hendon each summer from 1929 until 1936. No 3 Sqn's initial appearance in 1929 was repeated in 1930 and again in 1931, by which time it was accompanied by Nos 17, 32 and 54 Sqns. In 1932 it was the turn of Nos 41, 54 and 111 Sqns, together with the composite Bulldog/Hart Fighter formation of No 23 Sqn. In 1933 no less than five Bulldog squadrons participated (Nos 3, 17, 19, 41

and 54) and in 1934 it was No 29, joined by Nos 17, 19 and 54, which thrilled the crowds. Reduced to only two squadrons (Nos 3 and 17) in 1935, the Bulldogs returned in force for a final fling in 1936, being represented by Nos 17, 32, 54 and 56 just before they all went over to the new Gloster Gauntlets.

As was the case with nearly all the interwar fighter biplane squadrons, some distinguished names in RAF history were numbered among their pilots and commanding officers. E M 'Teddy' Donaldson, who later commanded No 151 Sqn on Hurricanes in France and the Battle of Britain, flew Bulldogs with No 3 Sqn. No 17 Sqn was commanded by Sqn Ldr A R Arnold DSO DFC, an ex-Naval Eight Sopwith Triplane pilot who downed five Albatros Scouts in World War 1, and also on the squadron was Jeffrey Quill, the famous Spitfire test pilot. In his engaging book *Spitfire: A Test Pilot's*

Left Built in 1929, Bulldog J9576 was delivered to No 3 Sqn in July 1929. On 7 November 1930 the aircraft crashed and overturned at Chipping Norton but was reconditioned. In this photograph the aircraft appears to be in No 3 Sqn mnarkings

Story (John Murray, 1983), Quill relates some marvellous anecdotes about life on a Bulldog squadron in the early 1930s, as does Air Vice-Marshal S F Vincent in *Flying Fever* (Jarrolds, 1972) on his many varied Bulldog experiences with No 41 Sqn at Northolt. Commenting on the extreme unreliability of radio telephony in those days, Air Marshal Vincent recalls that on a flight from Filton to Northolt his C Flight Commander disappeared from the massed No 41 Sqn ranks, and on eventually being contacted announced that he was 'Over Chipping Sodbury'.

RADIO BANTER

'The whole of our three flights then rocked up and down as the pilots laughed, and I answered, 'You would be!' So R/T had its lighter side and steadily improved to the Very High Frequency (VHF) reliability of the Battle of Britain time, nine years later.'

As a flight lieutenant, Air Chief Marshal Sir Harry Broadhurst flew Bulldogs with No 19 Sqn. Also with the squadron at this period was the pilot who is commonly credited with having fired the first shots in the Battle of Britain from his Hurricane of No 145 Squadron, Plt Off J R A Peel.

Right A trio of No 23 Sqn Bulldogs, with K2151 in the foreground, K1678 in the centre and K1687 in the background. The squadron's Bulldogs were based first at RAF Kenley and later at Biggin Hill

Sqn Ldr B E Baker DSO MC (later to become Air Marshal Sir Brian Baker) commanded No 32 Sqn when it flew Bulldogs at Kenley. During a distinguished career in World War 1 he gained 12 victories flying Bristol Fighters with No 48 Sqn, including a Gotha night bomber, and later commanded No 141 Sqn with Bristol Fighters on Home Defence duties at Biggin Hill.

Sqn Ldr S L G Pope DFC AFC commanded No 54 Sqn at Hornchurch: he had scored 6 victories flying Nieuport Scouts and S.E.5As with No 60 Sqn in World War 1. The celebrated athlete Donald Finlay was with No 54 piloting Bulldogs after a spell with No 41. The second Bulldog Squadron at Hornchurch (No 111) was under the command of Sqn Ldr M B Frew DSO MC AFC (who retired as Air Vice-Marshal Sir Matthew Frew in 1948), who had flown Sopwith 1½-Strutters and Camels with No 45 Sqn.

The roll-call of famous names associated with the Bulldog could be extended almost indefinitely, but the most outstanding example must surely be that of the late Douglas Bader, who as a young pilot officer with

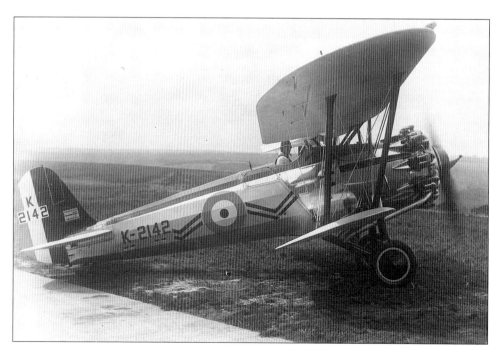

Left Bulldog IIA K2142 of No 17 Sqn was delivered during the second half of 1931 and remained with the squadron until it was struck off RAF charge in June 1934

Right A No 23 Sqn pilot leaps into a Bulldog to take part in air exercises at RAF Kenley on 21–22 July 1931

No 23 Sqn in December 1931 crashed his Bulldog
(K1676) from a low altitude roll – the accident in
which he lost his legs. In October 1932 he was back in
the air at the CFS in a Bulldog two-seater, which says
it all about his legendary courage and skill.

Bader's great prowess as an aerobatic pilot would
doubtless have led to his becoming a leading Bulldog
exponent if fate had not intervened. In the event, this
role was taken on by Flt Lt Harry Broadhurst of No 19
Sqn who, with Flg Off S F Godden and Sgts J Bignal,
R Parr and W J Rye, was responsible for what was to
become the definitive display of co-ordinated aerobatics with coloured smoke trails at Hendon in 1934.
Practically every pictorial review of the RAF's history
ever published carries photographs of this event.

However, if coloured smoke trail aerobatics were
aesthetically pleasing, bomber interception was what
fighters were all about, and in 1933 the Hendon
crowds were to witness one of the outstanding examples of the aerial fighting art. In that year, three
Bulldogs of No 3 Sqn flown by Flt Lt B W Knox, Flg
Off D Boitel-Gill and Sgt L James demonstrated a
spectacular dogfight with a Boulton Paul Sidestrand
twin-engined day bomber flown by Flt Lt A D Rogers
AFC of No 101 Sqn. For a medium-sized twin, the
Sidestrand was highly manoeuvrable and it gave the
Bulldogs a good run for their money.

AIR EXERCISES

During the Air Exercises of 1936, following the
formation of the newly established Fighter Command
structure, Bulldogs were to play an important role in
the air defences of the UK for the last time before
retirement. The contribution of No 54 Sqn at Hornchurch is well described in Air Vice-Marshal Arthur

Gould Lee's book *Fly Past* (Jarrolds, 1974), which includes a narrative on night interceptions of Handley Page Heyfords of Nos 10 and 97 Sqns from Boscombe Down and No 99 from Mildenhall. They were also up against Hawker Hinds flying daytime attacks from Bircham Newton. Among the visitors to the operations room at Hornchurch was Air Marshal Hugh Dowding – shades of things to come! By this period radio telephony procedures had been greatly improved and an increased percentage of interceptions were recorded.

As a flying machine, the Bulldog was popular with squadron pilots though, being much heavier than such types as the Gamecock, great care had to be exercised during low-level aerobatics, and problems were sometimes experienced with spin recovery. In the eight years it served with the RAF the usual quota of air collisions (with towed drogues during firing practice as well as with other aircraft in formation flying) were recorded, and it was difficult to taxy in crosswinds. There was also a tendency to nose heaviness in the landing configuration which produced many mishaps upon recovery. Most of these faults were alleviated by the retro-fitting of wider undercarriages, Bendix brakes, increased fin area and a tailwheel instead of the original skid.

One of the most interesting modifications which appeared on the Bulldog in squadron service was the experimental installation of short-chord polygonal cowling rings, which appeared briefly on K2206 and K2227 of No 56 Sqn, K1657 of No 32 Sqn and K1627 of No 111 Sqn – they were never standardised. Handley Page leading edge wing slots were also tried

Below A Bulldog cockpit, photographed during factory assembly

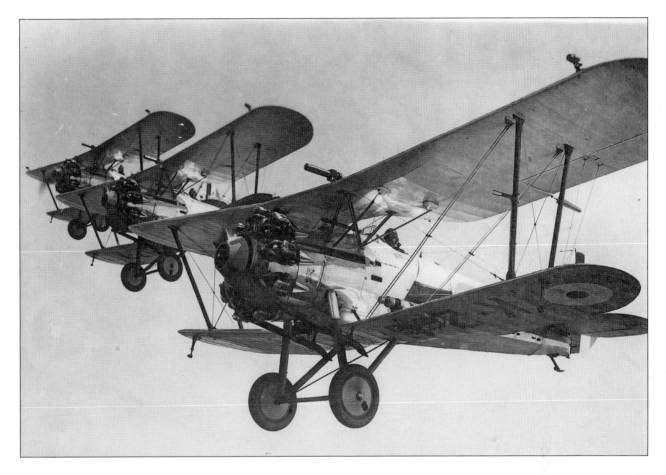

Above A trio of No 41 Sqn Bulldogs up from Northolt. The squadron leader's aircraft is nearest the camera

on a few Bulldogs (including K1653 of No 54 Sqn) but again, never entered general use.

In 1932 the Air Ministry decided to introduce a dual-control training version of the Bulldog, and K2188 was converted at Filton to meet Spec T.12/32 for tests at the CFS. With sweep-back on both upper and lower mainplanes and a revised tail assembly (eventually with increased rudder area), the first Bulldog TM reached the RAF in December 1932, followed by a further 58 airframes, some of which remained active until 1939. Production continued until May 1935, these being the last Bulldogs to be built for the RAF. Their serial numbers were in three production batches, namely K3170–3186, K3923–3953 and K4566–4576.

In the Flying Training Schools, the Bulldog TM superseded the dual Siskins and were mainly to be seen at Cranwell, Grantham and Sealand, although a few were also on the strength of RAF Abu Sueir in Egypt. Early in their careers, the Bulldog TMs

acquired a poor reputation for their spinning characteristics, but this was largely overcome by the introduction of a larger rudder, and there were very few accidents with the type. The TMs were much favoured by senior officers as personal transports, and Air Marshal Sir Robert Brooke-Popham made extensive use of K3172.

NO SURVIVORS

Sad to relate, not a single Bulldog survives in the United Kingdom today, which leaves a glaring gap in the RAF Museum's fine collection. From June 1961 until its final demise in a crash at Farnborough on 13 September 1964, Bristol's renovated factory demonstrator (G-ABBB finished to represent K2227 in No 56 Sqn livery) was a popular item on the post-war flying display circuit, and had also been featured in the film *Reach for the Sky*.

Is it perhaps too much to hope that the booming aircraft replica industry of today will turn its attention to this design, returning Bristol's arguably most famous fighter to the skies once again?

Right *Festooned with bolt-on extras, a No 41 Sqn Bulldog motors along at altitude during a sortie from its Northolt base. This aircraft wears the squadron's distinctive 'crown and cross' motif on its fin*

Below *Bulldogs K2227 and K2206 fitted with short-chord polygonal cowling rings. This modification was never standardised*

Bulldog Units in the RAF

No 3 Squadron *Upavon, May 1929 to May 1934*
Kenley, May 1934 to October 1935
Khartoum, October 1935 to January 1936
Aboukir, January 1936 to August 1936
Kenley, October 1936 to July 1937

Markings: Emerald green bar along fuselage sides from engine to tailpost and between the roundels on the upper mainplanes. Later, the fuselage stripe was broadened slightly and, ahead of the roundel, terminated just below the cockpit. On the rear of the fuselage it stopped level with the leading edge of the tailplane

Serials: J9567, 9568, 9569, 9570, 9571, 9572, 9573, 9574, 9575, 9576, 9577, 9578, 9579, 9580, 9581, 9582, 9583, 9584
K1079, 1090, 1626, 1628, 1633, 1634, 1640, 1649, 1651, 1670, 1682, 2140, 2150, 2172, 2216, 2219, 2225, 2226, 2232, 2233, 2234, 2479, 2486, 2487, 2494, 2495, 2860, 2863, 2869, 2870, 2947

No 17 Squadron *Upavon, October 1929 to May 1934*
Kenley, May 1934 to August 1936

Markings: Black parallel zig-zag stripes along the fuselage and between the roundels on the upper mainplanes. Initially, the zig-zag ahead of the fuselage roundel continued to a point just below the forward centre-

section strut, but was later terminated just below the cockpit. Behind the roundel, the zig-zags stopped ahead of the serial number

Serials: J9585, 9586, 9587, 9588, 9589, 9590, 9591
K1079, 1080, 1081, 1082, 1085, 1086, 1088, 1094, 1096, 1607, 1623, 1632, 1645, 1649, 1654, 1659, 1661, 1671, 1689, 2137, 2142, 2153, 2156, 2159, 2173, 2199, 2216, 2482, 2483, 2491, 2863, 2864, 2865, 2872, 2947, 2950, 3177

No 19 Squadron *Duxford, September 1931 to January 1935*

Markings: Blue and white squares each side of the fuselage roundel and across the upper mainplanes between the roundels. The commanding officer's aircraft repeated the blue and white checks on the fin and elevators

Serials: K2138, 2155, 2156, 2157, 2158, 2159, 2160, 2161, 2162, 2163, 2164, 2165, 2166, 2167, 2168, 2169

No 23 Squadron *Kenley, July 1931 to September 1932*
Biggin Hill, September 1932 to April 1933

Markings: Alternate red and blue squares before and aft of the roundel on the fuselage and across the upper mainplanes between both roundels. On the rear fuselage, the red and blue squares overlapped the serial number, which was displayed on a superimposed silver rectangle

Serials: K1633, 1670, 1671, 1672, 1673, 1675, 1676, 1677, 1678, 1679, 1687, 2149, 2151, 2152

Above With less than 20 hours on its Jupiter engine, K1080 poses for factory photographs in late 1929. Built as a Mk II, this machine served for some time with No 17 Sqn

No 29 Squadron *North Weald, June 1932 to April 1935*

Markings: Red 'XX' markings between two parallel red bars on the fuselage and across the upper mainplanes between the roundels.

Serials: J9587, K1081, 1085, 2210, 2211, 2215, 2220, 2866

No 32 Squadron *Kenley, January 1931 to September 1932*
Biggin Hill, September 1932 to July 1936

Markings: Blue band with diagonal inter-sections fore and aft of roundel on fuselage extending from just below cockpit to leading edge of tailplane with serial number outlined in silver on rearmost band. Wide blue bar with three diagonal inter-sections across upper mainplanes between roundels

Serials: J9587
K1606, 1615, 1616, 1617, 1619, 1620, 1622, 1623, 1631, 1657, 1665, 1680, 1690, 2147, 2155, 2170, 2171, 2192, 2480, 2481, 2493, 2963

No 41 Squadron *Northolt, October 1931 to August 1934*

Markings: Single red bar along fuselage from the cockpit to the leading edge of the rudder hinge. Serial number superimposed in black on rear bar without any silver outline. Single red bar repeated across upper mainplanes between the roundels

Serials: K2176, 2177, 2178, 2179, 2180, 2181, 2182, 2183, 2184, 2185, 2186, 2187, 2189, 2194, 2209

No 54 Squadron *Hornchurch, April 1930 to September 1936*

Markings: Single yellow bar along fuselage and across the upper mainplanes between the roundels. Initially, the yellow bar on the fuselage started below the cockpit and extended to the leading edge of the tailplane, but later this was reduced to aft of roundel only, with serial number superimposed in black and outlined in silver
Serials: K1090, 1091, 1092, 1093, 1094, 1095, 1097, 1099, 1100, 1101, 1604, 1605, 1607, 1608, 1611, 1623, 1624, 1641, 1645, 1646, 1651, 1652, 1653, 1655, 1660, 1661, 1663, 1664, 1665, 1666, 2135, 2141, 2145, 2146, 2149, 2150, 2165, 2197, 2203, 2204, 2207, 2488, 2860, 2861, 2867, 2868, 2960

No 56 Squadron *North Weald, October 1932 to May 1936*

Markings: Red and white squares on fuselage either side of the roundel and across the upper mainplanes between the roundels

Serials: K1662, 1665, 2205, 2206, 2210, 2211, 2215, 2216, 2219, 2223, 2224, 2225, 2226, 2227, 2228, 2229, 2231, 2492, 2495, 2871, 3513

No 111 Squadron *Hornchurch, January 1931 to July 1934*
Northolt, July 1934 to June 1936

Markings: Single black bar along fuselage, tapering from broad below the cockpit to narrow beneath the tailplane, terminating at the rudder hinge. Narrow black bar repeated across the upper mainplanes between the roundels. Serial number on rudder only

Serials: K1613, 1624, 1625, 1626, 1627, 1628, 1629, 1630, 1633, 1634, 1672, 1681, 1683, 1684, 1685, 2139, 2149, 2197, 2208, 2209

Meteorological Flight Aldergrove
K1660, 1686, 1687, 2144, 2213, 2493, 2861, 2951

Meteorological Flight Duxford
K2170, 2213, 2963

Central Flying School
K1636, 1668, 1693, 2167, 3505

RAF College Cranwell
K1667, 2166, 2195, 2196, 2212, 2862, 3175

No 3 FTS Grantham
K2952, 2953, 2954, 2955, 2956, 2962

Air Armament School
K1648, 1669, 1670, 1638, 2168

A&AEE Martlesham
K2191, 2193, 1603, 1659, 2201, 2215, 2221

Left The Bulldog trainer featured sweepback on both upper and lower mainplanes, and a modified empennage. A total of 59 trainers was built. This dual-control aircraft was attached to No 19 Sqn at Duxford

Left Mass jostling for positions as No 3 Sqn depart Upavon on a summer exercise in 1929. Squadron groundcrew are helping to keep the aircraft apart by physically manhandling the Bulldogs in the right direction - try doing that with a Harrier GR.7, No 3's front line fighter of today!

Bulldog Trainer

The Bulldog TM dual-control version was allocated to:

Central Flying School
K3170, 3174

RAF College Cranwell
K3172, 3175, 3923, 3924, 3925, 3926, 3927, 3928, 3942

No 1 FTS Leuchars
K3175

No 3 FTS Grantham
K3176, 3936, 3937, 3938, 3939, 3940

No 5 FTS Sealand
K3929, 3930, 3931, 3932, 3933, 3935, 3936

Additionally, some Bulldog Trainers from the final production batch (K4566–4576) are believed to have been issued to No 4 FTS at Abu Sueir in Egypt. First-line fighter squadrons also had some dual Bulldogs on their strength, including No 3 (K3177), No 17 (K3177), No 19 (K3181 and 3947), No 32 (K3179), No 54 (3178) and No 56 (K3181 and 3182).

Bristol 105A Bulldog IIA data

Engine: Bristol Jupiter VIIF, nine-cylinder direct drive, supercharged; 490 hp at normal 1775 rpm, 8000 ft rated altitude.

Dimensions

Span	33 ft 11 in
Length (skid on ground)	25 ft 0 in
Height (skid on ground)	9 ft 10 in
Wing Area	306.5 ft²

Weights

Loaded	3503 lbs
Empty	2412 lbs

Performance

Maximum Speed	178 mph at 8000 ft
Time to 20,000 ft	14.5 min
Service Ceiling	29,300 ft
Range at 15,000 ft (incl climb)	350 miles

Armament: Two fixed, synchronized, 0.303 in Mk II or Mk IIIN, Vickers machine guns, using Constantinesco interrupter gear, 600 rounds ammunition per gun, four 20 lb Mk I, HE bombs

THE HAWKER FURY

IN THE SEEMINGLY far-off days of the late 1920s and early 1930s before radar became a reality, Britain's air defence was a fairly simple matter. There was not much of it and the first warning of an enemy bomber attack, should one have come, would have been the steady and increasing drone of approaching engines. In fact, that was exactly what happened during the Annual Air Exercises. The Fairey Fox two-seat day bomber, powered by a neatly-cowled American Curtiss D-12 liquid-cooled engine, appeared on the scene in Britain in 1925 and showed itself handsomely able

to outpace contemporary bombers at a good 150 mph. It was also capable of outrunning the fastest fighters in RAF service – a sobering thought.

The first of the Rolls-Royce 'F' series of engines (somewhat similar in general design to the American V12 and to become known as the Kestrel) was a timely and fortunate development and, when mounted in Sydney Camm's Hawker Hart bomber, added urgency to the need for a really fast fighter. The Hart was even quicker than the Fox – in fact 30 mph faster at 10,000 ft. This situation gave rise to a peculiarly British

Left Hawker Fury I K2048, the squadron commander's aircraft of No 1 Sqn, photographed in April 1933, up from RAF Tangmere. This machine also served with No 25 Sqn prior to its spell in Sussex

Right The unmarked Hawker Hornet photographed at Brooklands in January 1929. It was the true Fury prototype and later took up the serial number J9682

invention, the interceptor fighter, intended to eliminate as far as possible, the perceived need for standing fighter patrols. It obviously had to be fast, quick-climbing and capable of a rapid reaction to a high or low-level attack, for which the close proximity to the coast or major centres of population gave a minimum of warning time.

FIGHTER SPECIFICATIONS

A series of Air Ministry fighter specifications had succeeded F.9/26, the competition originating in 1926 being won by the Bristol Bulldog with its supercharged Jupiter VII engine. The Hart, with a high-compression but unsupercharged Kestrel, could outpace the Bulldog fairly comfortably at 10,000 ft, and this brought matters sharply to a head. Camm, seldom if ever outpaced, then produced an interceptor to Spec F.20/27 late in 1927, an unnamed prototype which achieved a creditable 202 mph powered by an uncowled Bristol Mercury VI radial engine. Despite this, the outstanding performance of the Hart almost

at once made the F.20/27 specification inadequate, and the fortunate dual availability of the Kestrel as an engine for use in fighters as well as bombers quickly changed all that.

The production by Rolls-Royce of a fully-supercharged version of the F.XI, the Kestrel IS, enabled Camm to mount it with a closely-fitting, streamlined cowling, in a derivative of the F.20/27. So was created the Hawker Hornet interceptor. At first it was only marginally faster at a slightly greater altitude than the F.20/27, but obviously had great potential and aroused much interest at the Olympia Aero Show in 1929. It was initially powered by the F.XIA, or Kestrel IA engine, a 490 hp unsupercharged development power-plant which was soon to be replaced by the new 480 hp supercharged Kestrel IS.

Several visits soon afterwards to the A&AEE confirmed initial impressions of the Hornet's excellent handling and performance. It had by then been given the serial J9682. Being largely of metal construction, it was also very strong but, perhaps more obviously, it was a most elegant aeroplane. It had a beautifully

Above and below Two views of K1927, the second
production Hawker Fury. This aircraft first went to the
A&AEE and then to the RAE, after which it joined No 43
Sqn before ending up as 1068M in 1938

cowled Kestrel IS, combining a sleekness with an
obvious air of aggression. When on the ground, its
rather narrow, stalky undercarriage gave little hint of
the appearance of the aeroplane in flight, and its

rocking motion when taxying over rough grass was anything but graceful. However, as soon as it got its tail up and off the ground (in little over 100 yards), its rakish and heavily staggered wings took charge under the impulse of the big Watts wooden propeller, and the wheels and struts of the undercarriage became more akin to the outstretched talons of a falcon.

The excellent assessment of the handsome Hawker Hornet at Martlesham led to its entry into competition for a production order as an 'interception day fighter', a contest which it won. The opposition had been the similarly-powered Fairey Firefly IIM. A production order was placed under Spec F.13/30. The engine was to be a fully-supercharged 525 hp F.XIIS, by then known as the Kestrel IIS. Under the 1927 Air Ministry policy of giving RAF fighters names beginning with 'F', the aircraft was renamed Fury. The first production aircraft K1926, was flown at Brooklands by P E G Sayer on 25 March 1931. The Fury's superb manoeuvrability and generally dazzling performance in flight (the first fighter in squadron service to exceed 200 mph in level flight) might have given the impression of its being a 'hot ship'. In fact, it was hardly more so than its stablemate the Hart, which in trainer versions cared (generally safely) for many hundreds of young pilots, as the writer can testify.

The Fury's airframe was similar to that of the

Above Hawkler Fury I K1926 was the first production aircraft. After a period with the A&AEE and the RAE, it flew with No 1 Sqn; it was finally grounded as instructional airframe 928M

Hornet but had been modified and slightly strengthened in places. The radiator area was greater and all water piping was of stainless steel, a novelty at the time. Oil and fuel supply pipes were similarly made. The construction was described as 'composite', that is to say the fuselage, complete tail unit skeleton, wing spars and struts were of steel, whilst the wing ribs were of wood. In accordance with standard Hawker practice, all tubes were cadmium coated and then stove enamelled. Light alloys, apart from the highly polished engine cowling panels, were anodically treated. The fuselage was principally of steel tube and duralumin, with fabric covering over light wooden formers and stringers. The fuselage side panels were warren girder structures, based on four tubular longerons, the stern frame being internally wire braced. Cross members were of tube with wire bracing. The fuselage was made in four parts; the front or engine mounting, with quickly-detachable and polished aluminium cowling panels; the centre containing the fuel and oil tanks, guns and cockpit (also with aluminium panels); and the rear section and stern frame.

Above The Kestrel VIS-engined Hawker High Speed Fury, with tapered lower wing and carefully-faired struts. The aircraft spent most of its life with Hawker, Rolls-Royce and the RAE and was used as a Kestrel and Goshawk engine test-bed

The centre portion contained the two fuel tanks, radiator, forward-firing synchronized guns and their ammunition boxes, together with the pilot's instruments, controls and adjustable seat (with Sutton harness Mk IV). The fuel was carried in two tanks, mounted behind a fire-proof bulkhead. The upper 27-gal gravity tank had its main axis fore and aft, with the upper surface deeply indented to accommodate the troughs for the twin Vickers machine guns. The lower, or main tank, containing 23 gal, was mounted beneath and at right angles to the other tank and fed to the carburettor by an engine-driven pump, via a non-return valve. Furies up to and including K2082 had entirely separate supplies from each tank to the carburettor. With this system, the gravity supply was liable to fail during certain negative-G manoeuvres, and some aircraft were modified so that the pump could draw supplies from either tank, the gravity tank being available should the pump fail. The oil tank was mounted beneath the main fuel tank, the five-element Vickers-Potts cooler mounted behind the venetian blind-type engine radiator shutters. Unlike the Hart series, the radiator, which was mounted between the undercarriage legs, was not retractable.

FUSELAGE CONSTRUCTION

The Fury's fuselage conformed to standard Hawker practice, the top fairing of the centre and rear portions being constructed of wood frames and stringers, covered with ply reinforcement at the rear of the cockpit and fabric, continuing the line of the top of the rear fuselage to the front fin post. The side and bottom panels were built in the same way. The undercarriage,

Above An unusual view of Hawker Fury I K1944 from the initial production batch. After service with No 43 Sqn it became an instructional airframe in June 1936 and was eventually struck off charge three years later

constructed of steel tube, was of the through-axle type, with Vickers oleo-pneumatic shock-absorbing legs and wire bracing for the trailing radius rods. The wheels were equipped with Palmer hydraulic brakes, operated by pedals on the rudder bar. The operation of each brake was through the inflation with fluid of an annular, rubberized fabric expansion chamber, round whose periphery a string of small asbestos brake blocks was bonded. The tail skid had compression-rubber shock absorbers and a limited swivelling arc.

The upper and lower wings differed in area, dihedral, even (very slightly) in their incidence, except for their RAF 28 aerofoil section. A wire-braced upper centre-section was supported by four struts and contained, on the starboard side, a 19-gal gravity fuel tank which provided an emergency supply for about 50 min duration. The spar booms were of rolled high-tensile steel strip, built up into an approximate figure of eight section. They were joined by longitudinally corrugated webs, this riveted assembly being both light and

strong. The ribs were built up of light alloy and all four wings were stabilized by internal drag struts and wire bracing. A single set of N-shaped interplane struts was mounted on each side, the whole interplane assembly being wire-braced. Frise-type balanced ailerons, differentially operated and giving 32° up and 24° down, contributed much to the Fury's good handling. Ailerons were mounted on the upper wings only. All wing surfaces were fabric-covered. Instead of tear-off patches over aileron inspection points, Hawker substituted small hinged doors, thus reducing the time to renew aileron control by 150 man-minutes – typical of the easy maintenance throughout the airframe.

The tail unit, including controls and stern frame, were of similar construction to the rear fuselage and

Below Hawker Fury Is of No 1 Sqn. Nearest the camera is K2043, delivered early in 1932 and relegated to an instructional airframe in November 1937. The other Furies are: K2040, which appears to have a replacement rudder; K5673, which has the squadron badge inside the standard spearhead surround on the fin (it crashed on landing at South Cerney on 7 December 1938 while with No 3 FTS); and, furthest from the camera, K2881, which was delivered in December 1932

wings. The braced tailplane was adjustable for incidence and therefore fore and aft trim, by a screw-jack attached to the sternpost and operated by the pilot's trimming wheel. The fin was offset 3° to port to counteract torque. On Furies up to K2082, the rudder bar was not adjustable in flight but, in later aircraft, the rudder bar was adjustable 4 in fore and aft, by means of a foot-operated star wheel.

It may come as a surprise to read that the *Air*

Publication for the Fury, dated 1931, specified the provision of a seat for an Irvin-type parachute. The long-overdue wearing of a parachute had only become compulsory in RAF flying in 1927 and, in this connection, the late Peter Lewis in his book *The British Fighter since 1912* (Putnam, 1965), deplored this delay and wrote '. . . an untold number of brave lives – those of dearly-loved sons, husbands and fathers – had been allowed to be lost needlessly over the years in the most scandalous manner, as though human life were of no value whatsoever to those in whose hands lay the responsibility for providing adequate equipment for the Nation's aircrew'.

In October, 1931, a detailed performance report on a production Fury emerged from Martlesham. This concerned K1927, the second aircraft to be built in the first production batch (together with 26 others, in three weeks, so straightforward were Hawker design

Above *Another atmospheric view of the High Speed Fury, the pilot banking his fighter towards the photographer, thus showing the modified upper wing to full advantage*

and assembly techniques). The A&AEE reports on the Fury were almost unstinting in their praise for the aircraft. The pilot's view was excellent and the cockpit was warmed from the engine radiator. Taxying was easy by means of the brakes, whose action was effective, progressive and easy in application. Cockpit controls and instruments were easily accessible.

In flying tests at all speeds and heights, the controllability and manoeuvrability were described as light and effective. Performance was a slight improvement on the Hornet, despite the engine rpm being well below the maximum permissible. Dive tests, to the limiting crankshaft speed of the engine (which had been increased from 2500 in the Hornet to 2700 rpm) were made at both fore and aft cg limits, the aircraft being steady in the dive, there being no sign of instability, flutter or undue vibration. Control move-

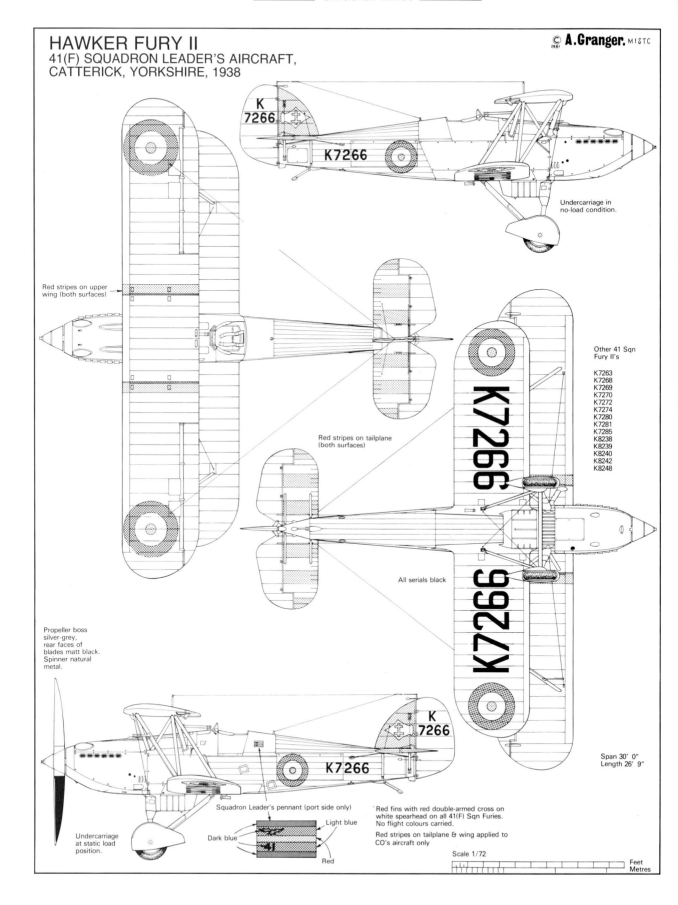

HAWKER FURY II
41(F) SQUADRON LEADER'S AIRCRAFT, CATTERICK, YORKSHIRE, 1938

© A.Granger. MISTC
1981

Undercarriage in no-load condition.

Red stripes on upper wing (both surfaces)

Red stripes on tailplane (both surfaces)

Other 41 Sqn Fury II's

K7263
K7268
K7269
K7270
K7272
K7274
K7280
K7281
K7285
K8238
K8239
K8240
K8242
K8248

All serials black

Propeller boss silver-grey, rear faces of blades matt black. Spinner natural metal.

Span 30' 0"
Length 26' 9"

Undercarriage at static load position.

Squadron Leader's pennant (port side only)

Light blue

Dark blue

Red

Red fins with red double-armed cross on white spearhead on all 41(F) Sqn Furies. No flight colours carried.

Red stripes on tailplane & wing applied to CO's aircraft only

Scale 1/72

Feet
Metres

ments during the dives gave proper response, and recovery was easy without alteration of the tail incidence set at the outset. The aircraft was simple to fly, the controls being good, although there was a marked swing to port on take-off.

The Fury Mk II was proposed by Camm in 1934. It was based on experiments with the airframe and engine which were undertaken to gain the maximum performance from this superbly clean design, and was originally built to Spec F.14/32, powered by a fully-supercharged 640 hp Kestrel VI fitted with automatic boost control. The design was cleaned up and wheel-spats were fitted at first, although operations from grass aerodromes (runways were almost unheard-of) tended to clog the spats with mud and they were often removed. Production Fury IIs were built to Spec

F.6/35 at the General Aircraft factory at Hanworth, as well as at Kingston, where the first (K7263) was completed in 1936. The Hawker fighter showed an adaptability to accommodate a variety of different engines, both British and foreign. This feature contributed to successful exports to five countries, although it must be admitted that few, if any, engine installations were as successful as that of the Kestrel.

FURIES IN SERVICE

The modern word is charisma. Can there ever have been a British fighter aeroplane (with the possible exception of the Spitfire) of the piston-engine era which possessed more of this mysterious but immediately recognisable quality? The Fury was the perfect

Right *Fury squadrons gained masses of publicity for the RAF in the 1930s, their slick airshow routines at the Hendon pageants impressing hundreds of thousands. One of the chief exponents of Fury formation flying was No 1 Sqn, who were photographed here by* Flight *practising over Sussex in the mid-1930s*

Left A flight of No 25 Sqn Furies land tied together at the 1934 RAF Display at Hendon on 30 June. Three flights of three landed in this way, and all but one of the rubber cables remained unbroken

Below Early in 1930 J9682 flew trials with No 1 Sqn, but on 11 April 1930 it collided with Siskin J7959 at 3000ft, shed its top wing and crashed near Chichester, Sussex

Above No 43 Sqn take off from Brooklands

vehicle for all the pre-war fighter pilots who flew it to exude the glamour which came to be associated with the life-style of the breed who, all too soon, were to be involved in the brutal realities of air combat in World War 2 in Hurricanes, Spitfires and Typhoons.

Historically, the Fury was the first RAF fighter to exceed the magic 200 mph, but even more exciting was its official description (arising from its design parameters) of interceptor, meaning in effect rapid climb and short endurance. This of course was long before the days of ground-controlled interception and radar, but it always had a certain ring to it. At all events it helped it to gain the publicity which it enjoyed as a star performer of the RAF, never less than in its triumphant performances at the annual RAF Displays at Hendon and, indeed, at international air displays.

The concept of the interceptor fighter, as embodied in the Fury, had its earliest origins in Air Ministry Specification F.20/27, which called for a fast single-seat day fighter with the 'capability to overtake, in the shortest possible time, an enemy passing vertically overhead at 20,000 ft and 150 mph'. In essence, this philosophy was getting close to the concept of 'point defence' as understood today, and stood in stark contrast to the practice of standing patrols familiar from World War One and maintained by RAF fighters throughout the 1920s and, indeed, by the Bulldog until as late as 1937. The design problem for manufacturers turned on the need to dramatically improve the power to weight ratio (hence a better climb) and to clean up the aerodynamic qualities. This is exactly what Hawker was able to achieve by utilising the smooth entry lines of a powerful Rolls-Royce in-line engine in place of a bulky drag-inducing air-cooled radial such as had hitherto reigned supreme in standard RAF fighters like the Gamecock, Siskin and Bulldog.

Air Staff thinking on these matters had been given greater impetus by (ironically enough) the entry into service of Hawker's own light bomber, the Hart, which exemplified the improved state of the art among attacking aircraft.

HORNET TO FURY

It was against this background that the Fury first emerged, following satisfactory trials with its immediate progenitor, the Hornet (J9682), during 1930. The change of the name to Fury from Hornet resulted from a new Air Ministry attempt to rationalise its nomenclature policy so that all land-based fighters had names beginning with 'F', and at one period (horror of horrors!) actually contemplated such bizarre and unsuitable names as Flash, Flicker and Foil. So it came about that the first Fury to full production standards, reaching 207 mph with its 525 hp Kestrel IIS engine, made its first flight from Brooklands on 25 March 1931. It met Specification 13/30, which was written around the design, and could reach 10,000 ft in just over four minutes, thus becoming the crack fighter of the RAF. The Fury maintained this position until the arrival of the Gauntlet in 1935.

HAWKER FURY I

SINGLE-SEAT FIGHTER
ONE 525 h.p. ROLLS-ROYCE KESTREL ENGINE

KEY

1 Stainless steel spar-boom and web
2 Outer plane attachment point
3 Wooden ribs
4 Dural tube outlines
5 Ply leading edge
6 Fuel bay provision on starboard side
7 Frise aileron (up 32°, down 24°)
8 Aileron control run
9 Aileron balance "streamline" rod
10 Dural strut
11 Steam condenser on Mk II
12 Rolls-Royce Kestrel IIS; power at max power altitude 575–590 b.h.p.
13 Watts wooden propeller, 10ft 6in dia, 15ft pitch
14 Coolant header tank (total 13gal)
15 Steel tube fuselage construction
16 Stainless steel jointing-plates
17 Starting-handle fitting
18 Air intake
19 Fireproof bulkhead (aluminium/asbestos sandwich)
20 Tinned-steel fuel tanks (50gal)
21 Fuel filler
22 Fuel contents gauge
23 Aluminium oil tank (4½gal)
24 Radiator
25 Vickers-Potts oil cooler
26 Engine controls
27 Radiator shutter controls

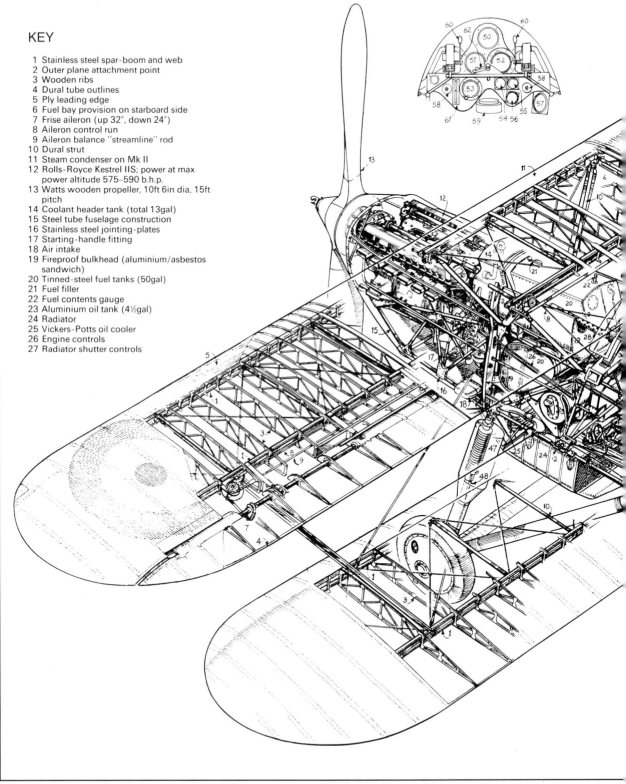

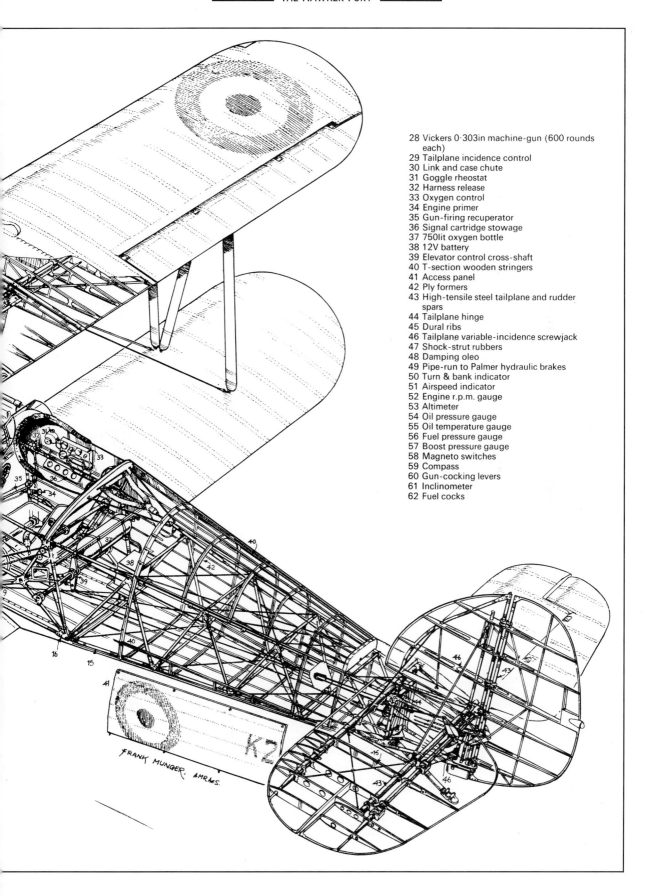

28 Vickers 0·303in machine-gun (600 rounds
each)
29 Tailplane incidence control
30 Link and case chute
31 Goggle rheostat
32 Harness release
33 Oxygen control
34 Engine primer
35 Gun-firing recuperator
36 Signal cartridge stowage
37 750lit oxygen bottle
38 12V battery
39 Elevator control cross-shaft
40 T-section wooden stringers
41 Access panel
42 Ply formers
43 High-tensile steel tailplane and rudder
spars
44 Tailplane hinge
45 Dural ribs
46 Tailplane variable-incidence screwjack
47 Shock-strut rubbers
48 Damping oleo
49 Pipe-run to Palmer hydraulic brakes
50 Turn & bank indicator
51 Airspeed indicator
52 Engine r.p.m. gauge
53 Altimeter
54 Oil pressure gauge
55 Oil temperature gauge
56 Fuel pressure gauge
57 Boost pressure gauge
58 Magneto switches
59 Compass
60 Gun-cocking levers
61 Inclinometer
62 Fuel cocks

FRANK MUNGER. AMRAeS.

Since the Fury out-performed the contemporary fighter squadron equipment of the period – the Bulldog – the question might well be asked as to why it equipped far fewer squadrons? Part of the answer is undoubtedly that it cost more to produce; allegedly about £5400 compared with £4600 for a Bulldog, at least at the outset, and at a time when the Treasury was struggling with a recession (then called a depression) in the British economy. In the event, a total of 230 Furies were built to RAF requirements in eight batches between October 1930 and April 1937. All but the last 89 were built by Hawkers, the remainder by General Aircraft of Hanworth. Details are as follow:

Hawker Fury Production for the RAF

Fury Mk 1	K1926–1946	Hawker
	K2035–2082	Hawker
	K2874–2883	Hawker
	K2899–2904	Hawker
	K3730–3742	Hawker
	K5663–5682	Hawker
Fury Mk II	K7263–7285	Hawker
	K8218–8306	General Aircraft

The Fury II, which made its first appearance in RAF service in November 1936, featured an up-rated Kestrel VI engine and had increased fuel tankage, which allowed it to reach a top speed of 223 mph. The initial production batch had rather elegant wheel spats, but these were discarded on later aircraft,

leaving only a tailwheel as a distinguishing feature. Early examples were built to Spec 6/35 and later production to Spec 19/35.

Although over the course of its RAF career the Fury equipped six first-line fighter squadrons, it is with three pre-eminent units that its fame is associated – the elite Nos 1, 25 and 43 Sqns. No 43 Sqn ('The Fighting Cocks') was the first to receive Fury fighters in May 1931 at the historic Tangmere airfield, where they had previously flown Siskins. Their companion squadron at Tangmere – No 1 Fighter Sqn – retained their Siskins until February 1932, as did No 25 Sqn at Hawkinge, before receiving Furies. The friendly rivalry between these three squadrons undoubtedly generated a notable standard of efficiency, as was well reflected in their performance year after year in competitive activities such as successful interceptions in Air Exercises, prowess in individual and formation aerobatics in air displays and gunnery. The high spirited activities of their very gifted young pilots are entertainingly recorded in a number of excellent accounts which the reader is recommended to seek out, notably Michael Shaw's *Twice Vertical* (No 1 Sqn), Roy Humphreys' *Hawkinge 1912–1961* (No 25 Sqn) and J Beedle's *No 43 Sqn* history. A flavour of the activities off-duty is well-conveyed by the very irreverent description of No 43 Sqn as 'Mother Meyrick's Own', named after a well-known London night club patronised by the boys from Tangmere.

However, No 43 Sqn could work hard as well as play hard. In the annual Air Exercises of 1931, Furies

Right Fury II K7284 was
attached to the Station
Flight at RAF Northolt.
Delivered towards the end
of 1936, it was lost in a
forced landing at Fulmer,
Bucks, in September 1939

Left Three flights of No 43
Sqn Furies up from RAF
Tangmere in June 1932

of No 43 Sqn alone achieved more interceptions against the raiding bombers than all the Bulldog squadrons put together. The unit also had the honour of presenting the Fury before the public at the 1931 Hendon Air Display, where a team of three led by Flt Lt E T Carpenter AFC included a formation roll in their repertoire. Furies were subsequently to be star performers at every annual RAF Hendon Display until the series came to an end in 1937. In 1933 it was the turn of No 25 Sqn (led by Sqn Ldr A L Paxton, universally known as 'Tony' Paxton) to earn top

billing, and to provide a footnote in RAF history with its outstanding team of nine Furies which began its show with a nine-aircraft take-off, all tied together. The most spectacular feature of their routine was a nine-aircraft formation roll whilst tied together! No 25 Sqn then broke into three flights, still tied together, for a series of individual aerobatics sequences, all topped-off by a 'Prince of Wales Feathers' break with the leading flight pulling up and looping after a

Below K2902 was delivered in January 1933

Left Camouflaged No 43 Sqn Furies up from RAF Tangmere in October 1938. From September 1938 all the squadron's Furies were painted thus, with squadron markings deleted from the Munich Crisis onward

vertical climb and the other two flights rolling to port and starboard.

In RAF Display annals the 1934 event became known as 'the Year of the Fury'. All three squadrons surpassed themselves and dominated the show. No 25 Sqn repeated its tied-together routine, No 1 Sqn performed magnificent synchronised aerobatics by two aircraft, augmented by a memorable exhibition of individual aerobatics by Flg Off J L M Davys in K2881, and No 43 Sqn contributed 17 manoeuvres in two flight sections before a triumphant finale over the Royal Box.

In 1935 it was the turn of No 1 Sqn to demonstrate the Fury's actual air combat skills as a change from aerobatics, however exciting. Three Furies piloted by Flt Lt C R Hancock DFC, Flg Off E A Douglas-Jones and Sgt Pearson engaged in an aerial dogfight with the very agile Overstrand twin-engined day bomber of No 101 Sqn, a spectacle which recalled memories of the encounter between Bulldogs and a Sidestrand in 1932 and the even earlier fight between two Nighthawks and a Boulton Paul Bourges in 1923.

The year 1937 witnessed the emergence of what was arguably the finest of all the Fury aerobatic teams, namely that of No 1 Squadron led by Flt Lt E M 'Teddy' Donaldson in his familiar K5673, accompanied by Flg Offs H E Boxer, 'Johnnie' Walker and 'Prosser' Hanks. This was the team which gained international renown for the RAF by exhibiting the skill of pilots during its historic appearance at the International Air Meeting at Zurich. This event

followed close on the heels of the team's standing ovation performance at the final Hendon Air Display in the presence of HM King George VI. The display in Switzerland, which even brought congratulations from General Milch of the *Luftwaffe* and outclassed the best that the crack Fiat CR.42 team could do from the *Regia Aeronautica*, was flown by Furies K5673 (leader), K2043, K2089 and K2881. Without question, these four (by 1937 standards) rather obsolescent biplanes had made a strong impression on their future enemies at a time of rapidly increasing international tension, and struck a blow for the prestige of RAF fighter skills which was to be fully confirmed during the events of 1940.

'Teddy' Donaldson, who later added to his laurels in September 1946 by raising the World Air Speed Record to 616 mph in RAF High Speed Flight Meteor EE549 (and on leaving the Service became the *Daily Telegraph*'s Air Correspondent), was but one among a host of memorable personalities associated with the elite world of the Fury. Sqn Ldr F R D Swain AFC, who commanded No 1 Sqn in 1937, already merited an entry in the history books for his achievement of the World Altitude Record of 49,967 ft in a Bristol 138A in September 1936. One of No 25 Sqn's commanders in Fury days was, in 1953, to become Chief of the Air Staff, namely Marshal of the RAF, Sir William Dickson GCB KBE DSO AFC. Another future air marshal in No 25 Sqn was Flt Lt K B 'Bing' Cross, later to become Air Vice-Marshal Sir Kenneth Cross, a stalwart commander of the Bomber Command V-Force

Right No 1 Sqn Furies up from Tangmere in July 1933. Like several other Sussex Furies, the lead aircraft in this formation initially served with No 25 Sqn

until 1963. Many outstanding members of Fury squadrons were, alas, to lose their lives in the air fighting of 1940–45. The transition from peace to war for the fighter pilots of No 1 Sqn is well-captured in Paul Richey's classic account *Fighter Pilot* (Jane's, 1980). He describes the traumatic business of hastily camouflaging the beautifully groomed silver Furies to drab war paint during the Munich Crisis of September 1938, and the dismay which greeted Sqn Ldr Bertram's announcement, 'Gentleman, our aircraft are too slow to catch the German bombers: we must ram them.'

Happily, as events turned out, no such desperate measures were required as No 1 Sqn gave up its Furies for Hurricanes in November 1938, as did No 43 Sqn in January 1939.

FRONTLINE SERVICE

The popularity of the Fury as a flying machine and aerobatic mount has been sufficiently well-rehearsed in the foregoing account and some comments must be made on its capacity as a fighting machine. Although, with the RAF, it never fired its guns in anger, some 29 examples were exported to the South African Air Force (22 of them ex-RAF) between 1939 and 1941 and some of them saw action in East Africa in May 1940. Records show that at least two Caproni Ca 133s were shot down but they proved inferior in the climb to the Fiat CR.42 fighter. As already mentioned, Furies performed well during the earlier Air Exercises of the 1930s in the UK, but the squadrons reported consistent trouble with stoppages on the twin Vickers guns during air firing training camps, especially at higher altitudes, and it has to be concluded that by about 1937 their true effectiveness was over with the introduction of such types as the Blenheim and modern foreign adversaries such as the Heinkel He 111 and Dornier Do 17. Naturally enough, all this had been foreseen, but at this date only a trickle of Hurricanes was coming from the factories and, as new Fighter Command Squadrons were being formed, late production Furies built in 1936–37 which had not been earmarked for training duties were used to provide interim equipment for first-line squadrons such as No 41 (actually scheduled for Spitfires which were not to arrive until January 1939), and Nos 73 and 87 which were to be equipped with Gladiators. The upshot was that the Fury did not actually disappear from Fighter Command's Order of Battle until as late as January 1939. No 43 Sqn had the last six Furies flown away to storage at Kemble on 2 February 1939.

With Munich clouds fast approaching, the Fury had its final fling in the atmosphere of pre-war air display glory at the *Daily Express* flying show held at Gatwick in June 1938. No 43 Sqn flew up from Tangmere to treat the public to a nine-aircraft line-abreast fly-past in atrociously bumpy weather and this was followed by a typically dashing exposition of individual aerobatics by one of the great characters of the squadron, Flt Lt Caesar Hull, a Rhodesian who had joined the RAF in 1935. Hull went on to serve in World War 2 in Gladiators in the short-lived Norwegian Campaign, before returning to join his old squadron (by that time on Hurricanes) which he commanded very briefly from 1 September 1940, before being shot down and killed on 8 September, having logged at least 10 victories over the *Luftwaffe*.

As a vehicle for imbuing confidence in the flying skills of budding fighter pilots the Fury was unsurpassed, and it is therefore no surprise to note that, in addition to its fame as a fighter with first-line squadrons, it played a key part in the training programme during the 1930s. Beginning with No 2 FTS Digby in

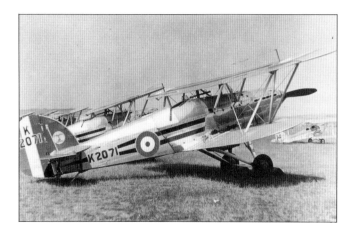

Above Wearing the solid fin colours synonymous with a flight commander's mount, K2071 of No 25 Sqn heads a line-up of Fury Is resting at an unknown civil airfield in Kent. Following the unit's re-equipment with Demons in October 1937, this veteran machine was passed onto No 3 FTS at South Cerney

1933 it served with no less than nine FTSs in addition to the CFS and the RAF College, Cranwell, offering advanced training to pupils who had already passed through the dual-control Hart phases. With their polished aluminium nose panels in stark contrast to the yellow-painted fabric surfaces, the training Furies were just as aesthetically satisfying to look at as their more warlike counterparts in the first-line squadrons.

A large proportion of future Battle of Britain pilots had their first experience of flying fighters in the cockpit of a Fury, and the memories were always vivid and pleasurable. One of the best writers on this subject is John Nesbitt-Dufort DSO, who recorded in his book, *Open Cockpit* (1970), that the Fury's 'performance and behaviour can be summed up in two words, perfectly delightful. Possibly the Gloster Gauntlet ran it a close second for sheer joy in flight, but even the Spitfire and the Hurricane did not possess its extremely light positive 'feel'. It had the sparkle of a Bugatti coupled with the docility of an Hispano-Suiza'.

Altogether, about 140 Furies served with the various training establishments. Some of them were passed on from first-line units, but the majority were from late production batches direct from the factory, or from reserve stocks at maintenance units. Some examples were still flying around in 1940, including those serving with No 1 Air Armament School and No 2 Anti-aircraft Co-operation Unit, although these well-used fighters were soon grounded.

It is a matter of the greatest regret that today not a single example of an ex-RAF Fury survives in this country. The late and much missed collector and *aficionado*, the Hon Patrick Lindsay, had a beautiful reproduction built and flown just prior to his death but this was recently sold abroad. Readers who have been inspired by the legend of the fabulous Fury cannot do better, therefore, than to seek out the reproduction Fury II bearing the serial K7271 and the insignia of No 25 Sqn, which was displayed at the Aerospace Museum at Cosford for some years, but is now likely to move to Tangmere.

Fury Units in the RAF

No 1 Squadron *Tangmere, February 1932 to November 1938*

Markings: Two red parallel bars (joined at each end) between roundels on upper mainplanes. Parallel red bars ahead of roundel and tapering aft on the fuselage. On early aircraft, the fuselage bars were more widely spaced than on later aircraft. Top decking on early aircraft painted in flight colours which were duplicated on spinners and wheel covers and on fins for flight leaders. Later aircraft had squadron badge inside standard spearhead surround on fins. Camouflage finish was applied at the time of Munich in 1938, but there is no evidence that the code letters issued (NA) were ever displayed

Serials: K1926, 1931, 1940, 1943, 2035, 2036, 2037, 2038, 2039, 2040, 2041, 2042, 2043, 2044, 2045, 2046, 2047, 2048, 2049, 2050, 2051, 2052, 2055, 2060, 2061, 2062, 2063, 2064, 2065, 2066, 2067, 2069, 2074, 2075, 2878, 2881, 8247, 8248, 8249, 8255, 8272, 8289, 8290, 8291, 8296, 8303

No 25 Squadron *Hawkinge, February 1932 to October 1937*

Markings: Two black parallel bars on upper mainplanes between roundels and on the fuselage ahead of the roundel and tapering aft. Later aircraft had squadron badge inside standard spearhead surround on the fin

Serials: K1930, 1945, 2041, 2048, 2050, 2051, 2052, 2053, 2055, 2056, 2057, 2059, 2060, 2062, 2066, 2067, 2068, 2069, 2070, 2071, 2072, 2073, 2076, 2077, 2078, 2079, 2877, 2878, 2882, 2883, 5677, 7263, 7264, 7265, 7266, 7267, 7268, 7269, 7270, 7271, 7272, 7273, 7274, 7275, 7276, 7277, 7278, 7279, 7280, 7281, 7282, 7283

No 41 Squadron *Catterick, October 1937 to January 2939*

Markings: No specific squadron markings were carried on mainplanes or fuselage, but a red fin surrounded the standard fighter spearhead outline which in turn enclosed the squadron badge. Formation leader displayed two red longitudinal stripes across upper mainplanes and red stripes longitudinally on tailplane

Serials: K7263, 7264, 7265, 7266, 7268, 7269, 7270, 7271, 7272, 7274, 7275, 7276, 7277, 7278, 7280, 7281, 7282, 7283, 7285

No 43 Squadron *Tangmere, May 1931 to January 1939*

Markings: Black squares in a checkerboard pattern against the aluminium dope finish between the roundels on the upper mainplanes and ahead of the roundel on the fuselage. By 1937, the standard fighter spearhead surrounded the squadron badge on the fin. From September 1938 all aircraft were camouflaged and squadron markings disappeared. Squadron code letters (NQ) were officially allocated but it is doubtful if they were ever applied as there is no photographic evidence to support this theory

Serials: K1927, 1928, 1929, 1930, 1931, 1932, 1933, 1934, 1935, 1936, 1937, 1938, 1939, 1940, 1941, 1942, 1943, 1944, 1945, 1946, 2035, 2050, 2051, 2052, 2053, 2054, 2070, 2074, 2075, 2076, 2080, 2081, 2082, 2882, 3730, 3731, 3732, 3733, 3734, 3735, 3736, 3737, 3738, 3739, 3740, 3741, 3742, 5671, 5672, 5674, 5675, 8250, 8251, 8252, 8253, 8254, 8256, 8257, 8299

No 73 Squadron *Mildenhall, March 1937 to July 1937*

Markings: No squadron markings applied as the aircraft were merely interim equipment for the short period before Gladiators arrived

Serials: K8247, 8248, 8249, 8257, 8258, 8270, 8271, 8272

No 87 Squadron *Tangmere, March 1937 to June 1937*

Markings: No squadron markings applied in the brief period of service before the planned Gladiator equipment arrived

Serials: K2052, 2062, 2066, 2878, 2882, 2883, 8256, 8257, 8258, 8270, 8271, 8273, 8274, 8275, 8276, 8277, 8278, 8279, 8280, 8281

Training Units

No 2 FTS Digby and Brize Norton
K2877, 2903, 3730, 3731, 3732, 3741, 8269

No 3 FTS South Cerney
K1928, 1929, 1941, 2035, 2058, 2067, 2071, 2876, 2880, 2882, 3740, 5673, 5676, 5678, 5680

No 5 FTS Sealand
K1941, 2050, 3733, 3734, 3735, 3736, 5663, 5669, 5670, 8226, 8251

No 6 FTS Netheravon
K2040, 3737, 3738, 3739, 5667, 8225, 8234, 8237, 8258

No 7 FTS Peterborough
K5663, 5668, 5669, 5670, 8270, 8278, 8288, 8299

No 8 FTS Montrose
K2050, 5672, 8227, 8228, 8229, 8252, 8253, 8261, 8262, 8263, 8265, 8266, 8267, 8293

No 9 FTS Hullavington
K2879, 8218, 8219, 8220, 8221, 8222, 8223, 8224, 8254, 8264, 8271, 8289, 8290, 8303, 8305

No 10 FTS Ternhill
K2082, 8230, 8231, 8232, 8233, 8282, 8283, 8284, 8285, 8286, 8287, 8299

No 11 FTS Shawbury
K1937, 1938, 2062, 2878, 2883, 5666, 5679, 8235, 8236, 8256, 8275, 8294, 8295, 8304

RAF College, Cranwell
K5664, 5665, 5678, 5680, 5681, 5682, 8242, 8259, 8260, 8268, 8297, 8298, 8300, 8301, 8302

Central Flying School, Upavon
K2875, 2904, 8238, 8239, 8240, 8241, 8243, 8244, 8245, 8250, 8259, 8260, 8268, 8292, 8297, 8298, 8300, 8302

No 1 Air Armament School
K2899, 8243, 8244, 8245, 8246, 8255, 8306

No 2 Anti-Aircraft Co-operation Unit
K8273, 8274, 8280

Hawker Fury I & II data

Engine: Rolls-Royce Kestrel, V12 cylinder, fully-supercharged

	Kestrel IIS	Kestrel VI
Max power	550 hp, 2700 rpm	696 hp, 2900 rpm
	+1.75 boost at 11,500 ft	+1.5 boost at 11,000 ft
Dimensions		
Span	30 ft 0 in	30 ft 0 in
Length	26 ft 9 in	26 ft 9 in
Height	10 ft 2.5 in	10 ft 2.5 in
Wing Area	251.8 ft²	251.8 ft²
Weights		
Loaded	3490 lbs	3609 lbs
Empty	2623 lbs	2743 lbs
Performance		
Max Speed	207 mph at 14,000 ft	223 mph at 16,400 ft
Time to 10,000 ft	4.5 min	3.8 min
Service Ceiling	28,000 ft	29,500 ft

Armament: Two fixed, synchronized Vickers 0.303 in Mk II, or Mk IIID machine guns, each with 600 rounds

Right Possibly the saddest photograph in this book. With their wings clipped, four forgotten Furies are abused by apprentice engine fitters somewhere in the Midlands in 1941. The second Fury in this shot had earlier served with No 8 FTS in Montrose as K8293. Hiding in the background is a propellerless Hampden

THE HAWKER DEMON

FOR SOME YEARS (around 1930) as a boy, I was the proud 'owner' of a red and blue panel which had dropped off an aeroplane on to the lawn of our garden. This was on the edge of Kenley aerodrome, at that period a busy fighter station south of London. The exact origin of the panel is now forgotten (other than coming from No 23(F) Sqn), but was either from a Gamecock or a Bulldog and it bore the legend 'W/T'. When A Flight of the squadron began to re-equip with Hawker Hart Fighters, the station commander arrived at our house requesting my father to allow the trees on the boundary to be lopped. These days, the very necessity for such a request would probably cause a 'green' uproar. Then, we were used to fairly narrow

clearances over our roof by landing aircraft and accepted the proposal with stoicism (or enthusiasm, according to age). To say more, other than to add that my knowledge of Bulldog serials was rather better than my sums at school, would be to trespass unduly on Owen Thetford's territory.

The Hawker Hart day bomber, designed by Sydney Camm, chief designer of H G Hawker Engineering Co Ltd at Kingston, Surrey, to Specification 12/26, first flew in June 1928. It was powered by a 490 hp high-compression, unsupercharged Rolls-Royce F.XIB (Kestrel IB) and entered RAF service two years later. Like the sleek Fairey Fox which had preceded it by three years, the Hart immediately caused conster-

Left This photograph shows the prototype Demon, built as a Hart bomber in 1929, taking off from Brooklands featuring the Frazer-Nash 'lobster-shell' turret, fitted in May 1934

nation. It proved to be so fast that the existing interceptors were hard-pressed to keep up with it, let alone adequately fulfil their defense function of catching it. An improved fighter response was demanded. Camm therefore proposed a fighter version of the Hart, to be powered by a supercharged, high-altitude, engine and armed with twin forward-firing Vickers machine guns in place of the bomber version's single gun. Specification 15/30 was therefore drafted initially to suit the requirement. As in the Hart, the gunner in the rear cockpit was provided with a single Lewis weapon on a ring mounting, modified to slope upward aft, so as to give him an improved field of fire and, in theory, a slight amount of protection from the airstream.

Two early production Harts, J9933 and J9937, were thus modified to take the fully-supercharged Kestrel IIS and were sent for testing to the A&AEE at Martlesham Heath near Ipswich early in 1930. The wisdom of adopting this solution, rather than going immediately for a similarly armed and powered single-seater, may be questioned. It suggests that a fixation persisted in Air Ministry circles of the idea used very successfully in World War 1 with the Bristol F.2B Fighter of similar layout. Hindsight also suggests that the significant increase in speed made possible by the doubling of engine power, though far from being linear, was improperly understood and certainly not put to the best use. Sadly, to a great degree it was also wasted. It was as a 'weapons system', in present parlance, that the Hart Fighter failed. Whatever the motive at the time for retaining the two-seat fighter in this form as a method of attacking bomber formations, the pursuance of this concept led, ultimately, to the initial disasters which befell the unfortunate Boulton Paul Defiant during 1940.

CREW DISCOMFORT

Early squadron service and concurrent experience of pilots and gunners at Martlesham pointed to serious shortcomings in the aeroplane's layout. Not least of these was the great discomfort and difficulty of the gunner in achieving accuracy in beam gunnery directed at bombers in formation at the relatively high speeds then being achieved. Some protection for him was essential, without obstructing his field of fire, although an interim solution did just that. Despite this, the Hart Fighter (not named Demon until July 1932) was an admirable aircraft, like its forebear. Quick, easy and relatively cheap to build, production orders were issued, to Spec 6/32, for the aircraft powered by the Kestrel IIS, the first of them being flown on 10 February 1933. The Royal Australian Air Force then stated a requirement for a Demon powered by a de-rated Kestrel V of 584 hp, for which Spec, 1/34 was issued.

The RAF followed suit and, with the amount of work in hand at Kingston, sub-contracting became necessary, the contract being allocated to Boulton Paul. The initial success of the Demon did not mask the continuing concern about the effectiveness of the gunner, to say nothing of his discomfort in the exposed cockpit. Electrically-heated clothing and gog-

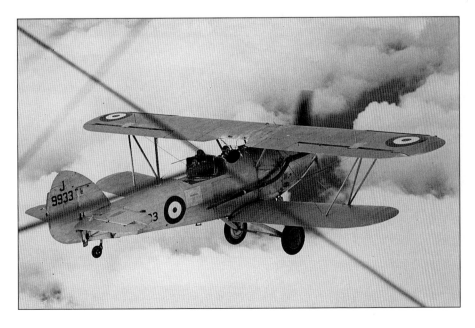

Left Another view of the Demon prototype fitted with the Frazer-Nash turret. J9933 eventually became an instructional airframe in August 1938

Left and below Two views of the Frazer-Nash 'lobster-shell' turret fitted to the Hawker Demon. Though operation of the turret was satisfactory, accurate aiming of the Demon's front guns was difficult when the turret was moved laterally

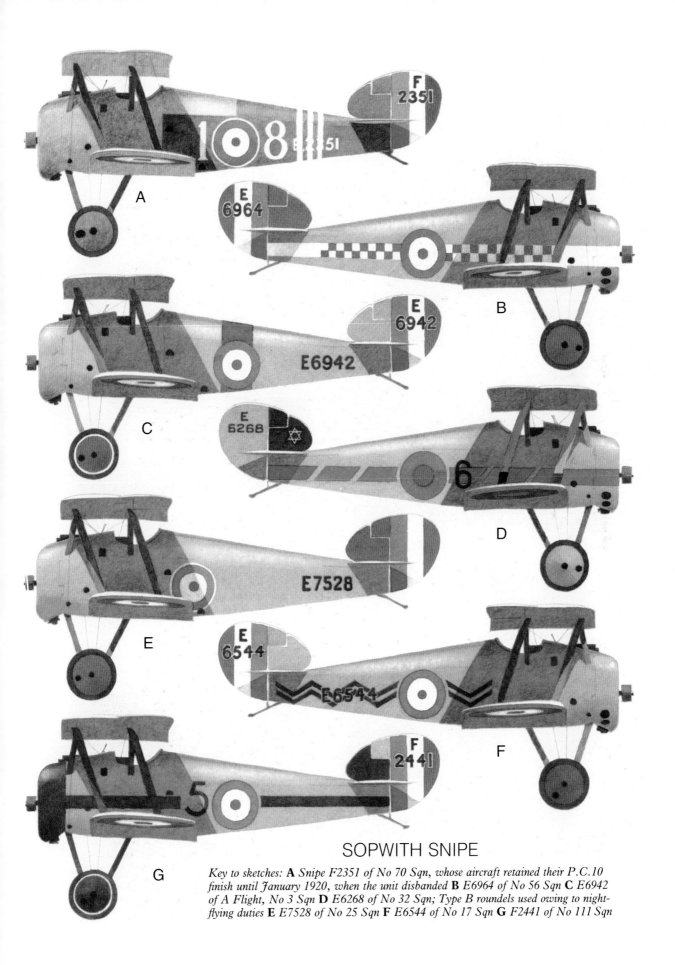

SOPWITH SNIPE

Key to sketches: **A** *Snipe F2351 of No 70 Sqn, whose aircraft retained their P.C.10 finish until January 1920, when the unit disbanded* **B** *E6964 of No 56 Sqn* **C** *E6942 of A Flight, No 3 Sqn* **D** *E6268 of No 32 Sqn; Type B roundels used owing to night-flying duties* **E** *E7528 of No 25 Sqn* **F** *E6544 of No 17 Sqn* **G** *F2441 of No 111 Sqn*

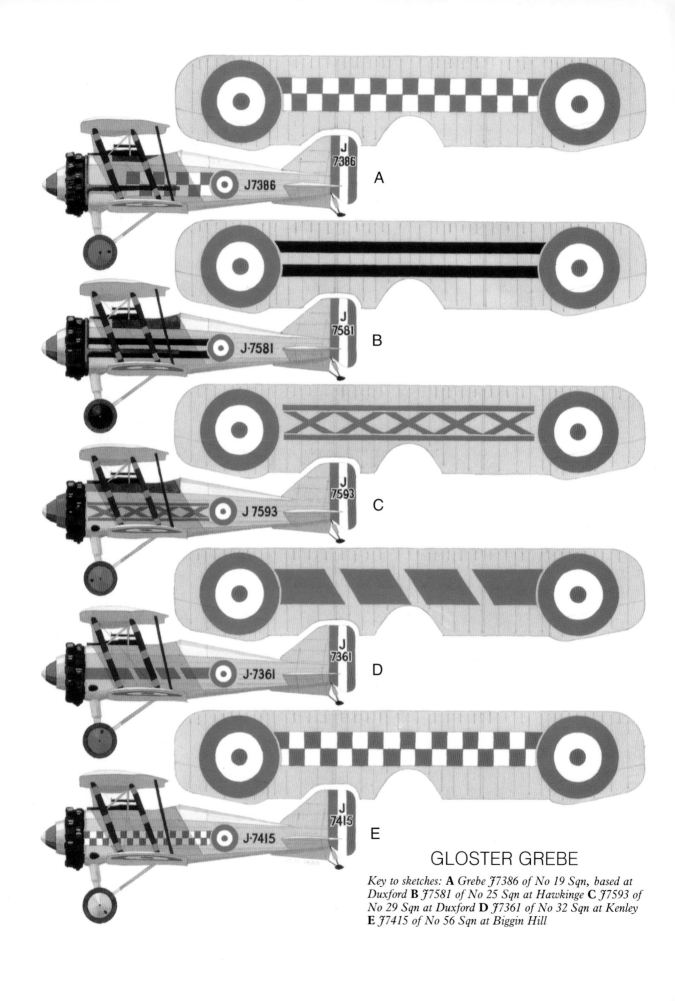

A

B

C

D

E

GLOSTER GREBE

Key to sketches: **A** *Grebe J7386 of No 19 Sqn, based at Duxford* **B** *J7581 of No 25 Sqn at Hawkinge* **C** *J7593 of No 29 Sqn at Duxford* **D** *J7361 of No 32 Sqn at Kenley* **E** *J7415 of No 56 Sqn at Biggin Hill*

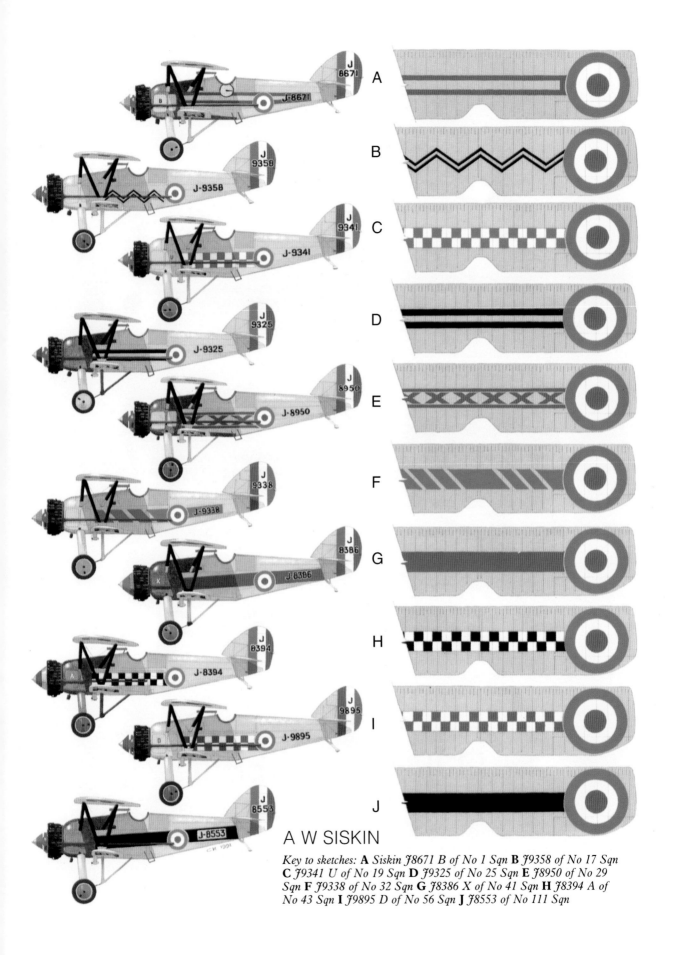

A W SISKIN

Key to sketches: **A** *Siskin J8671 B of No 1 Sqn* **B** *J9358 of No 17 Sqn*
C *J9341 U of No 19 Sqn* **D** *J9325 of No 25 Sqn* **E** *J8950 of No 29*
Sqn **F** *J9338 of No 32 Sqn* **G** *J8386 X of No 41 Sqn* **H** *J8394 A of*
No 43 Sqn **I** *J9895 D of No 56 Sqn* **J** *J8553 of No 111 Sqn*

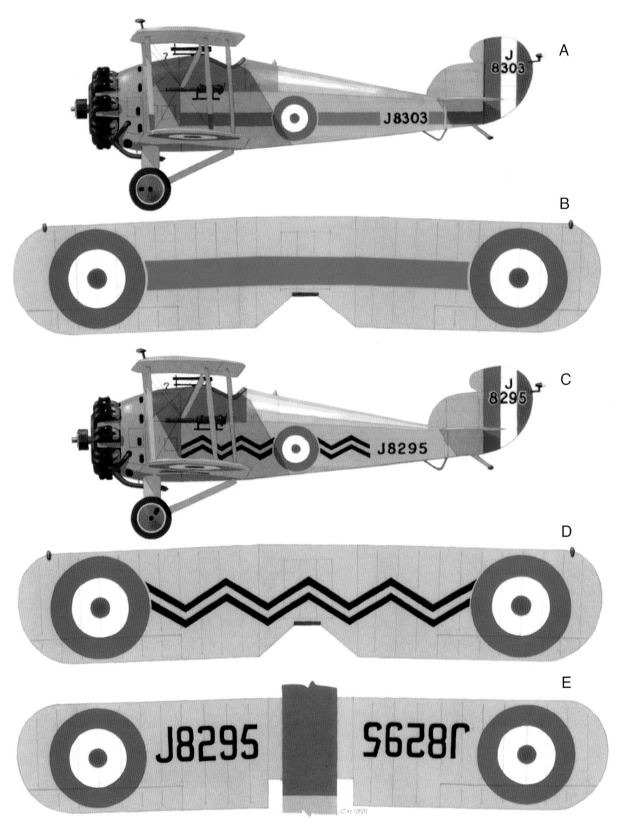

A

B

C

D

E

HAWKER WOODCOCK

Key to sketches: **A** *&* **B** *Woodcock J8303 No 3 Sqn, Upavon, 1926* **C, D** *&* **E**
J8295 of No 17 Sqn, Upavon, 1927. This was the aircraft used by Charles
Lindbergh in June 1927 after his transatlantic flight

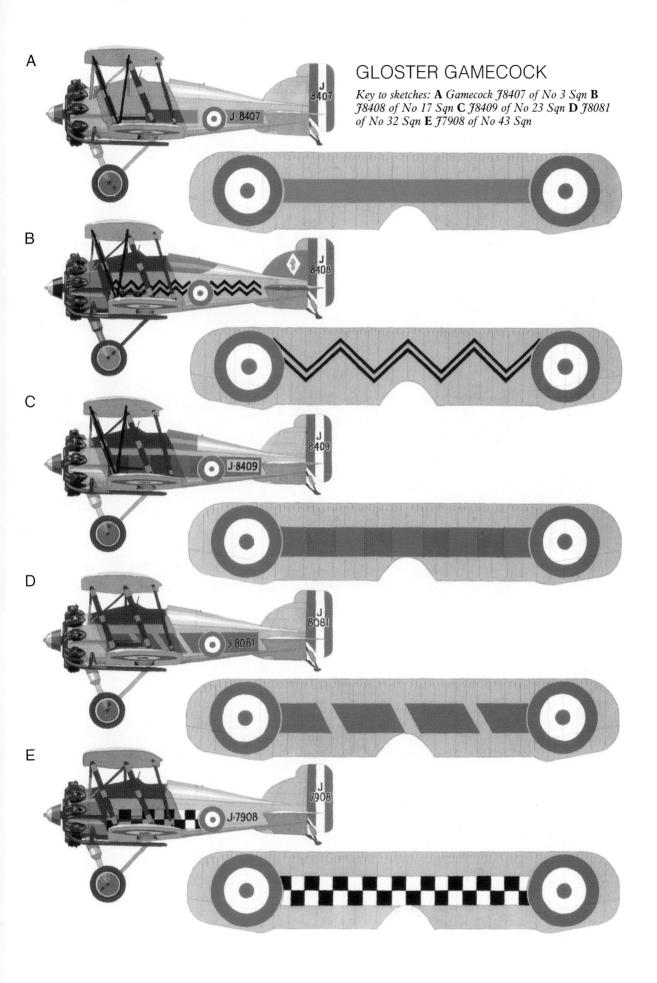

GLOSTER GAMECOCK

Key to sketches: **A** *Gamecock J8407 of No 3 Sqn* **B** *J8408 of No 17 Sqn* **C** *J8409 of No 23 Sqn* **D** *J8081 of No 32 Sqn* **E** *J7908 of No 43 Sqn*

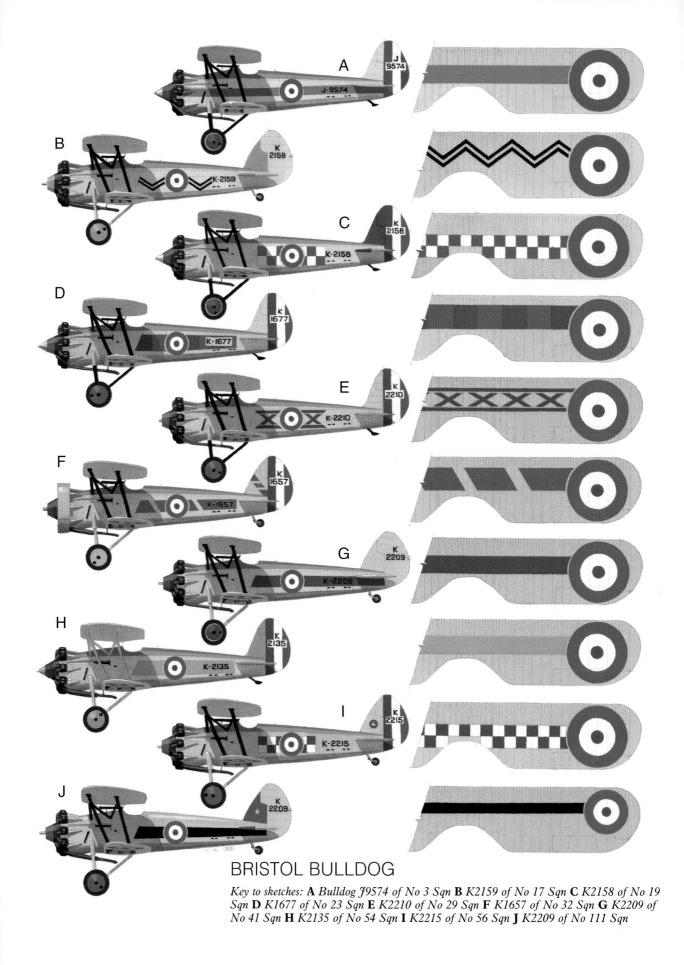

BRISTOL BULLDOG

Key to sketches: **A** *Bulldog J9574 of No 3 Sqn* **B** *K2159 of No 17 Sqn* **C** *K2158 of No 19 Sqn* **D** *K1677 of No 23 Sqn* **E** *K2210 of No 29 Sqn* **F** *K1657 of No 32 Sqn* **G** *K2209 of No 41 Sqn* **H** *K2135 of No 54 Sqn* **I** *K2215 of No 56 Sqn* **J** *K2209 of No 111 Sqn*

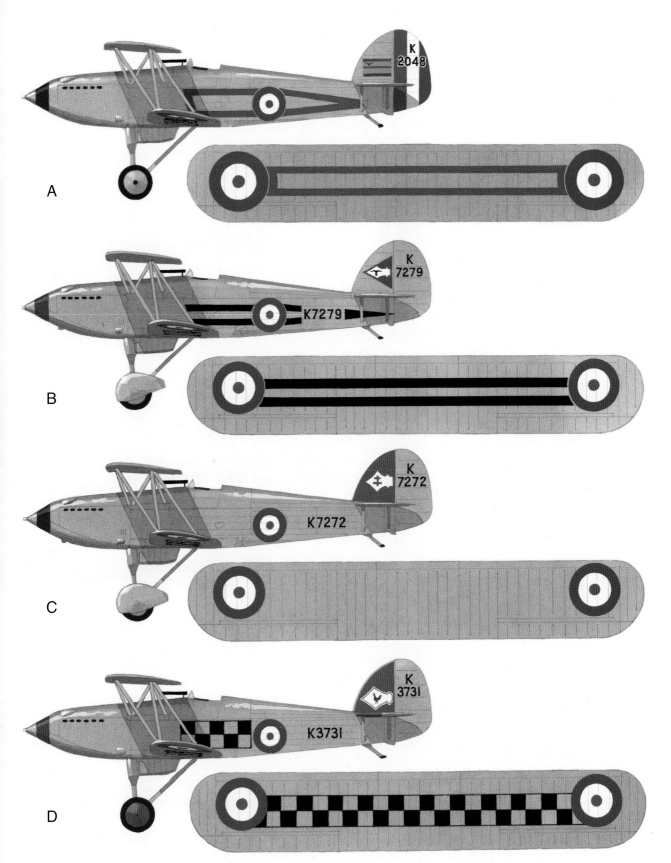

HAWKER FURY

*Key to sketches: **A** Fury K2048 of No 1 Sqn (squadron leader's aircraft) **B** K7279 of No 25 Sqn **C** K7272 of No 41 Sqn **D** K3731 of No 43 Sqn*

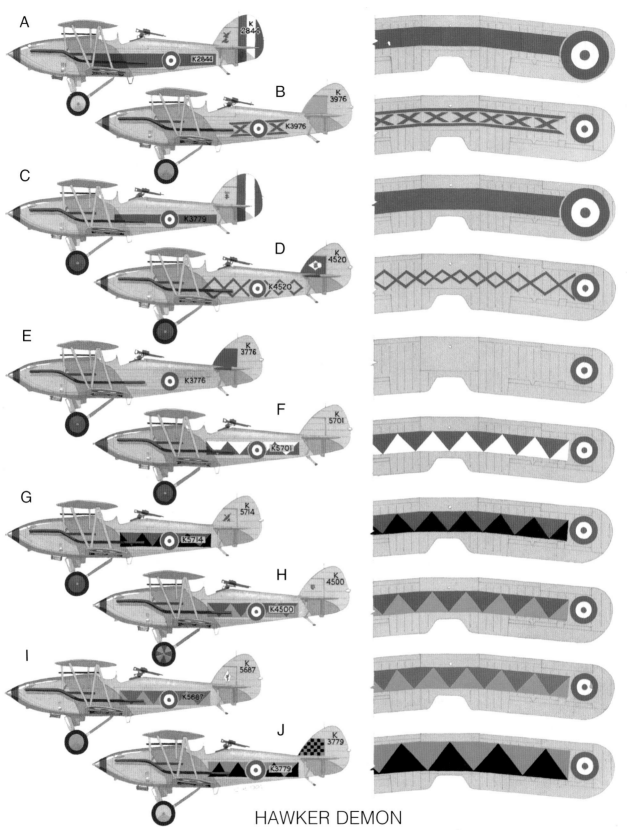

HAWKER DEMON

Key to sketches: **A** *Demon K2844 of No 23 Sqn, 1933* **B** *K3976 of B Flight, No 29 Sqn* **C** *K3779 of No 41 Sqn, September 1934* **D** *K4520 of A Flight, No 64 Sqn* **E** *K3776 of C Flight, No 65 Sqn* **F** *K5701 of A Flight, No 600 Sqn* **G** *K5714 of C Flight, No 601 Sqn* **H** *K4500 of No 604 Sqn* **I** *K5687 of B Flight, No 607 Sqn* **J** *K3779 again, this time with No 608 Sqn, 1937–38*

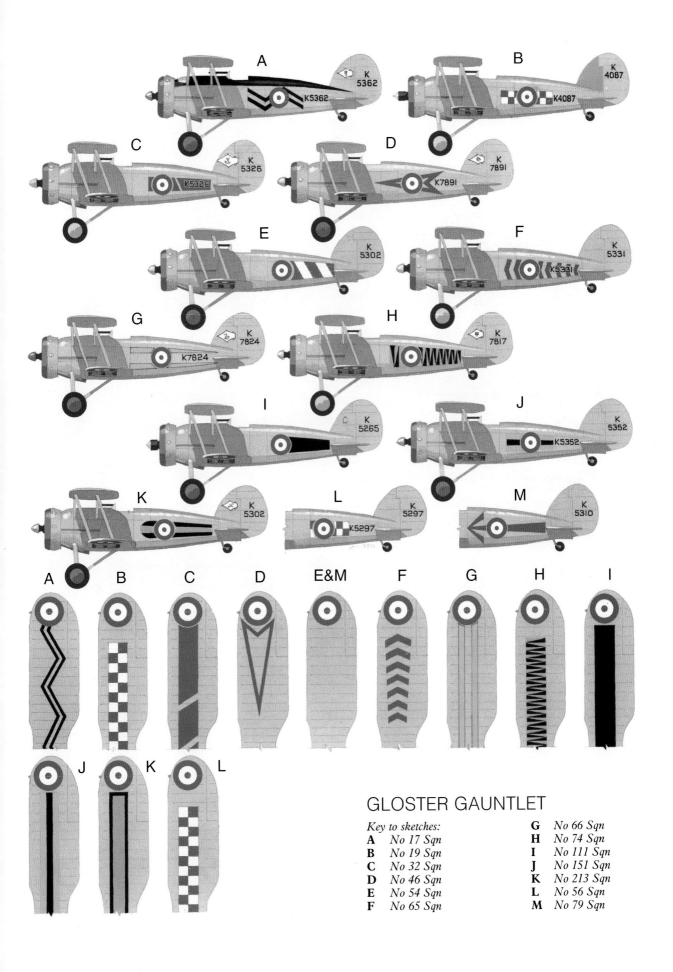

GLOSTER GAUNTLET

Key to sketches:

A	*No 17 Sqn*	**G**	*No 66 Sqn*
B	*No 19 Sqn*	**H**	*No 74 Sqn*
C	*No 32 Sqn*	**I**	*No 111 Sqn*
D	*No 46 Sqn*	**J**	*No 151 Sqn*
E	*No 54 Sqn*	**K**	*No 213 Sqn*
F	*No 65 Sqn*	**L**	*No 56 Sqn*
		M	*No 79 Sqn*

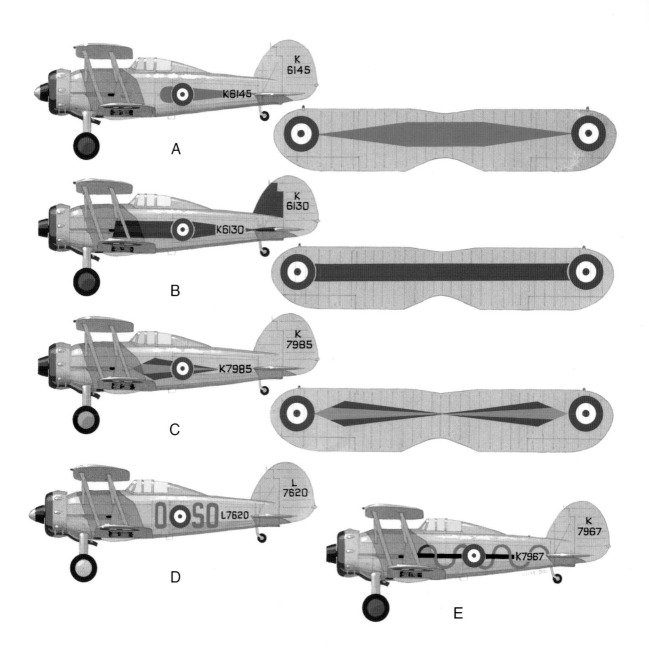

GLOSTER GLADIATOR

Key to sketches:

A A Flight No 3 Sqn
B A Flight No 72 Sqn
C B Flight No 73 Sqn
D O of No 33 Sqn
E A Flight No 87 Sqn

*The illustration **below** of a No 65 Sqn Gloster Gladiator has previously been depicted as an artist's impression. Although the scheme is perfectly plausible and has been verbally described before, it has not been possible to uncover any photographic evidence of its existence.*

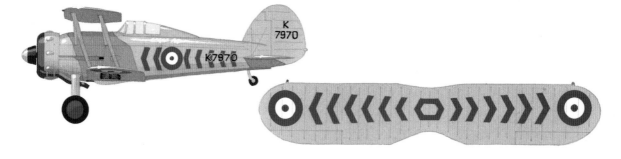

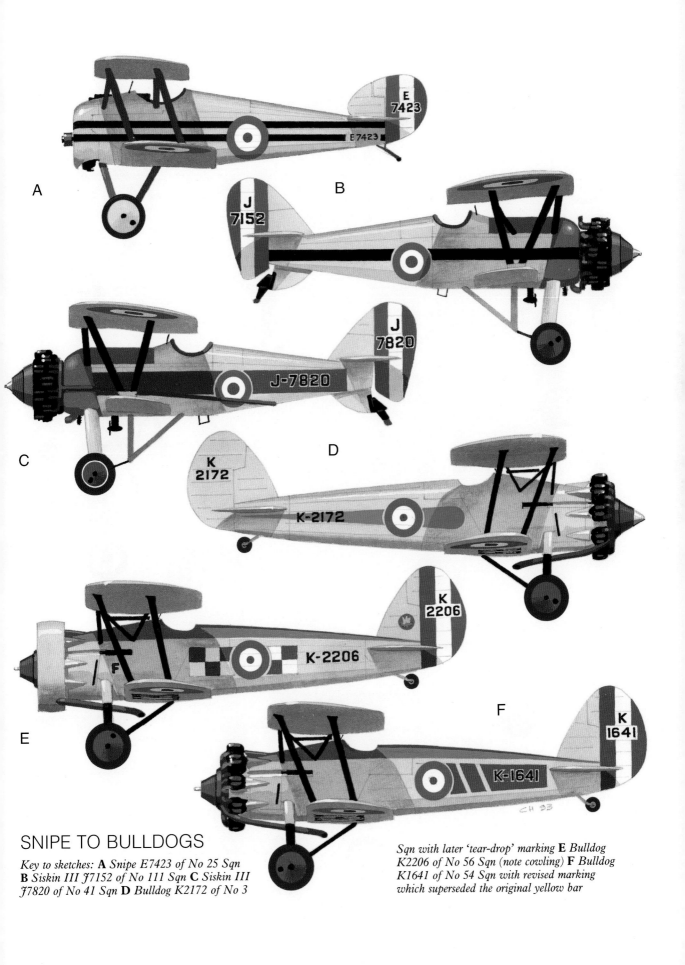

SNIPE TO BULLDOGS

Key to sketches: **A** *Snipe E7423 of No 25 Sqn*
B *Siskin III J7152 of No 111 Sqn* **C** *Siskin III*
J7820 of No 41 Sqn **D** *Bulldog K2172 of No 3*

Sqn with later 'tear-drop' marking **E** *Bulldog*
K2206 of No 56 Sqn (note cowling) **F** *Bulldog*
K1641 of No 54 Sqn with revised marking
which superseded the original yellow bar

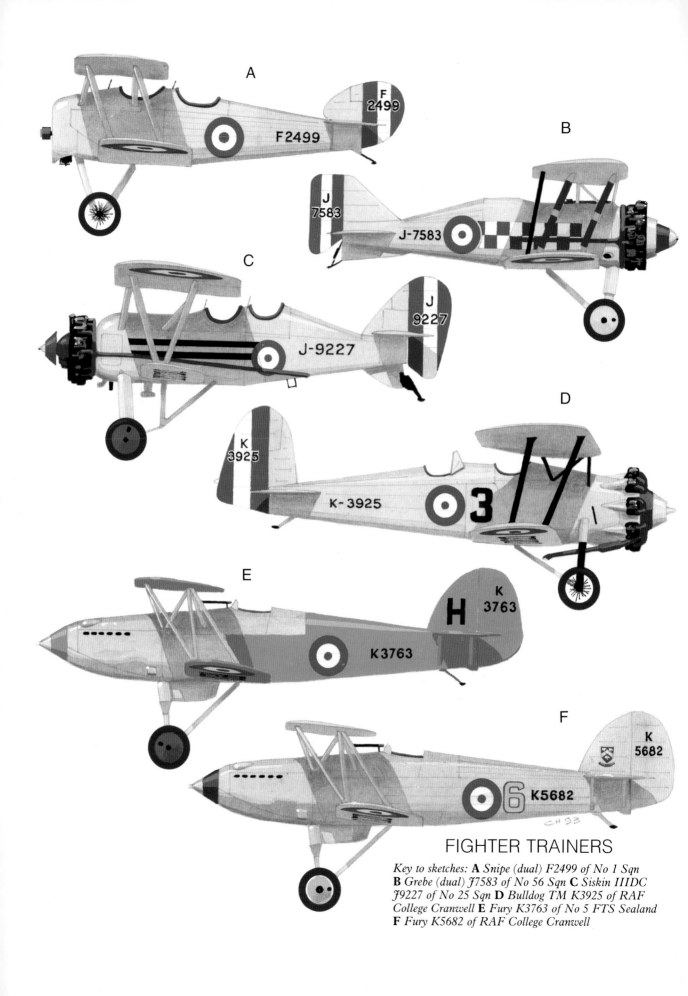

FIGHTER TRAINERS

Key to sketches: **A** *Snipe (dual) F2499 of No 1 Sqn*
B *Grebe (dual) J7583 of No 56 Sqn* **C** *Siskin IIIDC*
J9227 of No 25 Sqn **D** *Bulldog TM K3925 of RAF*
College Cranwell **E** *Fury K3763 of No 5 FTS Sealand*
F *Fury K5682 of RAF College Cranwell*

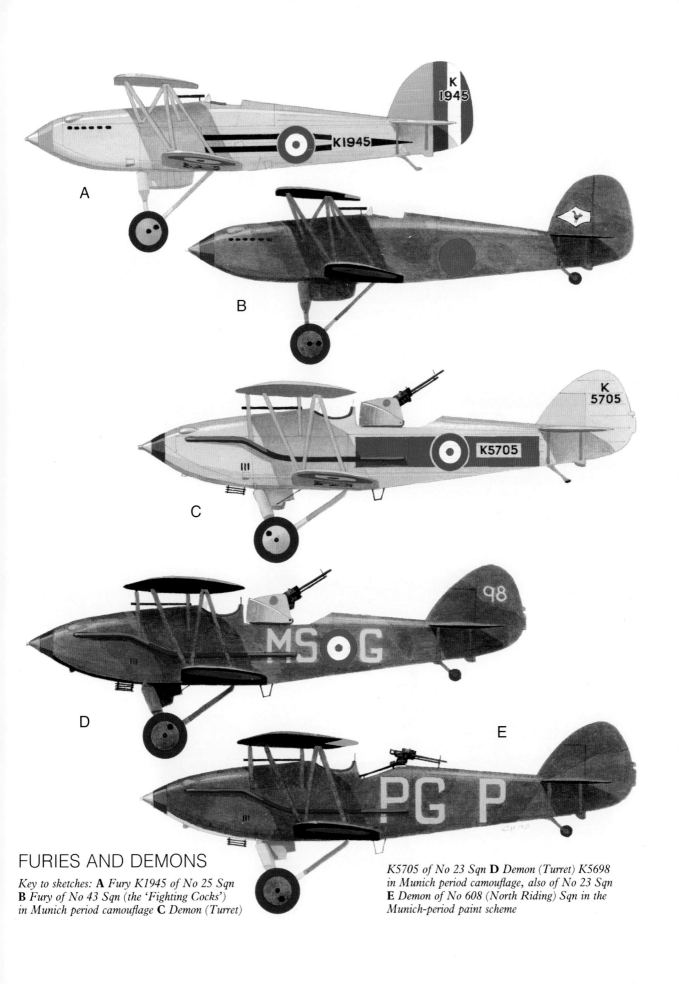

FURIES AND DEMONS

Key to sketches: **A** *Fury K1945 of No 25 Sqn*
B *Fury of No 43 Sqn (the 'Fighting Cocks')*
in Munich period camouflage **C** *Demon (Turret)*

K5705 of No 23 Sqn **D** *Demon (Turret) K5698*
in Munich period camouflage, also of No 23 Sqn
E *Demon of No 608 (North Riding) Sqn in the*
Munich-period paint scheme

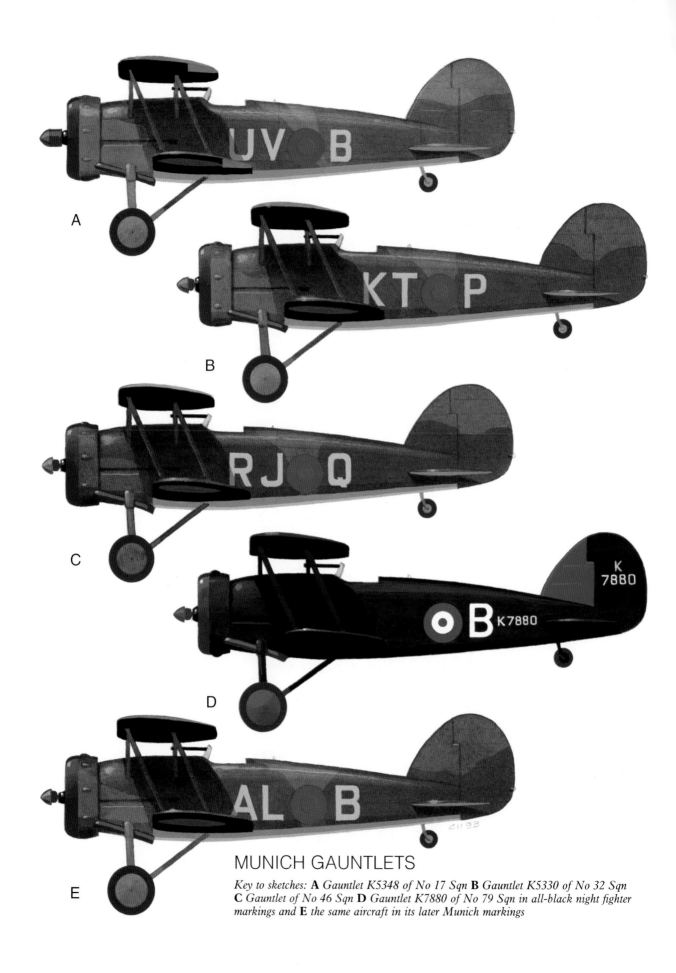

MUNICH GAUNTLETS

Key to sketches: **A** *Gauntlet K5348 of No 17 Sqn* **B** *Gauntlet K5330 of No 32 Sqn* **C** *Gauntlet of No 46 Sqn* **D** *Gauntlet K7880 of No 79 Sqn in all-black night fighter markings and* **E** *the same aircraft in its later Munich markings*

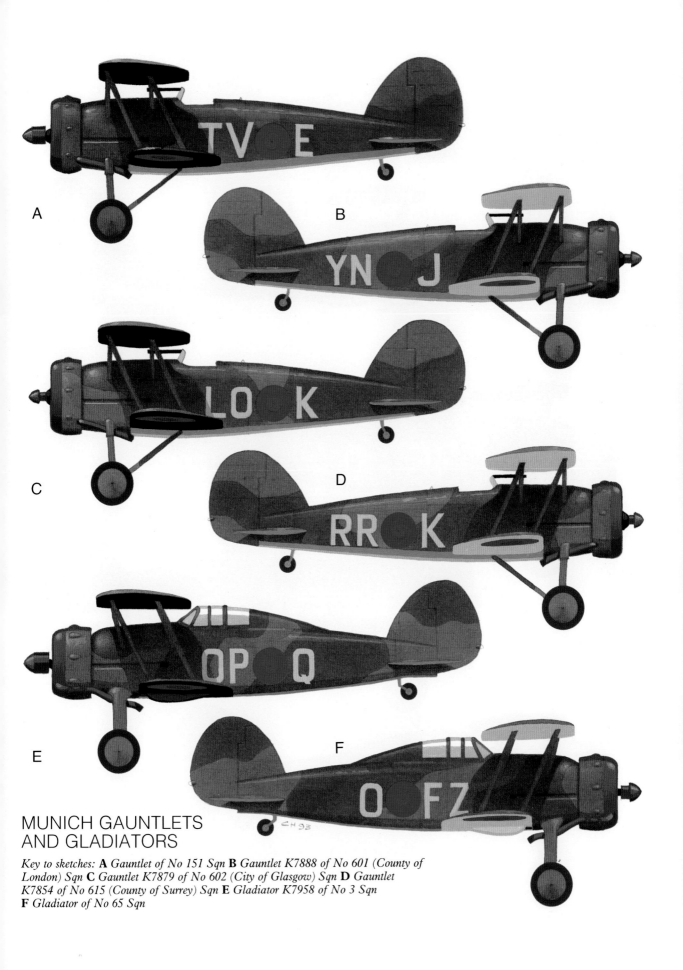

MUNICH GAUNTLETS
AND GLADIATORS

Key to sketches: **A** *Gauntlet of No 151 Sqn* **B** *Gauntlet K7888 of No 601 (County of London) Sqn* **C** *Gauntlet K7879 of No 602 (City of Glasgow) Sqn* **D** *Gauntlet K7854 of No 615 (County of Surrey) Sqn* **E** *Gladiator K7958 of No 3 Sqn* **F** *Gladiator of No 65 Sqn*

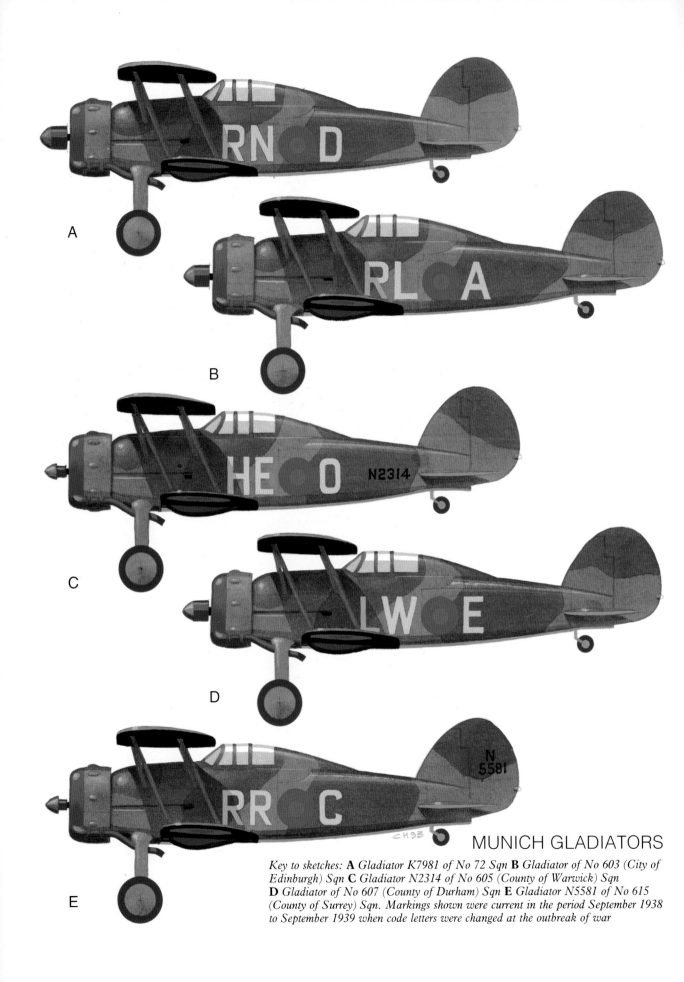

A

B

C

N2314

D

E

N 5581

MUNICH GLADIATORS

Key to sketches: **A** *Gladiator K7981 of No 72 Sqn* **B** *Gladiator of No 603 (City of Edinburgh) Sqn* **C** *Gladiator N2314 of No 605 (County of Warwick) Sqn* **D** *Gladiator of No 607 (County of Durham) Sqn* **E** *Gladiator N5581 of No 615 (County of Surrey) Sqn. Markings shown were current in the period September 1938 to September 1939 when code letters were changed at the outbreak of war*

Right Hawker Demon K2842 served with Nos 23, 601 and 604 Sqns after trials with the A&AEE. In April 1940 it became an instructional airframe. This first production Demon is fitted with standard tilted Scarff gun ring

gles were but an inadequate palliative. By comparison, the pilot was relatively warm, thanks to air deflected from the engine radiator beneath his feet. The well-known firm of motor engineers, Frazer-Nash, made a significant contribution towards solving the problem by designing a rudimentary turret for the gunner. This took the form of a hydraulically-rotated protective shield, segmented in four sections, like a lobster's shell. Though this was barely adequate, and the added weight put the Demon's cg at its aftmost limit, it paved the way to the fully-enclosed multi-gun Defiant turret, and to the large family of turrets which all too soon became commonplace festooned all over the multi-engined bombers of World War 2.

The Demon's all-metal construction, in accordance with standard Hawker practice, was of steel tube and duralumin, with fabric covering over light wooden formers and stringers. The fuselage side panels were warren girder structures, based on four tubular longerons, the only wire bracing in them being in the stern frame. Cross members were of tube with wire bracing. The fuselage was made in four parts; the front or engine mounting; the centre containing the cockpits; the rear section and the stern frame. The centre portion contained the main 63-gal fuel tank, retractable radiator, forward-firing synchronized guns and their ammunition box, together with the pilot's instruments, controls and adjustable seat (with Sutton harness Mk IV), as well as the gunner's installation.

The plain gun-ring installation of early Demons conformed to standard practice and included six 97-round ammunition drums for the single Lewis machine gun.

The top fairing of the centre portion was robustly constructed of wood to carry the gun ring, and was covered with ply and fabric. A similarly-built top fairing continued the line of the top of the rear fuselage to the front fin post. This top fairing, which rested on the upper longerons, was made of spruce and ply formers, the spruce stringers being covered by fabric. The side and bottom panels were built in the same way. The undercarriage, constructed of steel tube was of the through-axle type, with Vickers oleo-pneumatic shock-absorbing legs and wire bracing for the trailing radius rods. The wheels were equipped with Palmer hydraulic brakes, operated by pedals on the rudder bar. The operation of each brake was through the inflation with fluid of an annular, rubberized fabric expansion chamber, round whose periphery a string of small asbestos brake blocks was bonded. The tail skid (replaced by a wheel in late-production Demons) had compression-rubber shock absorbers and a limited swivelling arc.

The upper and lower wings were different in almost every respect – area, dihedral, sweepback – except for their RAF 28 aerofoil section and incidence. A wire-braced upper centre-section was supported by four struts and contained, on the starboard side, a 19-gal gravity fuel tank which provided an emergency supply for about 50 minutes duration. The spar booms were of rolled high-tensile steel strip, built up into an approximate figure of eight section. They were joined by longitudinally corrugated webs, and this riveted assembly was both light and strong. The ribs were built up of light alloy and all four wings were stabilised by internal drag struts and wire bracing. A single set of N-shaped interplane struts was mounted on each side, the whole interplane assembly being wire-braced. Frise-type balanced ailerons were differentially operated, giving 22° of up and 18° of down movement, and contributed much to the Demon's good handling. Ailerons were mounted on the upper wings only, which also featured automatic slats, the slats themselves being 6 ft long. All wing surfaces were fabric covered.

The tail unit, including controls and stern frame, was of a similar construction to the rear fuselage and wings. The braced tailplane was adjustable for incidence to the sternpost and operated by the pilot's trimming wheel. The fin was offset $2\frac{1}{2}$° to port to counteract torque, and the rudder bar was adjustable 4 in fore and aft, in flight, by means of a foot-operated star wheel.

It was not until April 1934 that a performance

Below Hawker Demon K5695 was delivered to the RAF towards the end of 1936 and served initially with No 23 Sqn. It later passed to No 9 Bombing and Gunnery School and No 14 FTS before being struck off charge in December 1940

report on a production Demon emerged from Martlesham. This concerned K2857, one of the early aircraft, which was to remain at the A&AEE and Farnborough for trials purposes until 1940. Taxying was easy by means of the brakes, whose action was effective, progressive and easy in application. Cockpit controls and instruments were easily accessible and functioned normally. The pilot, though adequately warm, had an uncomfortable seat. In flying tests at all speeds and heights, the controllability and manoeuvrability were described as light and effective. Dive tests to the limiting crankshaft speed of the engine of 3000 rpm were made at both fore and aft cg limits, at a weight of 4452 lbs. The aircraft was very steady in the dive and there was no sign of instability, flutter or undue vibration. Control movements during the dives gave proper response, and recovery was easy without alteration of the tail incidence set at the outset. The aircraft was easy to fly, the controls being good, despite a marked swing to port on take-off. It was highly manoeuvrable and the pilot's view good.

GUN PLATFORM

As a flying platform for the forward-firing guns, the Demon was steady at all speeds up to the maximum tested of 240 mph. An appreciable quantity of engine oil penetrated the ammunition tank in flight, making rounds very oily when fed to the gun. The ammunition tank, when full with 1200 rounds, was very heavy, requiring three men to mount it, and would

Above *Another photograph of K2842, the first production Hawker Demon*

have been better if divided in two. The gunner's equipment, apart from his physical difficulties and discomfort, was satisfactory. Firing the Lewis gun to starboard resulted in the empty cases passing over the port tailplane or striking it with slight chipping of paint, whereas, when firing to port the cases passed clear. Before empty case chutes or containers were fitted, cases from the front guns caused considerable damage to the rear fuselage and tail surfaces, causing gashes and bruises up to 3 in long. As for the effectiveness of the gunner, above speeds of 130 mph air pressure made operation of the gun very uncomfortable and tiring, also causing helmet and goggle flutter. So restricted was the gunner's operation, that effective fire was only possible upward and to the rear, reducing progressively to a small cone at 200 mph.

In September 1935, over a year after the publication of the first Martlesham report on Demon K2857, another appeared concerning the same aircraft, but by now modified to Spec. 8/34. It was powered by a Kestrel V, rated at 600 hp, boost being maintained at +1.5 lbs to 11,000 ft. It suffered a failure in the composite water cooling system, caused by ice forming at 20,000 ft but this was corrected by a small modification. Earlier in the year, Frazer-Nash had produced a prototype power-operated, shielded 'lobster-shell' mounting for the gunner and this was flown in J9933. As might be expected, the added weight aft had pushed the centre of gravity to the extreme limit. Despite this, spinning tests were successfully completed. However, there were continuing doubts about the cg position. An experimental Hawker-built Demon, K4496, designated Demon I (Turret), to 'Spec 8/34 and 40/34' visited Martlesham in mid-1936, following which a report dated 10 December stated that there was a considerable variation in the cg figures, as determined by the Establishment and Hawker, and that another Demon was to be sent to Martlesham for cg checks, it being suspected that the location was further aft than expected in production aeroplanes. It was even suggested, unofficially of course, that the cg could not be found because it was towed at the end of a long piece of string.

Above Hawker Demon I K3974 of No 29 Sqn, 15,000 ft above Epping, Essex, on 22 July 1935. After passing to No 41 Sqn, this Demon crashed while landing at Catterick on 6 September 1937

The turret, though a novelty and still somewhat primitive, was designed to give the gunner, when seated, control of the gun without appreciable effort and to give him protection from the airstream under all conditions. Rotation and the combined movements of the seat, gun elevation and hood were made through a hydraulic system, receiving pressure from an engine-driven pump and controlled through valves operated from a handlebar by the gunner. The turret drum rested on rollers on a circular track and was rotated by a motor driven by oil under pressure, instant reversal of rotation being effected by control of the direction of the oil supply. The gun, valve box and handlebar

formed one unit which moved in conjunction with the gunner's seat. A pair of double-acting rams raised or lowered the seat by oil pressure controlled by the valve box connected by links to the seat. As the latter rose or fell, so the gun was depressed or elevated through a range of about 180°, the back of the seat remaining vertical. Operation of the turret was satisfactory, although all movements tended to produce opposite reactions in the aircraft's trim in yaw and (during elevation and depression), longitudinally. This made accurate aiming of the front guns difficult when the turret moved laterally.

The second turret Demon to be sent to Martlesham was a production aircraft (K8182) and, like K4496, was powered by a derated Kestrel V running on 87 octane fuel. Three reports were produced by the A&AEE between February and May 1938. Despite the most careful checks of the two aeroplanes and of

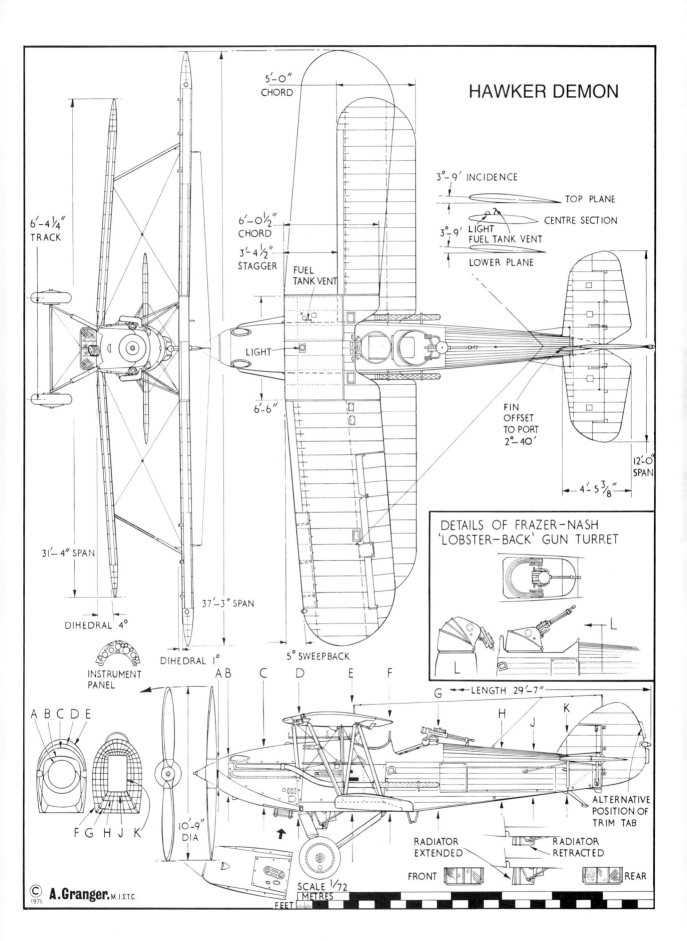

HAWKER DEMON

5'-0" CHORD

3°-9' INCIDENCE

TOP PLANE

CENTRE SECTION

3°-9' LIGHT FUEL TANK VENT

LOWER PLANE

6'-0½" CHORD

3'-4½" STAGGER

FUEL TANK VENT

LIGHT

6'-6"

FIN OFFSET TO PORT 2°-40'

12'-0" SPAN

4'-5⅜"

6'-4¼" TRACK

31'-4" SPAN

DIHEDRAL 4°

37'-3" SPAN

DIHEDRAL 1°

5° SWEEPBACK

INSTRUMENT PANEL

DETAILS OF FRAZER-NASH 'LOBSTER-BACK' GUN TURRET

L

L

A B C D E

F G H J K

10'-9" DIA

A B   C   D   E   F

G   LENGTH 29'-7"

H   J   K

ALTERNATIVE POSITION OF TRIM TAB

RADIATOR EXTENDED

RADIATOR RETRACTED

FRONT

REAR

SCALE 1/72
METRES
FEET

© A.Granger. M.I.S.T.C.
1971

Above Three of a first production batch of Hart fighters – K1952, K1955 and K1951 – supplied to No 23 Sqn

the weighbridge, there were still differences of cg between the two aircraft, despite there being no increase in the empty weight. The Demon was considered to be satisfactory up to speeds of 270 mph ASI, within the approved cg limits, whether fitted with a tail skid or the later wheel. It was also considered that the extreme aft cg position was not likely to occur often with weight sheet summary loads, as that entailed zero fuel load but with all ammunition remaining. The spinning characteristics of the aircraft were satisfactory within the approved loadings and cg limits, whether the machine was fitted with a tailskid or wheel, following certain elevator modifications. Brakes should be maintained in an efficient condition, as the tendency to swing on the ground could only be checked by use of brakes, especially when fitted with a tail wheel – a matter requiring great care when night-flying.

The tail trimming gear needed revision to prevent the risk of a pilot attempting to take-off with it wound too far back. Also, because at extreme aft cg loading the Demon climbed with the trimming wheel fully forward, it was suggested that six inches of cord should be fitted to the upper trailing edge of each elevator. This simple device finally overcame the trim

problem and permitted the trimming wheel to be wound a quarter turn back from fully forward, and reduced the nose-heaviness in subsequent dives. Thus the Hawker Demon appeared in RAF service – if not Cinderella, certainly not an Ugly Sister.

In the heyday of the RAF's biplane fighter era in the inter-war years, no aeroplane could better exemplify the combination of economy-led compromise enforced by the Treasury, and the Air Staff's flawed tactical concepts, than the Demon. Its period of service came at a time when the RAF was sometimes jokingly described as 'the Hawker Air Force' – a time, that is, when the predominance of the Hawker Hart family was so striking. The very excellence and adaptability of the Hart had enabled it to be mass-produced (spreading work throughout the aircraft industry and leading to lower unit costs per airframe) and supplied under many different names according to role for day bomber, Army co-operation, colonial policing overseas, advanced pilot training, reconnaissance with the Fleet and, as the Demon, as a Home Defence or overseas day or night fighter.

In performance terms, at the outset, the Demon was only marginally inferior to its single-seat biplane equivalents and fully capable of all fighter manoeuvres (as many a long-suffering rear gunner would testify). With hindsight, it is difficult to see how the Air Staff's stubborn faith in the concept of the two-seat fighter (a latter-day revival of the World War 1 Bristol Fighter) could sensibly have been sustained to the point where the Boulton Paul Defiant two-seater was thrown into action in 1940 with such disastrous consequences in fighter versus fighter operations. The suspicion is bound to arise that the very existence of the Demon was to lead fighter tacticians up a tragic blind alley.

The answer to some of these imponderables might reside in the fact that in the 1930s the RAF's fighter defences were geared towards interception of slower moving bomber formations, and the notion of joining combat with fighter escorts had simply not been envisaged. This would certainly account for the introduction of power-operated turrets for the rear gunners, pioneered by Demons.

Although it was not to be given the name of Demon until July 1932, the type's genesis was in the Hart Fighter, proposed by Sydney Camm (Hawker's chief designer) in 1930. As Bulldogs of the time had some difficulty in catching Hart bombers, the idea was conceived that a fighter variant of the Hart with twin front guns and an up-rated Kestrel engine might do the job better. Two prototypes thus converted (J9933 and J9937) were followed by an Air Ministry contract for six Hart Fighters (K1950 to K1955), which were delivered to No 23 Sqn at Kenley, where from July 1931 they equipped one flight alongside two flights of Bristol Bulldogs. In April 1933, by which time No 23 Sqn had moved to Biggin Hill, the Bulldogs were discarded in favour of more two-seaters, thus becoming the first wholly-equipped Demon squadron. By the summer of 1933, No 23 Sqn had worked up to a high state of proficiency and gave a polished display of formation air drill at the annual Hendon Display.

By this time, the Demon was in full production at Hawker's Kingston factory (the first off the line, K2842, had flown on 10 February 1933), and Hawker received four more contracts before production was transferred to Boulton Paul in 1936. The RAF was to take delivery of 232 Demons before production ceased in January 1938 and details are as follow:

Demon Production for the RAF

Manufacturer	Serials
Hawker	K2842–2858
	K2905–2908
	K3764–3807
	K3974–3985
	K4496–4544
Boulton Paul	K5683–5741
	K5898–5907
	K8181–8217

Above *Dramatic photograph of No 64 Sqn Demons demonstrating dive bombing for* Flight's *cameraman in June 1937. The squadron was then based at Martlesham Heath*

The transfer of production to Boulton Paul (caused chiefly by Hawker's requirement to concentrate on Hurricanes) coincided with the decision to equip Demons with power-operated gun turrets, although it was not until October 1936 that the Turret Demon made its appearance with front-line units. This was No 29 Sqn at North Weald, to be followed by No 23 Sqn at Northolt in May 1937 and No 64 Sqn at Martlesham in February 1938. The renowned aviation writer and editor H F 'Rex' King has written very vividly of his experiences flying in the gunner's position of Demons in his excellent book, *Armament of British Aircraft 1909–1939* (Putnam 1971), and comments on the extreme discomfort of trying to manipulate a manually-operated gun as compared with the protection from the slipstream afforded by the Frazer-Nash hydraulically-operated 'lobster-back' turreted version. Though it did little for the aesthetic appeal of the Demon, the turret undoubtedly improved the accuracy of the gunnery.

During its six years of service with the RAF as a first-line fighter, the Demon equipped no less than 12 squadrons (seven of them regular and five auxiliary), plus the partial equipment of two overseas squadrons (Nos 6 and 208). No 23 Sqn at Kenley and then Biggin Hill was the sole user until July 1934 when No 41 at Northolt exchanged its Bulldogs for Demons, closely followed by No 65 at Hornchurch in August 1934. No 23 Sqn was in the public eye more than most Demon squadrons by virtue of its appearance at Hendon Air Displays in 1933 and again in 1935, and it was also selected to participate in the Royal Review which marked HM King George V's Jubilee in a spectacular assembly of 356 RAF aircraft at Mildenhall, followed by a grand fly-past over the royal saluting base at Duxford. This comprised five separate formations which followed each other at two mile intervals, the heavy night bombers leading in a 98 mph stream, and terminating in a 150 mph stream of Furies and Gauntlets. No 23 Squadron's Demons suffered the minor indignity (for a fighter squadron) of being slotted in with the Army Co-operation stream at 115 mph!

Curiously enough, Demons of a regular air force

squadron were not to appear again before the public at the annual Hendon Display after 1935. In 1936 and 1937 the spotlight was to be on the Demons of the Auxiliary Air Force. In impeccable demonstrations of formation air drill, Nos 600 (City of London), 601 (County of London) and 604 (County of Middlesex) Sqns acquitted themselves well in a style which would have done credit to any regular squadron. In only a few short years the 'weekend airmen', as they were known, were to put their training and skills to good effect in the Battle of Britain.

AUXILIARIES

Two-seat fighters of the three London-based Auxiliary Air Force squadrons were to remain a familiar sight at Hendon aerodrome from 1933 until the close of 1938. On replacing their obsolete Westland Wapiti day bombers, each squadron received Hawker Harts, but these were soon to be re-cast in the role of fighters and embellished with the colourful squadron regalia later applied to Demons. In their fighter-style squadron

Above Five No 604 Sqn Demons off Worthing during the squadron's summer camp in August 1936

markings, the Harts were barely distinguishable from the later Demons, but the clue to their identity was the absence of the long exhaust pipes and the cutaway rear cockpits which characterised the Demon. Some 36 Harts were to serve in the fighter role between February 1933 and August 1937. Details of individual aircraft appear in the squadron tables at the end of this chapter.

By 1937, two additional Auxiliary Air Force squadrons (Nos 607 and 608) were also flying Demons from bases in North-East England. No 607 (County of Durham) Sqn retained their Demons until Gladiators arrived in December 1938 and continued as a fighter squadron, going on to earn many battle honours in World War 2; but No 608 (North Riding) Sqn ended its brief fighter career with their Demons, converting to Ansons for general reconnaissance duties in March 1939.

Meanwhile, in the regular service, the pioneer Demon squadron, No 23, had been followed by six further units, two of them (Nos 64 and 74) having been formed initially overseas before eventually coming back to the UK to join Fighter Command – this unusual sequence of events was brought about by the Abyssinian crisis of 1935/36.

The deployment of Demon squadrons overseas to meet the Abyssinian situation caused much disruption in the home defence fighter force in the mid-1930s. Following the re-organisation which led to the formation of Fighter Command on 1 July 1936, there were, in fact, only two (understrength) regular squadrons of

Left Three No 208 (Army Co-operation) Sqn Demons flying over Cairo, Egypt, in December 1935. They were based at RAF Heliopolis. Primarily equipped with Audax Army Co-operation aircraft, the squadron did not decorate their handful of Demons with fighter-style markings

Left Three No 29 Sqn Demons. Nearest the camera is K3982, which later flew with No 600 and 601 Sqns before being relegated to a maintenance unit in October 1940. K3983, in the background, collided with K4538 and crashed near Dover on 5 November 1937

Right Flight *photograph of* No 604 (County of Middlesex) *Sqn Demons flying from their RAF Hendon base in July 1936*

Demons in the Battle Order: Nos 29 and 41 Sqns had been sent overseas *in toto* and many of No 23 and 65 Sqn's aircraft had been shipped out as reinforcements. However, by September 1936 these units had returned to the UK, where they were joined by Nos 64 and 74 Sqns, providing Fighter Command with five regular Demon units. No 65 Sqn at Hornchurch had meanwhile exchanged its Demons for Gauntlets in July 1936, as did No 74 Sqn in April 1937. This left Demon frontline strength at four units, plus five Auxiliary Air Force squadrons.

It was not until October 1937 that the last Demon squadron came into service with Fighter Command. This was at Hawkinge, where the crack No 25 Sqn was dismayed to be told that it had to give up its beautiful Hawker Fury II fighters in exchange for No 41's old Demons at Catterick with which they soldiered on until receiving Gladiators in June 1938. This episode is well described in Roy Humphreys' book *Hawkinge 1912–61* (Meresborough Books, 1981).

By 1938, with war clouds already looming and the Munich Crisis to emerge in September, the Demon was seeing its last year of first-line squadron service and, despite its power-operated turret innovation, was clearly obsolescent. The author recalls seeing Turret Demons of No 64 Sqn performing at the opening of Ringway Airport in the summer of 1938 and, even then, gravely doubting their ability to take their place in the front line in any future conflict. In the event, they were all gone from the fighter squadrons by the beginning of 1939. In retrospect, it seems strange that their replacements should not have been the new Boulton Paul Defiant which was, after all, the 'state of

the art' two-seat turret fighter of its time, but this was not to be. Instead, the surviving Demons in their drab 'Munich camouflage' and sporting their ungainly turrets, were followed into service by the twin-engined Bristol Blenheim equipped as a night fighter. Nos 23, 29 and 64 Sqns all began to receive Blenheim IFs in December 1938 and the three auxiliary squadrons (Nos 600, 601 and 604) in January 1939.

OPERATIONS OVERSEAS

Largely because of the threat to British interests posed by Mussolini's invasion of Abyssinia in 1935–36, the Demon saw much more service overseas than was customary for a Home Defence fighter type, and at one period in the first half of 1936 there were four Demon squadrons stationed overseas, which represented roughly 40 per cent of the aircraft available. Additionally, No 65 Sqn at Hornchurch (which had been intended as a specialised night fighter squadron) lost most of its Demons and almost all its personnel to reinforce the squadrons in the Mediterranean area and North Africa. No 23 Sqn at Biggin Hill also sent Demons to Malta. These reductions in the air defences of the UK were not made public at the time – in those distant days media coverage of aircraft dispositions such as we enjoy today was quite unthinkable! Demons were also involved in Palestine operations, forming additional flights in Nos 6 and 208 Army Co-operation Squadrons.

During the course of their Service careers, many famous RAF names were associated with the Demon. This distinguished roll call includes a World War 1

fighter ace, two World War 2 night fighter aces, four future Chiefs of the Air Staff and even a future Air Minister (Aidan Crawley). In 1934, Sqn Ldr Frank Soden commanded No 65's Demons at Hornchurch; in World War 1 he had achieved 27 victories over the Western Front flying Nieuports and S.E.5as with Nos 60 and 41 Sqns. The world-famous night fighter pilot and later test pilot, John Cunningham, served with No 604 Sqn in the mid-1930s at Hendon and Wg Cdr J R D 'Bob' Braham DSO DFC AFC, famous for his wartime exploits on Beaufighter and Mosquito night fighters, was at Debden with No 29 Sqn when they

Above Hendon was 'Hell' when it came to Demons in the mid-1930s, the north London airfield hosting no less than three Auxiliary squadrons (Nos 600, 601 and 604 Sqns)

had Demons. In his book *Scramble* (Frederick Muller, 1961), he writes most entertainingly about his ill-concealed disappointment in December 1938 when, as a newly-fledged acting pilot officer he arrived on his first operational station expecting to fly Gladiators and saw to his dismay two-seater Demons waiting on the tarmac, and the tantalising sight of brand-new Hurricanes of rival squadrons peeping out of the hangars.

The celebrated North Weald station commander of 1940, Gp Capt Victor Beamish (killed whilst leading No 485 Sqn Spitfires on a sweep in March 1942), commanded No 64 Demon Sqn from December 1937 at Martlesham and from May 1938 at Church Fenton.

It was the socially fashionable (and highly efficient) London auxiliary squadrons at Hendon which probably laid claim to the most notable 'old boys' of all. That very gifted senior officer, Marshal of the Royal Air Force Lord Elworthy, served when a young pilot officer with No 600 Sqn, and another brilliant com-

mander, Marshal of the Royal Air Force Sir John Grandy, flew with No 604 Sqn as an instructor in 1935–36. Yet another celebrity in aviation circles and future Marshal of the Royal Air Force, Sir Dermot Boyle, served on Harts with No 601 Sqn at Hendon in 1933.

The name of Roger Bushell will be familiar to those who have read about the epic escape (and later execution) of RAF prisoners of war from *Stalag Luft III*. Sqn Ldr R J Bushell, an outstanding pilot who led No 92 Sqn Spitfires, was one of the most colourful characters of the pre-war No 601 Sqn, and performed a spectacular solo aerobatic display in a Demon at the 1938 Empire Day airshow. The Demons based at Hendon undoubtedly gained some remarkably good publicity for the RAF, but a sadder note has to be recorded in mentioning the widely-reported crash of K4502 on to the railway tracks near Colindale Station on 4 August 1935, which claimed the lives of Flg Off R L Nimmo and AC2 Mabbutt.

By 1938, with the days of the Demon as a first-line fighter rapidly approaching their end, the type was relegated to various training duties, mainly at Bombing and Gunnery Schools, and it was at one of these establishments that yet another budding Chief of the Air Staff, later to become Marshal of the Royal Air Force Sir Andrew Humphrey, served as a Demon pilot training gunners at Penrhos in North Wales before he joined 266 Sqn on Spitfires in 1940 (sadly, Sir Andrew died unexpectedly of pneumonia in January 1977, only three months after being appointed Chief of the Defence Staff).

Although it lacked the glamour of its single-engined fighter contemporaries such as the Bulldog, Fury and Gauntlet, the Demon was a good, reliable aeroplane and had no particular vices. About 30 were lost in flying accidents (including six with the Auxiliaries and three in Aden). There were several collisions, including two from No 25 Sqn (K3983 and 4538) which crashed at Dover on 5 November 1937. The worst single loss was of three aircraft from No 64 Sqn

(K8199, 8200 and 8201) abandoned in fog in August 1938.

In the aftermath of Munich, Demons gradually faded away from the fighter squadrons, and the type was officially declared obsolete in September 1939, but about 50 examples continued to serve with Bombing and Gunnery Schools, Air Armament Schools, Anti-Aircraft Co-operation Units and various Flying Training Schools. A few lingering aircraft continued to serve as target-tugs at Castle Camps and Langham until Hawker Henleys arrived and the last flying example is alleged to have been spotted in early 1944. Not a single example survives in this country today.

Below Sharing the green fields of Hendon with No 601 was No 600 'City of London' Sqn. This mass outing was photographed soon after the squadron had received their first Hart Fighters in early 1935

Demon units (including Hart Fighters) in the RAF

No 23 Squadron *Kenley, July 1931 to September 1932*
Biggin Hill, September 1932 to December 1936
Some aircraft detached to Malta 1935–36.
Northolt, December 1936 to May 1938
Wittering, May 1938 to December 1938
(Note: From July 1931 until March 1933 the Demon's immediate forerunner, the Hart Fighter, was in service)

Markings: Red and blue alternating squares along the fuselage and between the roundels on the upper mainplanes. Markings aft of the roundel on the rear fuselage had a rectangular cut-out superimposed to accommodate the serial number. Camouflaged from September 1938, displaying the squadron code letters 'MS'

Serials: The Hart Fighters used alongside Bulldogs were K1950 to K1955. Demons were K2842, 2843, 2844, 2845, 2846, 2847, 2848, 2849, 2850, 2851, 2852, 2853, 2854, 2855, 2857, 2858, 3786, 3789, 3796, 3797, 3798, 3799, 3802, 3804, 4500, 5694, 5695, 5698, 5699, 5700, 5705, 5710, 5712, 5716, 5718, 5719, 5725, 5726, 5727, 5729, 5730, 5731, 5732, 8194, 8195, 8196, 8197, 8198, 8217

No 25 Squadron *Hawkinge, October 1937 to June 1938*

Markings: Traditional black parallel bars not carried by Demons, but unit badge carried on standard fighter spearhead frame on the fins

Serials: K2905, 2906, 3770, 3791, 3976, 3979, 3983, 4525, 4526, 4529, 4532, 4538, 4539, 4540, 4542, 4543, 4544, 5694, 5722, 8183, 8186, 8190, 8203, 8204, 8205, 8206, 8208, 8211, 8212, 8213

No 29 Squadron *North Weald, March 1935 to October 1935*
Amiriya, October 1935 to March 1936
Helwan, July 1936 to August 1936
Aboukir, August 1936 to September 1936
North Weald, September 1936 to November 1937
Debden, November 1937 to December 1938

Markings: Two parallel red bars with two red 'X' between them on fuselage sides and eight red 'X' between them on the upper mainplanes. On return to the UK after Abyssinian crisis deployment in 1936, new Turret Demons carried no squadron markings other than the unit badge

Below *No 29 Sqn re-equipped with Turret Demons upon their return to North Weald following a two-year stint in North Africa in September 1936*

in the standard spearhead fighter frame on the fins. Received camouflage finish during Munich Crisis but no evidence of pre-war codes 'YB' being displayed

Serials: K2843, 2845, 3766, 3767, 3769, 3770, 3772, 3774, 3775, 3777, 3781, 3782, 3783, 3785, 3787, 3791, 3792, 3805, 3974, 3975, 3976, 3979, 3980, 3981, 3982, 3985, 4509, 4510, 5725, 5733, 5734, 5735, 5736, 5737, 5738, 5739, 5740, 5741, 5898, 5899, 5900, 5901, 5902, 5903, 5904, 5905, 5906, 5907, 8195, 8196, 8197

No 41 Squadron *Northolt, July 1934 to October 1935*
Khormaksar, October 1935 to March 1936
Sheikh Othman, March 1936 to August 1936
Catterick, September 1936 to October 1937

Markings: Single broad red band across the upper mainplanes between the roundels and along the fuselage sides. Squadron emblem on fin

Serials: K1952 (Hart Fighter), K2853, 2858, 2904, 2905, 2906, 2907, 2908, 3765, 3767, 3773, 3774, 3777, 3778, 3779, 3788, 3790, 3794, 3798, 3800, 3806, 3974, 3983, 4525, 4526, 4532, 4533, 4534, 4535, 4536, 4537, 4538, 4539, 4540, 4541, 4542, 4543, 4544

No 64 Squadron *Heliopolis, March 1936 to April 1936*
Ismailia, April 1936 to August 1936
Aboukir, August 1936 to September 1936
Martlesham Heath, September 1936 to May 1938
Church Fenton, May 1938 to December 1938

Markings: No markings when serving overseas, but on return to the UK in 1936 adopted an unusual red and blue 'trellis' design which appeared between the roundels on the upper mainplanes and along the sides of the fuselage. This was retained until the summer of 1938. At the time of the Munich Crisis in the autumn of 1938, the Demons were camouflaged and allocated the squadron code letters 'XQ', though it is not certain whether they were in fact embodied

Serials: K2850, 2906, 2907, 2908, 3765, 3773, 3786, 4507, 4508, 4509, 4510, 4511, 4512, 4515, 4516, 4517, 4518, 4519, 4520, 4521, 4523, 4524, 4527, 4528, 4529, 4531, 4532, 4543, 5719, 5727, 5729, 8181, 8182, 8183, 8184, 8185, 8186, 8187, 8188, 8189, 8194, 8195, 8198, 8199, 8200, 8201, 8202, 8203, 8214, 8215, 8216

No 65 Squadron *Hornchurch, August 1934 to July 1936*

Markings: As the squadron was tasked with the night fighting role it did not carry the colourful red chevrons which later adorned their successors, the Gauntlet and the Gladiator

Serials: K3774, 3775, 3776, 3780, 3782, 3784, 3787, 3788, 3789, 3796, 3800

Also assigned some Hart Fighters (ex-No 23 Sqn) serialled K1951, 1952, 1954

No 74 Squadron *Hal Far, September 1935 to September 1936*
Hornchurch, September 1936 to April 1937

Markings: During service in Malta, the Demons were camouflaged using locally-produced dopes. On return to the UK the standard silver finish was reinstated, but there is no evidence that the yellow and black tiger-skin squadron regalia (as used on Gauntlets from 1937 onwards) was ever applied to the Demons

Serials: K2846, 2847, 2850, 2853, 2905, 2906, 2907, 3767, 3769, 3770, 3772, 3773, 3777, 3784, 3791, 3792, 3793, 3794, 4535, 4536, 4537, 4539, 4540, 4542, 4543

Auxiliary Air Force

No 600 Squadron *Hendon, January 1935 to September 1938*
Kenley, October 1938
Hendon, October 1938 to January 1939
(Note: Hart light bombers carrying fighter squadron markings were used until February 1937 when Demons replaced them)

Markings: Red triangles against a white bar background across the upper mainplanes, between the roundels and along the sides of the fuselage. In September 1938 camouflage was introduced and the squadron code letters 'MV' applied

Serials: Demons: K2846, 2847, 2850, 2854, 3784, 3793, 3982, 4507, 4523, 5697, 5700, 5701, 5702, 5703, 5704, 5707, 5708, 5709, 5710, 8190, 8204
Harts: K2979, 2980, 2981, 2982, 2983, 2984, 2985, 2986, 2987, 2988, 3028, 3040, 3045, 3048

No 601 Squadron *Hendon, February 1933 to October 1938*
(Note: Hart light bombers carrying fighter squadron markings were used until replaced by Demons in August 1937)

Markings: Red and black interlocking triangles in a band across the upper mainplanes between the roundels and along the sides of the fuselage. In September 1938 during the Munich Crisis, the Demons were camouflaged but it is unlikely that the allocated squadron code letters 'YN' were utilised until the arrival of Gauntlets the following month

Serials: Demons: K2842, 2855, 3796, 3799, 3801, 3802, 3979, 3982, 4496, 4511, 4513, 4521, 4522, 4527, 4540, 5691, 5693, 5713, 5714, 5715, 5716, 5717, 5720, 5721, 5722, 5723, 5724, 5728, 8191
Harts: K2966, 2970, 2971, 2972, 2973, 2974, 2975, 2977, 2978, 3031, 3049, 3889

Left Hawker Demon K8189 flew with No 64 Sqn before passing to No 1 Air Armaments School. Many Turret Demons were only marked with squadron crests on the fin rather than full fuselage and upper wing markings

No 604 Squadron *Hendon, September 1934 to January 1939*
(Note: Hart light bombers with fighter squadron markings were in service until June 1935 when replaced by Demons)

Markings: Red and yellow interlocking triangles in a band between the roundels on the upper mainplanes and along the sides of the fuselage and the County of Middlesex Arms motif on the fin. In September 1938 the Demons were camouflaged, but the allocated squadron code letters 'WQ' were not embodied

Serials: Demons: K2842, 3786, 3789, 3797, 3800, 3801, 3980, 3985, 4496, 4497, 4498, 4499, 4500, 4501, 4502, 4503, 4504, 4505, 4506, 4514, 4528, 4529, 4530, 4534, 5709, 5715, 5721, 8192, 8207
Harts: K3893, 3894, 3895, 3896

No 607 Squadron: *Usworth, September 1936 to December 1938*

Markings: Mauve and stone interlocking triangles above the upper mainplanes between the roundels and along the sides of the fuselage. During the Munich Crisis in 1938, the Demons were camouflaged. The squadron code letters 'LW' were allocated but it is doubtful if they were ever used

Below *No 23 Sqn was issued with six Hart 'Fighters' (K1950 to 1955) prior to definitive Demons being delivered from Hawkers. Issued to a single flight within the then Bulldog-equipped unit, they commenced operations from Kenley in July 1931*

Serials: K2906, 3765, 3767, 3777, 3794, 3800, 3801, 3805, 3806, 3984, 4507, 4528, 4542, 5683, 5684, 5685, 5686, 5687, 5688, 5689, 5690, 5691, 5692, 5693, 5724, 5732, 5735, 8184, 8193, 8205, 8212, 8213

No 608 Squadron *Thornaby, January 1937 to March 1939*

Markings: Pale turquoise and black interlocking triangles in a band between the roundels on the upper mainplanes and along the sides of the fuselage. Rectangular panel superimposed on markings on rear fuselage to accommodate the serial number. In September 1938 during the Munich Crisis, the Demons were camouflaged and the squadron code letters 'PG' applied

Serials: K2844, 2848, 2849, 2851, 3768, 3771, 3772, 3777, 3779, 3783, 3795, 3796, 3807, 3977, 4508, 4510, 4515, 4533, 4543, 5687, 5688, 5728, 8193, 8205, 8206, 8208, 8209, 8210, 8211, 8212, 8213

Overseas Service

No 6 Squadron *Ismailia (with detachments at Ramleh and Semakh), October 1935 to November 1936. This was basically a Hart squadron, but it operated Demons in 'D' flight during the period indicated*

Serials: K4509, 4514, 4518

No 8 Squadron *Khormaksar, October 1935 to 1936*
Basically a Vickers Vincent unit, but one Flight of Demons (ex-No 41 Sqn) was operated during the Abyssinian Crisis. No details of serials

No 208 Squadron *Heliopolis (with detachments at Mersah Matruh and Ramleh) 1935–36. This was basically an Audax squadron but it operated Demons in 'D' flight during the Abyssinian Crisis.*

Serials: K4515

Training and Miscellaneous

No 1 Air Armament School
K4496, 5726, 5727, 5736, 5741, 5900, 5902, 5904, 5907, 8181, 8182, 8184, 8188, 8194, 8202, 8216, 8217

No 9 Bombing & Gunnery School
K5694, 5695, 5735, 5737, 5738, 5898, 5905, 5906, 5907, 8183, 8195, 8197, 8198, 8203, 8214

No 9 Air Observer School
K5706, 5710, 5725, 5899, 5905, 8198, 8203

No 24 E & RFTS
K3789, 4514, 4522, 5702

No 3 FTS
K5735

No 6 AONS
K4522

No 14 FTS
K5695, 5706

A&AEE
K2842, 2905, 3764

No 1 AACU
K8182

RAE
K2856, 2857 (target-tug)

Above A formation of No 41 Sqn Demons up from RAF Northolt in 1935

Hawker Hart Fighter/Demon I (Turret) data

Engine: Rolls-Royce Kestrel, V12 cylinder, fully-supercharged

	Kestrel IIS	Kestrel VDR
Max power	581 hp, 2700 rpm at 11,500 ft	696 hp, 2900 rpm at 11,000 ft

Dimensions		
Span	37 ft 3 in	
Length	29 ft 7 in	
Height	11 ft 0 in	
Wing Area	348 ft^2	

Weights		
Loaded	4668 lbs	
Empty	3336 lbs	

Performance		
Max Speed	181 mph at 13,000 ft	202 mph at 15,000 ft
Time to 15,000 ft	11.3 min	8.8 min
Service Ceiling	24,500 ft	28,580 ft

Armament: Two fixed, synchronized, 0.303 in, Mk V, Vickers machine guns, using interrupter gear, 600 rounds ammunition per gun. One 0.303 in, Mk III Lewis machine gun in gunner's Frazer-Nash turret. Six 97-round ammunition drums, eight 20 lb Mk I HE bombs

THE GLOSTER GAUNTLET

THE GAUNTLET WAS, arguably, the best-looking fighter to emerge from the distinguished firm of Gloster Aircraft Co Ltd. It is all too easy to wax lyrical about such an attractive, well-rounded aeroplane. The early-model, short-chord Townend ring which surrounded the big Bristol Mercury radial engine led naturally towards the fuselage lines and gave the Gauntlet a graceful air, which the song of its engine did nothing to dispel. Neither the Gauntlet's fairly stalky, but neatly faired undercarriage, nor the plain fact of it being, unusually, a two-bay biplane, detracted from its purposeful elegance. To return to earth, the Gauntlet was also an effective war machine, very fast for its day, despite the relatively modest power of its Mercury VI, a fully-supercharged engine which gave its maximum power of 645 hp at 15,500 ft. Thanks to careful fairing and streamlining, the aircraft achieved 230 mph at its rated altitude, and its service ceiling of just over 33,000 ft was exceptional. With an open cockpit and despite the pilot's electrically-heated clothing, this could have been described as a debatable asset, but such a performance for an interceptor fighter was a first for the RAF.

Below The Gloster SS.19 taking part in the 1932 RAF Display at Hendon on 27 June. It was numbered '4' in the New Types Park and was flown by Howard Saint. Note the six-gun configuration

The distinguished designer H P Folland followed up his successes with the Grebe and Gamecock by submitting proposals for the Air Ministry's Specification F.9/26. None of the proposals submitted (including the Gloster Goldfinch) was selected. Never a man to be defeated, Folland proposed the all-metal framed Gloster SS.18 two-bay biplane, which first flew in January 1929. By this time, however, Spec F.20/27 had overtaken F.9/26 but, despite this, the SS.18 was still well up to the new requirements. The Bristol Bulldog eventually won the F.20/27 competition but, even so, Folland pressed ahead making further refinements to the SS.18. With modifications and varying engine installations, the aircraft became successively the SS.18A, SS.18B, SS.19 and SS.19A.

The final model, the SS.19B to Specification F.24/33 became the Gloster Gauntlet of 1933, subsequently to be used extensively as an interceptor fighter by the RAF. The Gauntlet, a compact all-metal two-bay biplane, was ultimately produced in two versions which were outwardly identical, using the same engine but differing significantly between the Mks I and II in the detail design of the structure itself. The Gauntlet I had a fuselage which was divided into three separate assemblies and had four tubular longerons. The front portion (or engine mounting), was built up from steel tubes on which was mounted a circular steel engine plate, a fireproof bulkhead and two jacking columns.

The centre part of the fuselage extended from the engine mounting to the rear of the pilot's cockpit and housed the fuel tanks, flying controls, the two machine guns, ammunition boxes and the synchronizing gear, pilot's seat (adjustable for height with Mk IV Sutton harness and release gear) and instruments. The joints between the longerons and side and cross-members were of the flat plate type, the top longerons consisting of single lengths of steel tube. The lower front longerons were built in three sections. The first of

Below Flight photograph of No 19 Sqn Gauntlets up from RAF Duxford on 17 June 1935. The squadron received its first Gauntlets in May and kept them until December 1938

Above *J9125, now the SS.19B, fitted with Mercury VIS2 and sporting a tailwheel, flying in April 1934*

Right *First production Gauntlet K4081 takes a break between trials at the A&AEE in early 1935. The stylish wheel fairings were soon dispensed with as muck and debris tended to build up very quickly within the covers when taxying on the standard grass airfields of the day*

these (from the engine mounting rearwards to the lower wing front spar attachment points) was of steel, rectangular in section and took compression loads from the engine and undercarriage. The remaining two portions of the front lower longerons, extending to the rear spar attachments were of square section steel tube, as were the vertical members and the bottom cross-struts of the front fuselage frame. All of the other cross struts were of round section steel tubes. The rear section of the fuselage, extending to the sternpost, carried the tail unit, tail wheel, radio installation and air bottles for engine starting and brakes.

The four rear longerons were of round-section steel tube, as far aft as the tailplane front spar mounting (for which there was a substantial vertical bearing beam at either side) and thence of square section. They were assembled into a frame by means of pressed-out steel plates which formed mounting sockets for the vertical and cross struts, as well as attachments for the cross-bracing wires. The rounded section of the rear fuselage was maintained by light metal formers and stringers mounted on the basic frame, covered with fabric aft of the cockpit, with large, detachable inspection panels. Elsewhere, the fuselage was covered by sheet metal panels, secured with quickly-detachable

fasteners. The through-axle undercarriage had Dowty oleo legs and Dunlop air-operated brakes. In Gauntlets K4083, K4087 and K4088, wheel spats were fitted but these tended to become clogged with mud in those days before hard runways (and therefore a hazard which could lead to turning over) and, in subsequent aircraft, Dunlop faired-in wheels were substituted, the spats not being fitted. A Palmer faired-in tail wheel was fitted, with a Dowty shock-absorber.

The two-bay wings had spars of riveted box-section in high-tensile steel, the main and light ribs being of duralumin. The interplane struts were fitted with fairings at the wing mountings. All four wings were fitted with Frise-type ailerons, the actuating levers being fitted to the lower wings only, the upper and lower units being connected by streamlined balancing wires. The wing assembly was entirely fabric-covered, as were the tail-plane and fin, which were wire-braced to the fuselage. The tailplane was built in two halves and was adjustable in incidence in the conventional way for altering fore and aft trim. Each half was attached, by a bearing at its front spar to the fuselage

Below The same aircraft now called the SS.19B, fitted with Bristol Mercury VIS engine and with provision for carrying small bombs beneath the lower wings

vertical beam and pivoted in the horizontal plane. When the pilot altered the tailplane incidence, the rear spar was adjusted vertically by a cable-operated screw-jack attached to a cross-beam to which each half tailplane was rigidly attached. The elevators were also in two portions, bolted together. The fin was not offset to counteract propeller torque, nor the rudder provided with a trimmer or bias.

The fuel system comprised two fuselage-mounted tanks. The lower, main tank, contained 58.5 gal and the gravity tank above it 21.75 gallons. Fuel was delivered from the main tank by an engine-driven pump which, in the case of failure, could be isolated by the fuel cock and the engine fed from the gravity tank. The oil system was cooled by a surface cooler mounted on the upper starboard side of the fuselage ahead of the pilot, the tank mounted ahead of the fireproof bulkhead. For engine starting, a Type A gas starter was installed or a Hucks starter could be used, by means of the propeller starter claw.

The two .303 in Mk III Vickers machine guns,

Below View of the first production Gauntlet, K4081. *Following trials at the A&AEE at Martlesham Heath, K4081 crashed in August 1936*

which fired through the propeller disc via Constantinesco synchronizing gear, were mounted with their muzzles snugly in external troughs along the fuselage sides, their breeches and feed mechanisms exposed inside the cockpit and adjacent to the two ammunition boxes. The guns were prone to jamming and their cocking levers were therefore easily reached by the pilot. The usual Aldis and ring sights were provided on the fuselage top decking. A G22 camera gun could be mounted on the top surface of the lower starboard wing. The equipment included a TR.9 H/F wireless transmitting and receiving set, mounted in a quickly removable crate aft of the cockpit, power being derived from a dry battery and a 2v accumulator. Other electrical supply for heating the pilot's clothing, the oxygen supply and both guns, as well as the necessary lighting for night-flying, was provided by a 12v 500-watt engine-driven generator.

As a result of the Gloster Aircraft Company having joined forces with Hawkers in 1934, as much as possible of the standard Hawker construction process was adopted for the Gauntlet II following completion of existing orders for the Mk I. It retained the overall framework pattern of the earlier aircraft, thereby avoiding a complete redesign. The all-metal construc-

tion, in accordance with standard Hawker practice, was of steel tube and duralumin, with fabric covering over light formers and stringers.

MK1 INTO MK2

The Gauntlet II differed from the Mk I version in that the vertical side frames of the rear fuselage were 'warren girder' (zig-zag) structures, rather than vertical struts stabilized by wire-bracing between them. Based on two pairs of tubular longerons, the whole vertical frame each side (from the cockpit to the stern frame) was bolted and riveted together as a unit, the only wire bracing being in the tail bay. Internal wire bracing was also used for stabilizing the top and bottom tube cross members. Many connections between tubes were made with ball-and-socket joints, stabilized by flat steel side plates and steel distance tubes or spacers, screwed, bolted or riveted together as required. Another example of the Hawker system being adopted was the design of the wing spars. These

were of riveted, dumb-bell section, high-tensile steel. The top and bottom booms were of polygon section and the vertical web was of corrugated drawn steel. This was a well-established practice at Hawker's, and was considered to be easier, faster and cheaper to assemble than any other method.

In view of the large number of Hawker-designed aircraft of the Hart and Fury families in RAF service, there was an obvious advantage in terms of familiarity of working practices, as well as common component parts. The carefully-faired undercarriage, with Dunlop or Palmer streamlined wheels (no spats), was constructed of steel tube (in the through-axle style) with Dowty oleo shock-absorbing legs and wire bracing for the trailing radius rods. The wheels were equipped with Dunlop pneumatic brakes, operated differentially by pedals on the rudder bar which could

Below *Side on view of K4081. It was completed in December 1934 and P E G Sayers made the first flight on the 17th of that month*

be adjusted by a 'star' wheel to suit the pilot's leg length. The tail wheel had an oleo shock-absorber, similar to the main undercarriage leg.

Light wing loading and clean design results in a considerable amount of float before touch-down and a fair degree of skill is needed to judge an accurate landing. The SS.37, which was intended to follow the Gauntlet, was to be an even cleaner single-bay biplane than the SS.18/19 series, with a low-drag cantilever undercarriage. Effective flaps were therefore needed and the new airframe was to incorporate split flaps on all four wings. To assess the operation of these flaps and to gain experience of them, Gauntlet I K4103 was fitted experimentally with such flaps in 1936, these devices at first being hydraulically operated. The installation was evaluated thoroughly by the A&AEE at Martlesham.

The initial installation, which allowed the flaps to be selected in any position from shut to 90° down, was simple and satisfactory, but took about 32 complete hand-pump movements to lower or raise completely. With flaps fully down, the Gauntlet's stalling speed was reduced by about 4 mph. A slight sluggishness occurred in the lateral control, giving plenty of warn-

ing before a spin occurred and there was no flicking beforehand. The gliding angle was increased by 7½°, much improving the pilot's view ahead and reducing the float after flattening out. At the high rate of descent, the change of attitude in landing was rather sudden. If an overshoot was needed with flaps fully down, the aircraft became disconcertingly tail-heavy when the throttle was opened. This was particularly noticeable at night, although with flaps down the increased gliding angle was a great advantage, the pilot being better able to see the flare path.

Martlesham concluded that the flapped Gauntlet was a much easier aircraft for an unskilled pilot to land on a small aerodrome, by day or night, but recommended fitment of a quicker-acting system. In October 1936, the aircraft was fitted with pneumatically operated flaps whose positions were either 'up' or 'down'. This was satisfactory, although Martlesham recommended that the rate of raising the flaps should

Below Misty morning view of a crowded flightline at North Weald in late 1936. The distinctive red and white chequers of No 56 Sqn were only worn by Gauntlets for a brief 14 months

Right *What the well-dressed Gauntlet pilot wore during the 1930s. Note the oil cooler just forward of the windscreen on the starboard side only. The Gladiator's radiator was located in a similar position*

be reduced so that the 'sudden dangerous drop is eliminated'.

The Gauntlet has frequently been quoted as having a Mercury VIS.2 engine. This is contrary to *Air Publication 1487* in versions applying to both the Gauntlet I and II. It also differs from surviving A&AEE reports from Martlesham which refer to the engine type. In every case it is stated to be a Mercury VIS with a reduction gear ratio of 0.5:1. The difference is quite important. Had a VIS.2 been fitted, by Bristol practice, this would have been 0.655:1, swinging the propeller slightly faster for a given crankshaft rpm. It may fairly be said that the difference was very small but it is also fair to assume that Folland and Fedden well knew how to match the airframe and engine with the big, fixed-pitch Watts wooden propeller initially fitted, and the Fairey-Reed three-blade metal propeller which was substituted later. The probability exists, of course, of normal comparative trials having taken place at Bristol or at Martlesham. Reduction gears in Bristol engines could be exchanged comparatively easily but official records refer simply to standard engines fitted to Gauntlets in service. In terms of achieved performance for its day, whatever the engine, the results speak for themselves and the Gauntlet was a superb interceptor.

SERVICE ENTRY

With the arrival of Gauntlets at the historic fighter station of Duxford early in 1935, the open cockpit fighter biplane, modelled on the classic World War 1 concept, reached its apotheosis. Its successor, the better known Gladiator, was somehow never the same with its enclosed canopy, and for the old-style fighter pilots the Gauntlet was definitely the end of an era. During its four years of service with the first-line squadrons, the Gauntlet became a much-loved aeroplane. A superb flying machine, it was widely regarded by its many exponents to be the finest example of the biplane fighter breed ever produced. When the proud name of Fighter Command first came into being in July 1936 the Gauntlet was, so to speak, the flagship of the fleet, being the fastest fighter in the RAF, and having bettered the renowned Fury in this capacity by about 15 mph, with a top speed of 230 mph. It was even faster than the improved Fury II, as well as

offering greater endurance and a higher ceiling. It was, however, not these specialised interceptors which the Gauntlet replaced, but rather the more numerous Bulldogs (in Nos 17, 19, 32, 54, 56 and 111 Sqns), where an even more notable advantage in top speed saw a dramatic advance from the Bulldog's long since inadequate 174 mph.

The long line of prototypes from which the production Gauntlet family emerged into squadron service from 1935 had in fact been close rivals of the Bulldog in earlier days. Indeed, it must have been a great source of satisfaction for Gloster's to have supplanted their old competitors at Bristol as the major suppliers of the RAF's most prolific fighter of the period. The major factor contributing to this successful long-term outcome was the develoment of the Gauntlet's powerplant – the original and unreliable Bristol Mercury IIA of the prototype SS.18 (J9125) had gradually evolved into the immensely satisfactory Mercury VIS2, delivering an impressive 645 hp housed in a very clean entry NACA cowling. An excellent performance resulted and, combined with the superlative handling qualities, gave the RAF a superb aerobatic aeroplane as well as a notably steady gun-platform much relished

Left *Gloster SS.19B being demonstrated by Howard Saint at the 1933 SBAC show at Hatfield. In the foreground is Wallace K3562, originally Wapiti IIA K1346*

1935 and a third for another 100 in September 1935, bringing total RAF deliveries to 228.

The vast majority of the Gauntlets in squadron service were designated Mk II, only the initial contract being Mk I. The difference between them resided in a change to the internal structure of the rear fuselage and the main wing spars following a company take-over by Hawker, although all the aircraft were built by Gloster's. Details of the serial batches are:

Gauntlet Production for the RAF

Gauntlet I	K4081 to K4104	Completed Aug 1935
Gauntlet II	K5264 to K5367	Completed Aug 1936
Gauntlet II	K7792 to K7891	Completed Feb 1937

Only one major change occurred to the configuration of the Gauntlet during its RAF service. This was in 1937 when the Watts two-blade wooden propeller was replaced by a Fairey-Reed three-blade metal type.

As already mentioned, the Gauntlet quickly established itself as an excellent gun platform, and as early as 3 June 1935 No 19 Sqn came top at the RAF's annual contest for the Sir Philip Sassoon Flight Attack Challenge Trophy. This triumph was quickly followed by the appearance of No 19 Sqn's Gauntlets at the historic Royal Review of the RAF held at the newly-opened Mildenhall aerodrome to mark the occasion of the Jubilee Year of King George V's reign. In a celebrated aerial photograph of this occasion, nine Gauntlets can be seen in pride of place with 36 Furies of Nos 1, 25 and 43 Sqns in the front row of a massed assembly of 356 aircraft awaiting His Majesty's inspection. They subsequently performed a special display of air drill prior to joining in a grand fly-past of 155 aircraft in wing formation over the saluting base at Duxford. The Gauntlets were the fastest fighters in the formation and this still remained the case when, two years later on 26 June 1937, Gauntlets took part in an even bigger 250 aircraft fly-past in the presence of HM King George VI at the RAF's 18th and last annual display at Hendon.

In 1936, the Gauntlets of No 19 Sqn were in the limelight again when three of their aircraft (K4094, 4097 and 4100) thrilled the crowds at the annual RAF Display at Hendon on 27 June with a polished display of 'tied-together' aerobatics. The formation leader was none other than Flt Lt (later Air Chief Marshal Sir

by luminaries in both fields such as Flt Lt Harry Broadhurst and 'Sailor' Malan, who flew it for many years.

No 19 Sqn (later to become the first Spitfire squadron) was selected to introduce the Gauntlet into RAF service following the Air Ministry's issue of a definitive Specification 24/33 in February 1934 and an initial production contract to re-equip one Bulldog squadron. The first production Gauntlet (K4081) took to the air at Hucclecote, flown by 'Gerry' Sayer, on 17 December 1934. No 19 Sqn received its first aircraft (K4086) for preliminary trials as early as 18 February 1935, and began full-scale re-equipment from 25 May. By July, No 19 had received its full complement of Gauntlets in their traditional blue and white check livery, and the type remained a familiar sight in the skies around Duxford until as late as January 1939, although from August 1938 they steadily gave way to Spitfires.

Right from the outset of its career, the Gauntlet was a huge success and the first order for 24 aircraft was quickly followed by a second contract for 104 in April

Harry) Broadhurst whose name became legendary in aerobatic circles in the 1930s. As a flight leader in No 19 Sqn, Harry Broadhurst had also won the Fighter Air Firing Challenge Trophy at Sutton Bridge in 1935, repeating this performance in 1936, and was noted as a crack aerial marksman as well as an aerobatic wizard.

Above A line of No 19 Sqn Gauntlets rise and fall in the warm summer air, in a symphony of whistling wires and the steady purring of Bristol Mercury radial engines. This priceless Flight photograph was taken on 17 June 1935 during formation practice from the squadron's Duxford base shortly after delivery of the type to the unit

AEROBATIC TEAMS

Aerobatics were to become the Gauntlet's forte and so it came as no surprise when, during what was to be the final display at Hendon in 1937, one of its highlights was a memorable display with coloured smoke trails by the Gauntlets of No 66 Sqn. Gauntlet aerobatic teams were still showing their prowess as late as 1938, notably two talented trios from Nos 17 and 151 Sqns. Their rivals at this time were the Gladiator teams of No 87 Sqn and the Furies of No 43 Sqn.

Steady replacement of Bulldogs by Gauntlets proceeded apace during 1936, and by the close of that year the transformation was completed in five more squadrons, namely No 17 at Kenley, No 32 at Biggin Hill,

No 54 at Hornchurch, No 56 at North Weald and No 111 at Northolt. In addition, No 65 Sqn at Hornchurch had forsaken its Demons for Gauntlets and three entirely new squadrons had been formed on Gauntlets as part of the RAF Expansion Scheme, these being No 46 at Kenley, No 66 at Duxford and No 151 at North Weald. It was also in 1936 that the new Gauntlet II was introduced into service, the first being issued to Nos 56 and 111 Sqns. Both these units were able to display their new mounts in the fly-past marking the unveiling of the Vimy Ridge memorial by King Edward VIII in July 1936.

The year 1937 witnessed the peak of the Gauntlet's career with Fighter Command, during which no less than 14 squadrons appeared in the Order of Battle.

Right Holding formation amidst a seemingly endless procession of silver aircraft, a Gauntlet five-ship from No 213 Sqn follow Demons and Ansons during Hendon Display rehearsals in 1937

Three of the last four regular Gauntlet squadrons to join the line of battle (Nos 79, 80 and 213) were in fact newly-formed Expansion Scheme units, but No 74 at Hornchurch (the famous Tiger Squadron) had already seen service with Demons out in Malta during the Abyssinian Crisis and, it is reported, was more than a little upset when it received Gauntlets as it had been scheduled to go on to the spanking-new Gladiator and was already starting to convert when, one day in March 1937, it was mysteriously switched over to Gauntlets instead. However, they quickly recovered their élan and swiftly compensated for their temporary disappointment by applying to their Gauntlets the most startling and original squadron markings ever seen on a biplane fighter. Their colourful squadron commander (Sqn Ldr D S 'Brookie' Brookes) authorised a system of alternate black and yellow triangles which symbolised a tiger's stripes, complementing the tiger's face incorporated in the squadron badge officially awarded in February 1937. The tiger stripe markings were emblazoned across the top wings and, uniquely, along the entire length of the fuselage aft of the roundel, thus obliterating the customary serial.

As it turned out, No 74 Sqn was to retain its trusty Gauntlets longer than most regular fighter squadrons, and did not go over finally to Spitfires until February 1939. Some wonderful anecdotes about this period of its distinguished history are to be found in Douglas Tidy's book *I Fear No Man* (Macdonald, 1972), one of the best being an account of No 74's Gauntlet operations during the grand fly-past of 250 aircraft over the saluting base at the final RAF Hendon Display in 1937. To quote briefly,

'The whole exercise called for very accurate navigation and timing. No 74 Sqn was leading the 50 fighters on the port wing, setting off from Duxford. The senior Duxford squadron, No 19, which had possessed Gauntlets since early 1935, tried not to look sour at being bossed about on their own aerodrome by the parvenu 74.'

Before finally relinquishing its Gauntlets, No 74 Sqn was to achieve the remarkable feat of winning the annual Fighter Attack Competition for the Sir Philip Sassoon Cup in November 1938, despite the fact that their (by now) obsolete biplanes were up against the Gladiators of Nos 54 and 65 Sqns and the Hurricanes of No 111 (the famous 'Treble One') Sqn. This was undoubtably due to the great emphasis on accurate air firing which No 74 had always cultivated during its Gauntlet days, and they were lucky to have in their midst as a flight commander a future Battle of Britain ace, the legendary 'Sailor' Malan, one of the best marksmen the RAF ever possessed.

FUTURE ACES

Many young pilots with the Gauntlet squadrons during those final peacetime years of the late 1930s were destined to earn their place in RAF history in the

ensuing air battles of World War Two. 'Al' Deere flew in Malan's flight with No 74 Sqn for a short period. Two future wing leaders, 'Mike' Crossley and 'Pete' Brothers, both flew Gauntlets with No 32 Sqn at Biggin Hill, and Ian 'Widge' Gleed, who became famous leading a Spitfire Wing in North Africa, served with No 46 Sqn at Kenley and Digby. Some amusing stories are related about Gleed's early days on Gauntlets in Norman Franks' excellent book *Fighter Leader* (William Kimber, 1978), including an embarrassing crash on 31 March 1937 when, during a landing approach at Hawkinge, he misjudged his glide and

swiped off his undercarriage on the roof of a house. Despite this *faux pas*, he survived to be selected for No 46 Sqn's Display Team at the RAF Hendon Display a few months later!

Gp Capt J A 'Johnny' Kent, another distinguished World War Two fighter ace, tells in his book *One of the Few* (William Kimber, 1971), about his experiences as a Gauntlet pilot with No 19 Sqn at Duxford in 1936 when, as a 'new boy', he had just been posted in from No 5 FTS at Sealand. In view of his later record, it comes as a surprise to learn that he was a very indifferent shot when on the ranges at Sutton Bridge,

Above Pleasing study of No 56 Sqn Gauntlet II K5296 on a sortie from RAF North Weald on 30 October 1936

but his air firing skills improved dramatically after some intensive instruction from his flight commander, Harry Broadhurst.

Yet another of the great fighter pilots in RAF history, Sqn Ldr M T St John 'Pat' Pattle, famed for his exploits on Gladiators and Hurricanes fighting in North Africa and Greece in 1940/41, began his career on Gauntlets with No 80 Sqn at Henlow in 1937.

Not often mentioned in accounts of the Gauntlet's contribution to RAF annals is the fact that, with No 32 Sqn, it was closely involved in secret trials of the radar-directed fighter interception techniques from November 1936 onwards, which were to make such a vital difference to Fighter Command's effectiveness against the *Luftwaffe* in the air battles of 1940. Three Gauntlets (K7797, 7799 and 7800) of No 32 Sqn were regularly directed to 'intercept' unsuspecting civil airliners by an experimental ground radar station at

Bawdsey Manor, thus initiating a quantum leap in the operational capacity of defensive fighters for ever afterwards.

Right up until the Munich Crisis of September 1938, the Gauntlet continued to perform well in squadron service and was remarkably trouble-free on the maintenance side apart from a brief interlude in 1937 when the Mercury engines had snags with sticking exhaust valves – this problem was soon rectified. They collected annual trophies with monotonous regularity (it was the turn of No 213 Sqn to win the Sir Philip Sassoon Cup in 1937) and even contributed a small footnote to media history when Gauntlets of No 151 Sqn from North Weald made a brief appearance on early television transmissions in

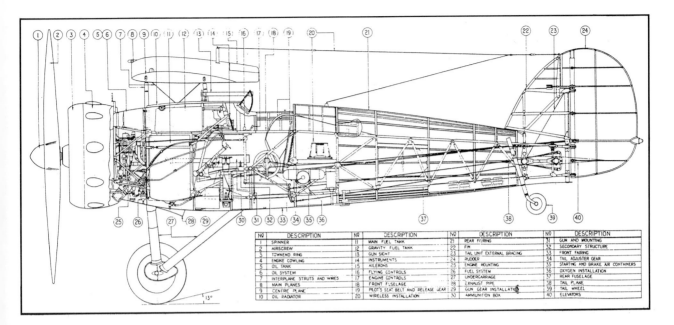

NO	DESCRIPTION	NO	DESCRIPTION	NO	DESCRIPTION	NO	DESCRIPTION
1	SPINNER	11	MAIN FUEL TANK	21	REAR FAIRING	31	GUN AND MOUNTING
2	AIRSCREW	12	GRAVITY FUEL TANK	22	FIN	32	SECONDARY STRUCTURE
3	TOWNEND RING	13	GUN SIGHT	23	TAIL UNIT EXTERNAL BRACING	33	FRONT FAIRING
4	ENGINE COWLING	14	INSTRUMENTS	24	RUDDER	34	TAIL ADJUSTER GEAR
5	OIL TANK	15	AILERONS	25	ENGINE MOUNTING	35	STARTING AND BRAKE AIR CONTAINERS
6	OIL SYSTEM	16	FLYING CONTROLS	26	FUEL SYSTEM	36	OXYGEN INSTALLATION
7	INTERPLANE STRUTS AND WIRES	17	ENGINE CONTROLS	27	UNDERCARRIAGE	37	REAR FUSELAGE
8	MAIN PLANES	18	FRONT FUSELAGE	28	EXHAUST PIPE	38	TAIL PLANE
9	CENTRE PLANE	19	PILOT'S SEAT BELT AND RELEASE GEAR	29	GUN GEAR INSTALLATION	39	TAIL WHEEL
10	OIL RADIATOR	20	WIRELESS INSTALLATION	30	AMMUNITION BOX	40	ELEVATORS

the London area in October 1938, defending the south-east from the seemingly imminent German invasion.

It is daunting in retrospect to think that in September 1938, when Britain seemed poised on the brink of war with Germany, almost half (45 per cent) of Fighter Command's single-seat fighter squadrons defending the UK were still equipped with two-gun open cockpit Gauntlets. Excellent as they had been in their heyday, they could no longer have been a match for the modern *Luftwaffe*. The nine squadrons of Gauntlets (Nos 17, 19, 32, 46, 66, 74, 79, 151 and 213) were accompanied in the Order of Battle by seven squadrons of Gladiators (Nos 3, 25, 54, 65, 72 and 85), two of Furies (Nos 1 and 43) and a mere three squadron of Hurricanes (Nos 56, 87 and 111). Spitfires had only just started to filter in to No 19 Sqn, which was still basically a Gauntlet unit.

FRONTLINE RETIREMENT

Twelve months later the situation had been transformed as deliveries of Hurricanes and Spitfires got into their stride. The Gauntlets (apart from a solitary auxiliary Squadron, No 616, which soldiered on until October 1939) had all departed, the last unit to relinquish them being No 17 Sqn at Kenley in June 1939. Of the nine squadrons deployed during the Munich crisis, six were operating Hurricanes and three were in the process of receiving Spitfires.

It was during that fateful month of September 1938 that, in common with most of the other silver-painted

Above An inboard profile of the Gauntlet from AP1487, the RAF manual on the aircraft

aircraft so typical of the peacetime RAF since the 1920s, the Gauntlets were hastily daubed in camouflage and colourful squadron heraldry replaced by grey code letters. It was in such uninspiring livery that the Gauntlet was to spend its final years on Home Defence duties with the 'weekend pilots' of the Auxiliary Air Force. This phase began in November 1938 with the issue of Gauntlets to No 504 (County of Nottingham) Sqn at Hucknall and continued in December 1938

Below Gauntlet II K7793 of No 46 Sqn is fitted with a three-bladed metal Fairey-Reed propeller. K7793 later passed to No 33 Sqn and was struck off in October 1941

with the equipment of No 601 (County of London) Sqn at Hendon and No 615 (County of Surrey) Sqn at Kenley in December 1938. Finally, in January 1939, No 602 (City of Glasgow) at Abbotsinch and No 616 (South Yorkshire) at Doncaster became Gauntlet squadrons. No 616, commanded by Sqn Ldr the Earl of Lincoln, were the very last Gauntlets to serve with a Home Defence fighter squadron, their veteran aircraft finally being replaced by Spitfires in October 1939. It was to be four-and-a-half years before they flew Gloster fighters again, the arrival of Meteors in July 1944 earning them the distinction of being the first jet fighter squadron in the RAF.

Although not on the same scale as its stablemate the Gladiator, the Gauntlet did see some service overseas when its days as a Home Defence fighter were over. The first Gauntlets sent overseas served with No 6 Sqn from August 1939, in Palestine, the aircraft being employed in the support of land forces policing the territory alongside Hardy and Lysander Army Co-op aircraft. Until the summer of 1940, some Gauntlets were also on the reserve strength of Nos 33 and 112 Sqns, which flew Gladiators in Egypt.

With the entry of the Italians into World War Two, the handful of Gauntlets in the Middle East were given a brief opportunity to get into the history books by participating in fighter-bomber operations with No 430 Flight in support of Vincent bombers in East Africa in August/September and Wellesley bombers in October 1940. The high point came on 7 September when Flt Lt A B Mitchell flying K5355 succeeded in downing a Caproni three-engined bomber when out on a strafing mission. Gauntlets were also to see front line service once more for a few days in the Western Desert in December 1940. These were ex-RAF machines passed over to No 3 Royal Australian Air Force Sqn to supplement their Gladiators.

MET DUTIES

Although no further offensive operations were carried out after 1940, a few Gauntlets are recorded as having served with No 1414 Flight on meteorological duties in Kenya in mid-1943. The Gauntlet was no stranger to Met duties, having previously operated in this demanding role with home-based units at Aldergrove, Duxford and Mildenhall between 1936 and 1939. They carried out daily climbs to high altitudes in all weather conditions just as Siskins and Bulldogs had in earlier years, and the final Gauntlet climb was made by K5280 on 6 December 1939.

By 1938, the increasing inability of the Gauntlet to catch the new generation of monoplane bombers had become painfully obvious and Gp Capt Hugh Dundas wrote in his memoirs about his dismay when, serving with No 616 Sqn, a Bomber Command Hampden from Finningley came alongside and passed his Gauntlet during a battle climb from Doncaster.

'The pilot made a rude and familiar sign. . . I opened the throttle wide but could not keep up . . . I then understood why the wiser and older pilots on the squadron were so passionately anxious for our delight-

Left *The aftermath of a ground loop at Kenley in 1937. This No 46 Sqn Gauntlet II appears to have suffered significant damage to its fin, undercarriage and wing leading edges. The Bristol Mercury engine has also been pushed in slightly with the impact. The clutch of mechanics on the port side of the Gauntlet have begun to dismantle the aircraft's crumpled nose section – the engine cowls have already disappeared*

ful little Gauntlets to be replaced by Spitfires or Hurricanes . . .'

Nevertheless, when the Gauntlet finally passed from the scene its departure was mourned by all who had relished the delights of open-cockpit fighters. The last word must be with Air Vice-Marshal Arthur Gould Lee who, in his book *Fly Past* (Jarrolds, 1974), remembers it with great affection.

Below Five No 56 Sqn Gauntlets up from RAF North Weald on 30 October 1936

'Instantly I fell in love with the Gauntlet. I had never piloted an aeroplane which responded with such docile yet eager obedience to my demands . . . here was my much-loved Pup grown into the Pegasus of my dreams.'

It is a matter of great regret that not a single Gauntlet survives in the United Kingdom today, and in fact the only example to be seen in the world is located in Finland. Once in service with the Finnish Air Force, it is the former RAF K5271, exported in December 1939.

Gauntlet units in the RAF

No 6 Squadron *Ramleh, Haifa and Ismailia, August 1939 to April 1940*
Some 15 Gauntlets were on charge with the squadron at various times alongside 2 Lysander and 18 Hardy aircraft

Serials: K4085, 4088, 4091, 4093, 4094, 4101, 4104, 5290, 5292, 5331, 7792, 7863, 7870, 7871, 7881

No 17 Squadron *Kenley, August 1936 to May 1939 and North Weald, May 1939 to June 1939*

Markings: Parallel black bars in zig-zags between the roundels on the upper mainplanes and alongside the fuselage. Top decking of fuselage painted in flight colours

Serials: K5267, 5270, 5276, 5289, 5296, 5333, 5343, 5344, 5345, 5346, 5347, 5348, 5349, 5350, 5356, 5357, 5358, 5359, 5360, 5361, 5362, 5363, 5367, 7798, 7821, 7822, 7823, 7836, 7867, 7877, 7878

Below Five No 111 Sqn Gauntlets brushing up on their formation-keeping. Nearest the camera is K5312. On 22 June 1937 this aircraft's career ended at Hendon when it collided with a tractor. The squadron was based at nearby RAF Northolt

No 19 Squadron *Duxford, May 1935 to August 1938*

Markings: Blue and white checks across the upper mainplanes between the roundels and along the sides of the fuselage

Serials: K4082, 4083, 4084, 4085, 4086, 4087, 4088, 4089, 4090, 4091, 4092, 4093, 4094, 4095, 4096, 4097, 4098, 4099, 4100, 4101, 4102, 4104, 5270, 5292, 5314, 5331, 7808, 7870

No 32 Squadron *Biggin Hill, July 1936 to October 1938*

Markings: Blue bar with diagonal white intersections across the upper mainplanes between the roundels and alongside the fuselage. Spearhead with badge on fin

Serials: K5273, 5275, 5293, 5294, 5295, 5301, 5319, 5320, 5321, 5322, 5323, 5324, 5325, 5326, 5327, 5328, 5330, 5342, 7797, 7800, 7818, 7819, 7820

No 33 Squadron *Mersah Matruh, February 1940 to June 1940. Taken in service as reserve aircraft alongside Gladiators which formed the squadron's basic equipment*

Serials: K5273, 5286, 5295, 5299, 5316, 5337, 5366, 7793, 7884

No 46 Squadron *Kenley, September 1936 to November 1937 and Digby, November 1937 to March 1939*

Markings: Red spearhead device on each of upper mainplanes between the roundels and on the sides of the fuselage

Left *The last Home Defence RAF fighter squadron equipped with Gauntlets was No 17 Sqn, who finally retired their Gloster fighters in favour of Hurricane Is at North Weald in June 1939. This Mk II was photographed at Kenley some time between August 1936 and September 1938, the aircraft boasting the familiar zig-zags as well as the No 17 Sqn gauntlet badge on its fin*

Serials: K5268, 5272, 5274, 5275, 5286, 5299, 5304, 5315, 5316, 5317, 5318, 5321, 7792, 7793, 7794, 7795, 7796, 7842, 7843, 7844, 7845, 7851, 7859, 7860, 7861, 7862, 7863, 7891

Below *Gauntlet K4097 was delivered to No 19 Sqn in 1934 and later served in the Middle East*

No 54 Squadron *Hornchurch, August 1936 to May 1937*

Markings: Red band with oblique white bars, possibly across the upper mainplanes between the roundels, and certainly on the sides of the fuselage

Serials: K5301, 5302, 5304, 5305, 5306, 5307, 5308, 5309, 5310, 5312, 5313, 5365, 5366, 5367, 7815, 7816, 7817

No 56 Squadron *North Weald, May 1936 to July 1937*

Markings: Red and white checks across the upper mainplanes between the roundels and on the fuselage sides

Serials: K5287, 5288, 5289, 5290, 5291, 5292, 5293, 5294, 5295, 5296, 5298, 5299, 5300, 5311, 7805, 7806, 7807, 7812, 7813

No 65 Squadron *Hornchurch, July 1936 to June 1937*

Markings: A line of red chevrons, slightly tapered, on the sides of the fuselage and on each upper mainplane, between the roundels

Serials: K5331, 5332, 5334, 5335, 7828, 7829, 7830, 7834, 7835, 7836, 7837, 7839, 7840, 7857, 7858, 7864, 7865

No 66 Squadron *Duxford, July 1936 to October 1938*

Markings: Two tapering pale blue bars with thin black border painted along the sides of the fuselage. There is no evidence that this appeared on the upper mainplanes but it seems not improbable. Squadron badge in standard spearhead on the fin

Serials: K5266, 5269, 5290, 5294, 5300, 5303, 5313, 5336, 5337, 5338, 5339, 5340, 7824, 7825, 7826, 7827, 7846, 7847, 7848, 7849, 7850, 7852, 7853, 7854, 7855, 7856, 7871, 7872

No 74 Squadron *Hornchurch, March 1937 to February 1939*

Markings: Narrow black and yellow vertical triangles formed into a continuous band across the upper mainplanes between the roundels and along the whole of the rear fuselage aft of the roundel, with no fuselage serial number exhibited. Badge in spearhead on fin

Serials: K5308, 5332, 5337, 5339, 5350, 5355, 5360, 5363, 7792, 7815,

7816, 7817, 7827, 7834, 7836, 7852, 7853, 7855, 7861, 7862, 7863, 7864, 7865, 7874, 7875, 7876

No 79 Squadron *Biggin Hill, March 1937 to November 1938*

Markings: Red arrow, with shaft ahead and aft of the fuselage roundel. This marking could have been repeated above the upper mainplanes, but no photographic evidence exists of this

Serials: K5265, 5299, 5310, 5336, 5357, 7797, 7799, 7823, 7876, 7880, 7881, 7882, 7883, 7884, 7885, 7886, 7887, 7888, 7889

No 80 Squadron *Kenley, March 1937. Henlow, March 1937 to May 1937*

Markings: Restricted to squadron crest on spearhead standard frame on fin

Serials: K5308, 5337, 5339, 5355, 5360, 5363, 7792, 7827, 7852, 7855, 7861, 7862, 7863

No 111 Squadron *Northolt, June 1936 to January 1938*

Markings: Solid black bar across the upper mainplanes between the roundels and on the fuselage sides behind the roundel. Squadron commander was distinguished by a black engine cowling, fin and tailplane and a black triangle above the centre-section.

Serials: K5264, 5265, 5266, 5267, 5268, 5269, 5270, 5272, 5273, 5274, 5275, 5276, 5285, 5286, 5309, 5312, 5334, 5341, 5342, 7809, 7810, 7811, 7814, 7829, 7864, 7877

No 112 Squadron *Helwan, March 1940 to July 1940*
Basically a Gladiator squadron, but had five Gauntlets allotted as reserve aircraft, including K5292 and 7843

Right *Scramble! No 56 Sqn Gauntlets about to get airborne from RAF North Weald on 30 October 1936. K5287 was posted to Northolt and No 213 Sqn following No 56's transition to Gladiators. K5288 stayed at North Weald, but swapped its chequers for the black and blue bars of No 151 Sqn. The aircraft eventually found its way to No 602 'City of Glasgow' Sqn at Abbotsinch in early 1939. The last Gauntlet in this photograph was passed on to No 17 Sqn at Kenley in July 1937*

No 151 Squadron *North Weald, August 1936 to December 1938*

Markings: Pale blue, black and pale blue bars across the upper mainplanes between the roundels and on the fuselage sides

Serials: K5276, 5288, 5293, 5305, 5309, 5319, 5351, 5352, 5353, 5354, 5355, 7831, 7832, 7833, 7841, 7858, 7865, 7866, 7867, 7868, 7869, 7870, 7873, 7890

No 213 Squadron *Northolt, March 1937 to July 1937*
Church Fenton, July 1937 to May 1938
Wittering, May 1938 to January 1939

Markings: Yellow bar encircled by black bars, across the upper mainplanes between the roundels and on the fuselage sides either side of the roundel with a rounded front edge forward. Badge in spearhead frame on fin

Serials: K5285, 5287, 5295, 5301, 5302, 5306, 5320, 5322, 5365, 5366, 7806, 7810, 7811, 7812, 7813, 7814, 7830, 7837, 7840, 7857, 7864, 7879

No 504 Squadron *Hucknall, November 1938 to August 1939*

Markings: See footnote on Munich Crisis

Serials: No records available

No 601 Squadron *Hendon, December 1938 to March 1939*

Markings: See footnote on Munich Crisis

Serials: K5265, 5273, 5311, 5325, 5329, 5334, 5336, 5342, 7797, 7799, 7819, 7837, 7881, 7883, 7884, 7885, 7886, 7887, 7888, 7889

No 602 Squadron *Abbotsinch, January 1939 to May 1939*

Markings: See footnote on Munich Crisis

Serials: K5287, 5288, 5293, 5301, 5305, 5309, 5319, 5352, 5354, 5364, 7831, 7833, 7837, 7841, 7858, 7865, 7869, 7873, 7879

No 615 Squadron *Kenley, December 1938 to September 1939*

Markings: See footnote on Munich Crisis

Serials: K5266, 5269, 5290, 5294, 5313, 5338, 5340, 5357, 7823, 7824, 7825, 7826, 7839, 7846, 7848, 7854

No 616 Squadron *Doncaster, January 1939 to October 1939*

Markings: See footnote on Munich Crisis

Serials: K5267, 5285, 5313, 5322, 5338, 5352, 5357, 5364, 7812, 7826, 7837, 7841, 7846, 7854, 7857

No 430 Flight *East Africa, September to November 1940*

Serials: K5265, 5284, 5295, 5355, 7881

Met Flight, Aldergrove K5279, 5280, 5282, 5283	**No 8 FTS, Montrose** K5281, 5282, 5283, 5284
Met Flight, Duxford K7801, 7802, 7803, 7804	**No 9 FTS, Hullavington** K4090, 5324
Met Flight, Mildenhall K7819, 7829	**No 10 FTS, Tern Hill** K5277, 5278, 5279, 5280
No 5 FTS, Sealand K5335	**No 11 FTS, Shawbury** K5334, 5336, 5342, 7799, 7883, 7886, 7889

Munich Crisis, September 1938
Footnote:
At this period all Gauntlets still in service, in common with other silver-painted biplanes, were hastily camouflaged in green and brown (with black and white undersurfaces to the wings, with red and blue roundels) and any squadron markings obliterated. For unit identity, code letters were introduced and these were as follows: 'UV' (No 17 Sqn), 'KT' (No 32 Sqn), 'RJ' (No 46 Sqn), 'JH' (No 74 Sqn), 'AL' (No 79 Sqn), 'TV' (No 151 Sqn), 'AW' (No 504 Sqn), 'YN' (No 601 Sqn), 'LO' (No 602 Sqn), 'RR' (No 615 Sqn) and 'QJ' (No 616 Sqn). No 79 Sqn, specialising in night fighter duties, had some Gauntlets painted all-black at one period.

Gloster Gauntlet II data

Engine: Bristol Mercury VIS, 590/620 hp, 2400 rpm, +2.5 lb boost take-off; maximum 615/645 hp, 2750 rpm, +1 lb at 15,500 ft

Dimensions

Span	32 ft 10 in
Length	26 ft 2 in
Height	10 ft 2 in
Wing Area	315 ft²

Weights

Empty	2770 lbs
Loaded	3970 lbs

Performance

Max Speed	230 mph at 16,500 ft
Stalling Speed	61 mph
Time to 20,000 ft	9 min
Ceiling	33,500 ft approx

Armament Two Vickers 0.303 in, Mk V machine guns, 600 rounds each, the spent cases and links being collected internally

THE GLOSTER GLADIATOR

ATMOSPHERE IS, PERHAPS, the most notable characteristic which has been common to all of the taut little biplane fighters in this series. In the 1920s and 30s, one of the most exciting things for a boy living on the edge of a Service aerodrome was the sudden awareness of a new noise gradually increasing in intensity beyond the trees at the end of the garden. It normally indicated the approach of a slowly taxying aeroplane,

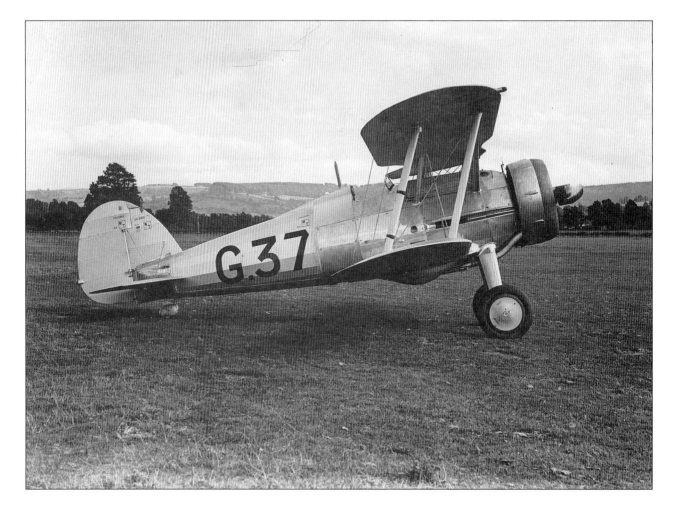

Above *View of the SS.37 as K5200. Utilising many Gauntlet components, the SS.37 was built in 1934 and first flown on 12 September that year. The following July it appeared at the Hendon Air Display, where it was allocated the Experimental Aircraft Park Number '1', painted just aft of the cowling in these pictures. After the display it went back to the factory for modification to production standard, which included the installation of an 830 hp Mercury IX engine in place of the 645 hp Mercury VIS*

Left *The Gladiator stemmed from the open-cockpit SS.37, a cleaned-up development of the Gauntlet. The SS.37 is seen here bearing the B Conditions marking G.37. It passed to the Air Ministry as K5200 in April 1935*

taking up position for take-off. Easily recognizable was the crackle of a Kestrel or the rumble of a pair of Lions. The tell-tale sound of a Bristol engine was a strange, but unmistakable mixture of rattling valve rockers, the swish of a big, slowly-turning wooden propeller and, sometimes, the faint grinding noise of the reduction gear. It all sounded rather agricultural, but was very different when the throttle was opened, the characteristic Bristol song differing little between the Jupiter and the later faster-turning Mercury, apart from a semi-tone higher pitch in the latter case heard

all too briefly with the sprightly ensuing acceleration.

Then, as now, atmosphere seemed important and this applied to colour as well as sound and the smell of burnt oil. The brilliant squadron colours were supplemented by Flight colours on wheel discs and propeller spinners, and Flight Commanders' aircraft often wore colours on their fins as well. These were as mentioned in a previous chapter and, in addition, sometimes Station Flight aircraft wore green. In the days before colour was banned from moving tail surfaces (to overcome balance problems caused by the added weight and consequent risk of tail-flutter), Gamecocks and Bulldogs sometimes had markings on the elevators as well, these indicating Flight Commanders' aircraft.

The Gloster Gladiator was superficially like its predecessor the Gauntlet, but it had three obvious distinguishing marks. These were its single-strut undercarriage with Dowty internally-sprung wheels, a single-bay wing layout and, of course, the cockpit cover. In those days it was called a hood, as fitted to a two-seater sports car in which any self-respecting fighter pilot might hope to take his girlfriend out to dine. Service flying was still fun when the Gladiator arrived on the scene but the fun, sadly, was not to last for long as the war clouds were all too obvious on the horizon.

When the Air Ministry issued the fighter Specification F.9/26, none of the proposals (including that from Gloster) was selected. However, H P Folland had up his sleeve as a backup the all-metal framed Gloster SS.18 two-bay biplane which first flew in January 1929. By this time, however, F.20/27 had overtaken the previous Spec but, despite this the SS.18 was still well up to the new requirements. Even though the Bristol Bulldog eventually won the F.20/27 competition, further refinements were made to the Gloster SS.18. With numerous modifications and variations in engine installation, the aircraft became successively the SS.18A, SS.18B, SS.19 and SS.19A. The final model, the SS.19B to Specification F.24/33, was the Gloster Gauntlet of 1933, described in the previous chapter and widely used by the RAF. Meanwhile,

Specification F.7/30 was announced by the Air Ministry at the end of 1930, by which time the Gloster Company was well advanced with the projected SS.37, a cleaned-up development of the Gauntlet. A top speed of at least 250 mph was required and the new Spec proposed the use of a Rolls-Royce Goshawk engine, a Kestrel derivative which was evaporatively cooled. In retrospect, this was an unsuitable choice.

UPGRADED ENGINE

By 1934, Bristol offered a new derivative of the Mercury VI, an 800 hp engine (later to become the Mk IX). Folland, therefore, offered a production version of the SS.37 to Spec F.7/30 with the new engine as a private venture, rather than using the Goshawk whose

Left The last of the silver biplanes. The Gladiator entered service in February 1937; this one, K7968, served with Nos 87, 65 and 112 Sqns

fire on target for long enough at rapidly increasing closing speeds was a serious problem.

The SS.19 design was revised in line with Spec F.7/30 and appeared at the RAF Display in 1931, with four Lewis guns, one under each wing, plus the two Vickers Mk IIIs, as well as four 20 lb bombs for good measure. Despite its added weight and suffering from increased drag, the remarkable 'Multi-gun fighter', as it was known, still managed a higher speed and a faster climb than any other air-cooled fighter used by the RAF. The way was clear for the development of the SS.37 in line with the Air Ministry's requirements. Light wing loading and clean design easily results in a considerable amount of float before touch-down, demanding a fair degree of skill to judge an accurate landing, particularly at night. The SS.37, a single-bay biplane, was even cleaner than the SS.18/19 series and boasted strengthened wings and struts, together with a very low-drag cantilever undercarriage and internally-sprung Dowty wheels. Effective drag-producing flaps were becoming a necessity and the airframe was therefore designed to incorporate split flaps on all four wings.

As related in the chapter on the Gauntlet, in order to assess their operation and to gain experience of the effect upon flight handling of such flaps (still something of a novelty), Gauntlet I K4103 was fitted experimentally with a hydraulically-operated set in 1936, initially allowing the flaps to be selected in any position to 90° down, by a hand pump. The flaps had reduced the Gauntlet's stalling speed by about 4 mph, and although the system was simple and satisfactory, it took too many pump movements to lower or raise the flaps completely. The gliding angle was greatly improved, giving the pilot a better view ahead and reducing the float, but causing a high initial rate of descent. At night, with flaps down, these combined effects were a great advantage, the pilot being better able to see the flare path when approaching at speeds down to 80 mph. However, because of the tail-heavy tendency when the throttle was opened with full flap, Martlesham recommended the installation of a system capable of acting more quickly. In October 1936, pneumatically-operated flaps were substituted but these then operated rather too abruptly and Martlesham recommended that the rate of raising the flaps should be reduced so that the 'sudden dangerous drop is eliminated'. This modification was adopted for the

attributes in wartime were doubtful. An armament of four machine guns was required, giving cause for much thought. The basic SS.19 airframe and the production Gauntlet were fitted for two Vickers Mk III machine guns firing along troughs in the fuselage sides. These guns, belt-fed from boxes containing 600 rounds of ammunition each, were prone to stoppages, but with their breeches within the cockpit, they could be cleared without too much difficulty by the pilot. The other standard British machine gun was the rather faster-firing Lewis which, though reliable, was handicapped by being fed from a drum which was heavy, cumbersome and only contained 97 rounds. There was not enough room within the fuselage for four such guns and, in any case, an interrupter gear cut the rate of fire substantially. To provide an adequate weight of

Gloster SS.37 and pilots of faster, hotter and similarly-equipped aeroplanes like the Spitfire had good cause to heed this.

Four machine guns were mounted in the SS.37, two new Vickers Mk IIIS (later to become the Mk Vs) in the fuselage and two drum-fed Lewis below the lower wings. The power promised from the new Mercury engine enabled Folland to feel confident of exceeding the F.7/30 requirements comfortably. As a result of the Gloster Aircraft Company joining forces with Hawker's in 1934, the standard Hawker construction process was used for the Mk II Gauntlet, the SS.37, and subsequently the Gladiator. In all major respects, other than those specified elsewhere, their design and construction were similar. The prototype

Below The second production Gladiator, K6130. Delivered to No 72 Sqn upon its formation in February 1937, it passed to No 112 Sqn and went out to the Middle East, crashing on 18 July 1940

SS.37, K5200, was built from a Gauntlet fuselage, with one surface-type oil-cooler on the top starboard decking and two Gallay-type units, used for cockpit-heating, mounted beside the main fuel tank. A head-rest was provided and the cockpit was still of the open type.

It was first flown by P E G Sayer on 12 September 1934, the engine being a 530 hp Mercury IV, later changed to a standard Gauntlet-type Mercury VIS. It first went to Martlesham early in 1935, being compared favourably with the other contenders for the F.7/30 Specification. The SS.37 thus appeared at the 1935 Hendon Air Display in July, bearing the Experimental Aircraft Park Number 1. In June, Gloster proposed details of the production version, with a Mercury IX of 830 hp, a sliding cockpit hood, revised tail and undercarriage and the Vickers Mk V gun in both fuselage and the lower wing positions. The chosen alternative to this layout was four British-built versions of the belt-fed American Colt-Browning

Above Gladiator K6131 shows off its planform above the fields of Gloucestershire for the benefit of Flight's camera

machine gun, modified to take standard British 0.303 in ammunition. This was a very fast-firing gun capable of 1200 rounds per minute which, thanks to its compactness, was adopted as a standard wing-mounted gun by the Air Ministry, an obvious successor to the time-honoured Vickers.

The re-armament scheme building up apace, the

Air Ministry ordered an initial prodution batch of 23 aircraft to Spec F.14/35, the formalities being completed within a couple of weeks and the name Gladiator bestowed on 1 July 1935. The prototype (K5200) began testing in its production form in September, by which time another batch had been ordered, fitted with three-blade Fairey-Reed propellers. On 23 October 1935 K5200 returned to Martlesham, where on landing, the port undercarriage leg sheared off and the lower wing was damaged. After quick repairs, tests

Above Gladiator K6132 served with No 72 Sqn, 13 Group Communications Flight and the RAE before being struck off charge on 26 April 1946. Note the lack of armament in this picture

were begun to evaluate the aircraft which, by then, had been fitted with a Fairey propeller.

Open cockpits were becoming unsuitable because the great increase in speed and the intense cold at high altitudes seriously reduced pilot efficiency. Covered cockpits were considered to be necessary, and the Gladiator had one of the earliest of these. Despite this, many pilots kept their hoods drawn back, preferring fresh air to the sometimes smelly confines of the Gladiator's cockpit. A report by the A&AEE in July 1936 noted that there were no noticeable effects on the

handling qualities, whether the hood was open or closed. Flying at over 30,000 ft with the hood closed, the pilot was quite warm, remaining at high altitude throughout the endurance of the aircraft in normal flying clothing without discomfort from the cold – there was no undue draught with it fully open either. The design and operation of the hood and windscreen were satisfactory, and did not appreciably obstruct the pilot's view. There was ample headroom without obstruction for a tall pilot with the hood closed, but there was a need for the hood to be capable of being locked in a series of positions. The noise with it open or closed was similar, and considered acceptable over an open R/T microphone.

One of the most interesting reports to emerge from Martlesham concerned Gladiator K7919. This aircraft was tested for the performance of the then new gyro-operated instruments which, with the ASI, altimeter and rate of climb instrument, were to feature in a cockpit panel layout which was standardized in all Service aircraft for two decades – a vital panel was adopted as standard by the RAF in 1937. In the Gladiator, the gyros of the Direction Indicator, Artificial Horizon and Turn & Bank Indicator were driven by a large venturi, mounted on the port rear centre section strut. All of the instruments worked satisfactorily, although the Rate of Climb was sluggish. The anti-vibration mounting was satisfactory as well, but the seat needed to be lowered fully by a pilot six feet tall in order to see the Artificial Horizon, as this was obstructed by the reflector gun-sight.

PROPELLER TRIALS

Martlesham, pre-occupied with comparative performances between different propellers, began a series of reports in October 1936 on tests carried out on K5200 fitted with a Mercury IX with a 0.5:1 gear ratio reduction gear, driving four different propellers – two two-blade wood, (sheathed and unsheathed) and two three-blade metal Fairey-Reed units. The sheathed propeller gave about 20 rpm less than the other in level flight. The second metal propeller was a replacement,

following damage to the first after the spinner came off in flight. Take-off, climb and level speeds were compared, with boost-control disconnected to ensure the maximum permissible boost. The climb was similar with both types of propeller. Level speed at full-throttle height was 4–5 mph greater with the metal airscrew, although the take-off was better with the wooden one, both sheathed and metal versions being satisfactory. In July 1937 vibration tests were published on two Fairey-Reed airscrews, the engine running smoother with the three-blader. While one was satisfactory, the other was only just so. Propellers which were nominally exactly similar could vary considerably and vibrations might develop to a degree which could preclude the use of this particular design.

The Gladiator was K7964, powered by a Mercury IX, with a 0.572:1 reduction gear. The same Gladiator was involved in a series of short performance trials in July, 1937 to investigate a reported tendency for the engine to cut out at high altitudes. A change of engine gear ratio from 0.5:1 was made in an attempt to obtain

Below A Gladiator being armed-up. Its armament comprised four .303 in machine guns: two were mounted in fuselage troughs, equipped with 600 rounds apiece firing between the engine cylinders and through the propeller arc; and two in the lower wings, each with 400 rounds

Above The second production Gladiator built, K6132

smooth running, this being a simple matter with the Mercury. The tests were made by K7964 and by the prototype K5200, first with a metal and then with a two-blade Watts propeller, the prototype still having the 0.5:1 reduction gear. The shortest take-off run was by K7964 at 150 yards, followed by K5200 with the Watts at 165 yd. The distance to clear a 50 ft screen was in similar vein, being 320, 330 and 450 yards respectively. Despite identical +3 lb boost at heights between 14,200 and 14,500 ft, and almost identical rpm (2725–2760), top speeds in level flight were different.

Gladiator K5200 with the metal propeller took the prize at 253 mph, the Watts coming second at 248 and K7964 marginally slower at 245.5 mph. The last achieved 1 mph faster with boost override giving +4.9 lb/in² at 12,400 ft. The increased gear-ratio of K7964 had the expected result of reducing take-off run and level speed. Afterwards, this aeroplane was climbed to

32,400 ft with no tendency for the engine to cut. The A&AEE sought opinions from squadron pilots on the relative merits of the three-blade propeller with 0.572 gear ratio and the two-blade Watts wooden unit and 0.5 ratio (as fitted to squadron aircraft). Two squadron aircraft with wooden airscrews and 0.5 gear ratio were compared with Martlesham aircraft with metal propellers and 0.572 ratio. There appeared to be little difference in vibration between the average wooden and the average metal unit, the latter being considered generally slightly superior. Reports issued in January, 1938 concerning vibration tests, with two average squadron Gladiators, concluding that the three-blade metal airscrew, in conjunction with the 0.572 reduction gear ratio, was in general superior to the two-blade unit.

The ultimate Martlesham report, issued in August 1938, concerned a Gladiator tested for the Portuguese government powered by a Mercury VIIIA engine with a 0.572:1 reduction gear – the Mercury VIIIA was similar to the Mk VIII, as used in the Bristol Blenheim

Above *The cockpit of the Shuttleworth Collection's preserved airworthy Gladiator L8032*

Right *The standard Gladiator instrument panel: 1 reflector gunsight, 2 artificial horizon, 3 airspeed indicator, 4 rate-of-climb gauge, 5 altimeter, 6 direction indicator, 7 turn-and-bank, 8 rpm gauge, 9 boost pressure gauge, 10 oil cooler control, 11 oil temperature gauge, 12 lighting rheostat, 13 oxygen gauge, 14 instrument lights, 15 magneto switches, 17 fuel contents gauge, 18 fuel cock, 19 fuel pressure gauge, 20 brake pressure gauge, 21 compass, 22 oil pressure gauge, 23 starting button, 24 primer, 25 carburettor cutout*

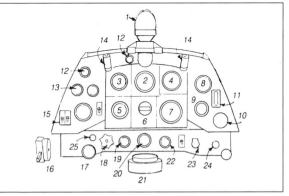

but with CC gun gear. Take-off tests compared wood and Fairey-Reed propellers, in the latter case 'retwisted' to $\frac{1}{2}°$ finer pitch. With the metal propeller, the Gladiator's weight was 4827 lb, 31 lb more than with the Watts. Take-off trials were made off tarmac into a steady wind of 19 mph, the pilot attempting the shortest possible ground run without regard to the subsequent climb. With the wooden airscrew it was 99 yd and with the metal 134 yd, the former giving 2000 rpm, marginally more than the metal – take-off speed

Right *Dramatic view of a formation of No 72 Sqn Gladiators put up specially for* Flight *from Tangmere soon after the squadron had become the first RAF unit to receive Gloster fighters in February 1937. The A Flight commander is flying the Gladiator on the extreme right*

was 60–62 mph. There was no measurable difference between the level speeds of 242 mph at 13,400 ft at $+3\frac{1}{2}$ lb/in² boost and 2750 rpm. The metal propeller gave a very slightly greater rate of climb to 15,000 ft, reached in 6.5 minutes as opposed to 7 minutes with the wooden unit. The vibration was worse with the metal airscrew, which was acceptable, but take-off with the wooden one was 'much superior'.

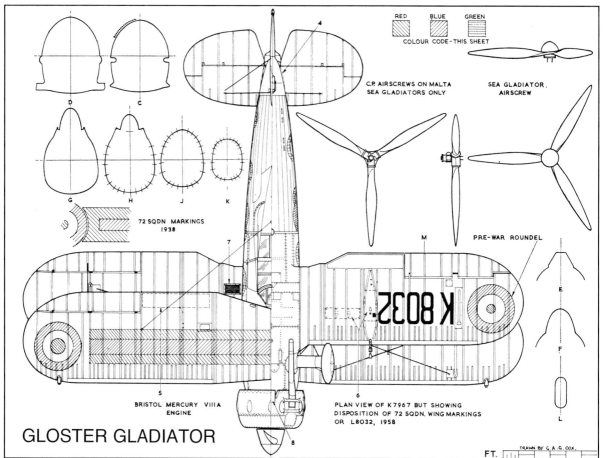

RED BLUE GREEN
COLOUR CODE-THIS SHEET

C.P. AIRSCREWS ON MALTA
SEA GLADIATORS ONLY

SEA GLADIATOR.
AIRSCREW

72 SQDN. MARKINGS
1938

PRE-WAR ROUNDEL

K 8032

BRISTOL MERCURY VIIIA
ENGINE

PLAN VIEW OF K7967 BUT SHOWING
DISPOSITION OF 72 SQDN. WING MARKINGS
OR L8032, 1958

GLOSTER GLADIATOR

FT.

DRAWN BY G.A.G.COX.

1/72nd scale drawing by G.A.G.COX

(ending an epoch which had begun with such stalwarts as the S.E.5, the Camel and the Snipe), but it contrived, against all the odds, to perform very creditably in combat against the enemy during the early phases of World War 2 when Britain's resources were stretched to the limit in such theatres as Northern France, Norway, Malta, North Africa and Greece.

OVERSEAS

In the more remote combat zones, such as Aden, Syria and Iraq, it remained in action well into 1941. Flown by determined and skilful pilots, it shot down an impressive number of enemy bombers (especially of the *Regia Aeronautica*), and frequently bested its nearest enemy equivalent, the marginally faster Fiat C.R.42 biplane. Indeed, in his classic book *The Gloster Gladiator* (Macdonald, 1964), Francis K Mason ventured to suggest that probably as many as 250 enemy aircraft were shot down by Gladiators, though not without some heavy losses in their own ranks. Two notable Gladiator exponents, Peter Wykeham-Barnes

Without any doubt the Gladiator deserves a place in the annals of RAF history scarcely less significant than that enjoyed by the Hurricane and Spitfire. Not only was it the very last of the long series of biplane fighters

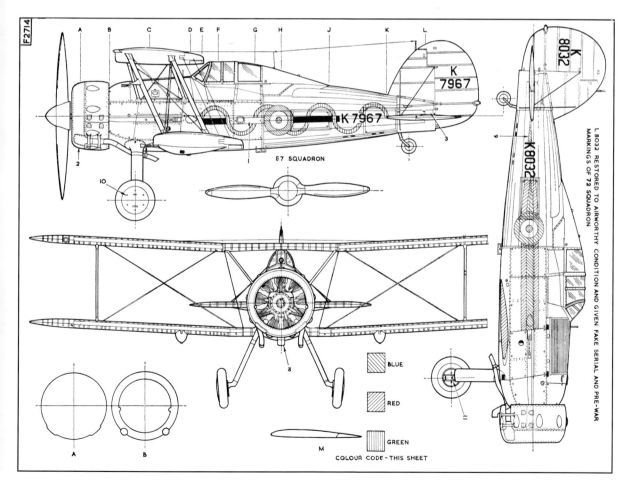

87 SQUADRON

K 7967

BLUE

RED

GREEN

COLOUR CODE - THIS SHEET

L 8032 RESTORED TO AIRWORTHY CONDITION AND GIVEN FAKE SERIAL AND PRE-WAR MARKINGS OF 72 SQUADRON (later to become Air Vice-Marshal Peter Wykeham-Barnes) and the legendary M T St John Pattle, were both shot down in Western Desert battles but escaped by parachute and went on to achieve high scores.

Just as with the Fleet Air Arm's Swordfish, the Gladiator seemed something of an anachronism in the World War Two environment. Patently a typical product of the RAF's biplane fighter era, the Gladiators which arrived in Northern France in the winter of 1939 must have brought back memories of their forebears on similar aerodromes against the same foe back in 1918. Notwithstanding its obsolescence, the Gladiator was still in full production and remained so until April 1940, by which time over 450 had been supplied to the RAF, making it their most prolific fighter biplane since the mass-production types of 1918.

Several factors had brought about this apparently paradoxical situation. Foremost among them was that the planned timetable for the phasing in of the Hurricanes and Spitfires had been set back by various production delays at the factories, and the small numbers becoming available were channelled into Metropolitan and South-East England defence, whilst the supplementary production flow of new Gladiators went to meet the newly expanding requirements overseas. Another element at work was the decision, following the Munich war-scare, to turn over all the part-time Auxiliary Air Force squadrons to fighter duties, and it was in this role that Gladiators made their first contacts with the *Luftwaffe* from Scottish bases in October 1939, and joined the British Expeditionary Force in France in November.

The Gladiator's first appearance before the public was by prototype K5200 in the New Types Park at the Hendon Air Display in July 1935. At this stage it still had an open cockpit – it remained for the production version to introduce enclosed cockpits to the pilots of Fighter Command. It was also to introduce four-gun armament, a sort of half-way house to the eight-gun monoplanes.

It was to be 22 February 1937 before the first Gladiators were collected by RAF pilots, the first production order having been placed on 1 July 1935. The pioneering squadron was No 72, commanded by Sqn Ldr E M Donaldson, which in fact retained them until Spitfires arrived in April 1939, the longest tenure of service in any Gladiator squadron. Next with Gladiators was No 3 Sqn at Kenley in April 1937, replacing its veteran Bulldogs which it had flown since 1931. By the close of 1937 the RAF possessed 202 Gladiators, of which 146 were in first-line squadrons.

By this time the Gauntlet re-equipment programme was in full swing (though 186 were still in squadrons) and Nos 54 and 65 Sqns at Hornchurch and No 56 Sqn at North Weald had all received Gladiators. Many fighter pilots lamented the passing of the earlier Gauntlet with its open cockpit and crisper handling qualities – the Gladiator's enclosed cockpit was not universally popular with the old hands and they frequently flew with it slid back. Undeniable, though, was its greater speed and doubled firepower, which far surpassed its Gloster forebear.

LAST DISPLAY

At the last of the RAF's annual air displays at Hendon on 26 June 1937, Gladiators of Nos 3 and 54 Sqns performed before an appreciative crowd and by the following year another Gladiator squadron, No 87, had put together a crack aerobatic team whose tied-together routines dazzled the audience at the Villacoublay Air Display on 10 July 1938. Flg Off G H J Feeny in K8027 was leading Plt Off R L Lorimer (K7972) and Sgt Dewdney (K7967).

Such perfection in close formation flying did not come easily, however, and during an exercise over Uckfield, Sussex, the RAF nearly lost one of its future aces of World War 2 when two Gladiators of No 65 Sqn (K7940 and K8014) collided in mid-air on 17 January 1938. The pilot in question was none other than 'Bob' Stanford Tuck, who escaped by parachute, the other pilot unfortunately losing his life.

From around March 1938, Gladiators began to appear with Fairey-Reed three-blade metal propellers. Their purpose was to eliminate the over-speeding experienced in dives with the large wooden two-blade propellers, which caused vibration and upset marksmanship. A similar change had earlier been effected on Gauntlets.

Gladiator strength in Fighter Command's pre-war battle order reached its peak in July 1938 when eight squadrons were equipped, namely No 3 (at Kenley), No 25 (at Hawkinge), Nos 54 and 65 (at Hornchurch), No 72 (at Church Fenton) and Nos 73, 85 and 87 (at Debden). No 56 Sqn, which had flown Gladiators until May 1938, then re-equipped with Hurricanes and No 80 Sqn, whose Gladiators had been a familiar sight at Henlow and Debden, went to Egypt to reinforce the growing RAF presence following the Abyssinian crisis.

September 1938 and the Munich Crisis signalled the end of Fighter Command's halcyon days – every-

Above A trio of No 87 Sqn Gladiators practising tied-together aerobatics over Debden in the summer of 1938

thing was sharply focused on states of readiness, intensive training and combat effectiveness. It witnessed the introduction of the drab warlike camouflage schemes supplanting the silver paint and colourful squadron heraldry familiar since the early 1920s, and hitherto central to the whole fighter squadron mystique. With only four Hurricane squadrons fully equipped, and no Spitfires at operational readiness, it saw the air defences of the UK dependent on six Gladiator squadrons, accompanied by eight still on Gauntlets, three of Furies and seven of Demons.

Right Gladiator I K7893 pictured at Kenley following an overshoot during landing. The No 3 Sqn aircraft subsequently flew with several other squadrons before being posted as lost on 20 July 1942, while flying with No 1411 Flight

As is now well known, the extra year of peace enabled Fighter Command to get its act together, not only in respect of the conversion to Hurricanes and Spitfires, but also in ensuring that the radar and fighter control systems were substantially in place. By April 1939, the Gladiators had disappeared from regular fighter squadrons and at the outbreak of war had been re-deployed for Auxiliary Air Force use by Nos 603, 605, 607 and 615 Sqns. Meanwhile, in the Middle and Near East, where new Gladiator II production was henceforth channelled, there were four squadrons, Nos 33, 80, 94 and 112. Altogether, 218 Gladiators were on strength in the UK and 178 overseas with the RAF when the war began.

It fell to No 607 Sqn, based at Acklington, Northumberland, to score the first Gladiator victory of the war. This was on 17 October 1939 when a flight led by Flt Lt J Sample downed a Dornier Do 18 flying-boat over the North Sea.

BACK IN THE FRONTLINE

During the same month, owing to the rapid expansion of Fighter Command, Gladiators were to make a re-appearance in regular squadron service when they equipped No 141 Sqn at Turnhouse, No 152 at Acklington and No 263 at Filton. No 263 Sqn was later destined to send its Gladiators to Norway, where they wrote a glorious chapter in RAF history fighting from a frozen lake, finally to be sunk with HMS *Glorious* on the voyage home.

By November 1939, as already mentioned, Gladiators of Nos 607 and 615 Sqns had been deployed to Northern France in support of the British Expeditionary Force. Few records survived of the Gladiator's gallant struggle against the *Luftwaffe* during the invasion of France, but No 607 Sqn, at least, is thought to have destroyed around 70 enemy aircraft.

As might be imagined, the Gladiator was not a leading contender in the Battle of Britain, but it did figure in a minor way by equipping a solitary squadron (No 247) which was formed at Roborough, Plymouth, in August 1940, primarily for the local defence of Devonport Dockyards. It was a descendant of the Sumburgh Flight which had served in the opening phases of the war in Scotland.

Meanwhile, with the entry of Italy into the war in June 1940, Gladiators found themselves responsible for the air defence of the entire Middle and Near East. Gladiators of Nos 33 and 80 Sqns had been active against Arab marauders in Palestine since 1938; the scene now shifted to the defence of Egypt and Aden and was to witness some classic air battles over the Western Desert against the *Regia Aeronautica*. The first victories were scored by No 33 Sqn on 14 June 1940 when Sgt Craig in N5768 shot down a Caproni Ca 310 and Flg Off E H Dean in N5782 accounted for a Fiat C.R.32. In the next six weeks, No 33 Sqn destroyed no less than 58 aircraft, including many Fiat C.R.42 fighters. With No 80 Sqn, the legendary M T St John 'Pat' Pattle (now widely recognised as the top-scoring RAF fighter pilot of World War Two) began his remarkable career on 4 July 1940 when, flying K7910, he shot down both a Breda 65 attack-bomber and a Fiat C.R.42. Pattle is thought to have shot down at least 40, and possibly 50 enemy aircraft before meeting his own death in the Greek campaign of 1941, where he flew Gladiators with No 33 Sqn.

Gladiators of Nos 33, 80 and 112 Sqns later fought heroically in the defence of Greece and Crete, before finally withdrawing from these actions in April 1941. The following month Gladiators (this time of No 94 Sqn) deployed from Aden saw action once again in defence of the RAF base at Habbaniyah, in Iraq, which had been invaded by a rebel army. They shot down two Messerschmitt Bf 110s and a Heinkel He 111, which had flown in to support the Iraqis.

No account of the Gladiator would be complete without mention of the defence of Malta during the dark days of June 1940. Much has been written about this, usually in the mistaken belief that three aircraft named *Faith*, *Hope* and *Charity* were solely responsible. In fact, no such names were ever used and the fighters in action against the Italian raiders were seven Sea Gladiators (with arrester gear removed) taken over by the RAF from Royal Navy stocks at Kalafrana. Eight more aircraft, in reserve, were drawn upon for spares by the hard-pressed ground maintenance personnel. Details are appended at the end of this chapter. At least one of the Sea Gladiators was adapted to take a non-standard Mercury engine removed from a Blenheim, complete with a variable-pitch airscrew and armour plate.

Below *Gladiator K6150 spun into Lyndhurst Road, Hove, Sussex on 24 January 1938. The pilot took to the silk and landed safely. K6150 had flown with Nos 3 and 74 Sqns since delivery to the RAF early in 1937*

With the supply of Hurricanes becoming more plentiful from the summer of 1941 (with the addition of Tomahawks from the USA), the Gladiator's fighting days in the Middle East were approaching their end, but No 261 Sqn continued to operate them during July and August on ground attack sorties, and for a brief period No 127 Sqn used them against Vichy-French Dewoitines in Syria. The very last enemy aircraft shot down by a Gladiator in Africa was almost certainly the Savoia-Marchetti S.M.81 *Pipistrello* bomber destroyed by Sgt Walter of No 6 Sqn in N5851 on 26 September 1941. No 6 Sqn retired its last Gladiator in January 1942.

Above This photograph of Sea Gladiator N5525 shows the ventral dinghy fairing and the deck arrester-hook just below and aft of the fuselage roundel. This Gladiator ended up in storage on Malta

Meteorological Flights and on radar calibration duties, providing essential intelligence for operational planning. These flights took place daily, in all weather conditions, the last by a Gladiator being from Ballyherbert in Northern Ireland by No 1402 Flight on 7 January 1945.

As already explained, the world events which engulfed the Gladiator from 1938 onwards, combined with unexpected delays in its replacement programme, resulted in much larger numbers entering service than would otherwise have been the case. As a result it became the most prolific of all the RAF's fighters which originated in peacetime, with a total quantity of 470 actually being manufactured for the Service, although the RAF deliveries were nearer to

WEATHER CHECKS

Back in the United Kingdom, the Gladiator had become extinct as a first-line fighter since No 247 Sqn had re-equipped with Hurricanes at the end of 1940, but it continued to give invaluable service with eight

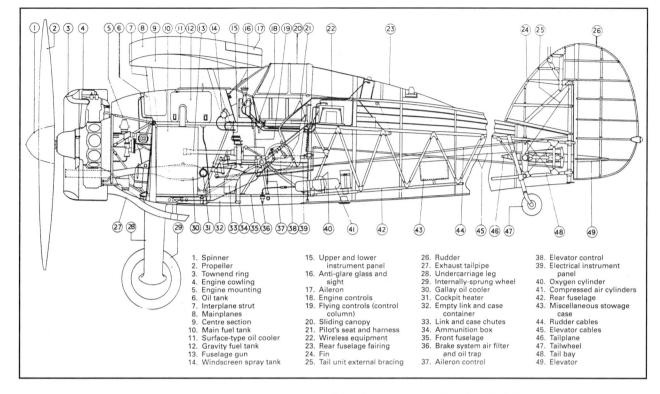

1. Spinner	15. Upper and lower	26. Rudder	38. Elevator control
2. Propeller	instrument panel	27. Exhaust tailpipe	39. Electrical instrument
3. Townend ring	16. Anti-glare glass and	28. Undercarriage leg	panel
4. Engine cowling	sight	29. Internally-sprung wheel	40. Oxygen cylinder
5. Engine mounting	17. Aileron	30. Gallay oil cooler	41. Compressed air cylinders
6. Oil tank	18. Engine controls	31. Cockpit heater	42. Rear fuselage
7. Interplane strut	19. Flying controls (control	32. Empty link and case	43. Miscellaneous stowage
8. Mainplanes	column)	container	case
9. Centre section	20. Sliding canopy	33. Link and case chutes	44. Rudder cables
10. Main fuel tank	21. Pilot's seat and harness	34. Ammunition box	45. Elevator cables
11. Surface-type oil cooler	22. Wireless equipment	35. Front fuselage	46. Tailplane
12. Gravity fuel tank	23. Rear fuselage fairing	36. Brake system air filter	47. Tailwheel
13. Fuselage gun	24. Fin	and oil trap	48. Tail bay
14. Windscreen spray tank	25. Tail unit external bracing	37. Aileron control	49. Elevator

400 since many had been diverted directly from RAF contracts to the air forces of Finland, Norway, Egypt and Portugal in 1939.

They also took into service (at Aden and Malta) 42 Sea Gladiators transferred from RN reserve stocks.

Gladiator Production for the RAF

Mk I	K6129–6151	L7608–7623
	K7892–8055	
Mk II	L8005–8032	N5680–5729
	N2303–2314	N5750–5789
	N5575–5594	N5810–5859
	N5620–5649	N5875–5924

It is gratifying to record that, today, a beautifully restored Gladiator, L8032, may still be seen flying from its base at the Shuttleworth Collection at Old Warden in Bedfordshire. Originally in No 72 Sqn's peacetime livery, it has since been camouflaged to represent an aircraft of No 247 Sqn in 1940. Another splendid (non-flying) example is on display in the 1938 colours of No 87 Sqn (K8042) at Hendon, this aircraft having originally served with No 61 OTU.

Right *Although not strictly an RAF aircraft, this unusual photograph nevertheless shows the hook-equipped Sea Gladiator in its element. This anonymous aircraft has just left the pitching deck of HMS* Furious

Gladiator units in the RAF

No 3 Squadron *Kenley: March 1937 to March 1938 and July 1938 to May 1939*
Biggin Hill: May 1939 to July 1939

Markings: Elongated green 'pendant' on fuselage sides with a rounded front ahead of the roundel. Above the mainplanes between the roundels was a green bar in an elongated diamond shape. Later, the markings were simplified, being confined to the display of the squadron numeral '3' ond the fin, superimposed on a green and white background (the squadron commander's aircraft had a green and black fin). From the time of the Munich Crisis in 1938, camouflage was introduced as described in the footnote

Serials: K6145, 6146, 6147, 6148, 6149, 6150, 7892, 7893, 7894, 7895, 7896, 7897, 7898, 7900, 7951, 7952, 7954, 7955, 7956, 7957, 7958, 7962, 7963, 7965, 7984, 7986, 8008, 8009, 8023, 8024, 8032, 8044

No 6 Squadron *Wadi Halfa: August 1941 to January 1942*
Primarily a tactical reconnaissance squadron, this unit also had some Gladiators on strength including N5820, 5821, 5828, 5830 and 5851

No 25 Squadron *Hawkinge, June 1938 to September 1938*
Northolt, September 1938 to October 1938
Hawkinge, October 1938 to December 1938

Markings: There is no evidence that the traditional black parallel bars associated with this squadron were ever applied to the Gladiators. From the time of Munich in September 1938 camouflage and code letters were applied
(see footnote)

Serials: K6147, 6149, 7961, 7982, 7983, 7988, 7989, 7992, 7995, 7996, 7997, 7998, 7999, 8000, 8019, 8030

No 33 Squadron *Ismailia, February 1938 to September 1938*
Heliopolis, September 1938 to October 1938
Ramleh, Mersah Matruh and Helwan, September 1938 to October 1940
Over the period February to June 1940, the Gladiators were reinforced by some Gauntlets

Markings: No distinctive squadron markings as with home fighter squadrons but code letters were painted in grey, at first against the silver finish and later with the desert camouflage. These were initially 'SO'. In 1939 they were changed to 'TN' and finally, with the outbreak of war, to 'NW'

Serials: K6140, 7897, 7954, 8006, 8007, 8013, 8018, 8025, 8031, 8034, 8035, 8036, 8037, 8038, 8039, 8047, 8048, 8050, 8054
L7608, 7609, 7611, 7612, 7613, 7614, 7615, 7616, 7617, 7619, 7620, 7622, 7623
N5513, 5535 (two ex-FAA Sea Gladiators used in Crete), N5750, 5751, 5752, 5761, 5763, 5764, 5765, 5766, 5768, 5769, 5770, 5773, 5774, 5775, 5776, 5777, 5779, 5780, 5781, 5782, 5783, 5784, 5785, 5786, 5825

No 54 Squadron *Hornchurch, April 1937 to April 1939*

Markings: No squadron markings were carried on the wings or fuselage but the squadron's crest was displayed inside the regulation spearhead frame on the fin superimposed on the appropriate flight colouring. From the Munich Crisis in September 1938, camouflage was applied and code letters (see footnote)

Serials: K7894, 7917, 7918, 7920, 7921, 7923, 7925, 7926, 7927, 7928, 7929, 7930, 7931, 7932, 7933, 7935, 7937, 7938, 7945, 7949, 7961, 7972, 7987, 7990, 8013, 8014, 8015, 8029, 8044

No 56 Squadron *North Weald, July 1937 to May 1938*

Markings: No photographic evidence has ever been produced to support the claim made in some accounts that the traditional red and white checks of this unit were painted on the Gladiators, but it remains a possibility

Serials: K6145, 6147, 6149, 7961, 7982, 7983, 7987, 7988, 7989, 7990, 7991, 7992, 7993, 7994, 7995, 7996, 7997, 7998, 7999, 8000, 8020, 8021, 8022, 8030

No 65 Squadron *Hornchurch, June 1937 to April 1939*

Markings: No records have come to light to support the claim, which remains a possibility, that the previous Gauntlet markings were repeated on the Gladiators. These consisted of a series of red chevrons either side of the roundel on the fuselage sides. Similar markings above the top mainplanes also remain unconfirmed. From the time of Munich, camouflage and code letters were introduced (see footnote)

Serials: K7895, 7936, 7939, 7940, 7941, 7942, 7943, 7945, 7950, 7961, 7970, 7979, 7983, 7996, 7997, 7998, 7999, 8001, 8002, 8013, 8014, 8015, 8016, 8033, 8040, 8044

No 72 Squadron *Tangmere, March 1937 to May 1937*
Church Fenton, June 1937 to April 1939

Markings: Red bars surrounding a blue rectangle appeared above the upper mainplanes between the roundels and on the fuselage similar markings were used, tapering aft of the roundel. Camouflage and code letters replaced these markings from September 1938 onwards (see footnote)

Serials: K6130, 6131, 6132, 6133, 6134, 6136, 6137, 6138, 6139, 6140, 6141, 6142, 6143, 6144, 6145, 7893, 7897, 7922, 7923, 7934, 7954, 7963, 7969, 7974, 7977, 7978, 7981, 7984, 7986, 8004, 8019

No 73 Squadron *Debden, June 1937 to November 1937*
Digby, November 1937 to July 1938

Markings: Two blue bands enclosing a yellow band (in the shape of a sword blade) appeared on each upper mainplane between the roundels and were repeated on the fuselage either side of the roundel

Serials: K6151, 7893, 7951, 7952, 7953, 7954, 7955, 7956, 7957, 7958, 7959, 7960, 7961, 7962, 7963, 7964, 7965, 7984, 7985, 7986, 8023, 8024, 8031, 8032

No 74 Squadron *Hornchurch, June 1937 to July 1937*
Five Gladiators (K6145–6148 and K6150) were allocated to this squadron but due to a change in policy were almost immediately re-assigned to No 3 Sqn, leaving No 74 to continue flying Gauntlets

No 80 Squadron *Henlow, March 1937 to June 1937*
Debden, June 1937 to April 1938
Egypt, May 1938 to November 1940
Greece, November 1940 to April 1941

Markings: No squadron markings on wings or fuselage but the unit badge (a symbolical bell) appeared inside the regulation spearhead frame on the fin. During initial service overseas, the Gladiators remained silver but introduced the code letters 'OD' in grey. As war approached, desert camouflage was introduced and the code letters were changed first to 'GK' and finally to 'YK'

Serials: K6146, 6148, 7829, 7893, 7900, 7901, 7902, 7903, 7904, 7905, 7906, 7907, 7908, 7909, 7910, 7911, 7912, 7913, 7914, 7915, 7916, 7923, 7937, 7971, 7973, 8003, 8008, 8009, 8010, 8011, 8012, 8013, 8017, 8020, 8021, 8022, 8036, 8047, 8051
L8009, 8010, 8011
N5583, 5761, 5763, 5776, 5784, 5785, 5788, 5811, 5812, 5814, 5816, 5819, 5823, 5827, 5832, 5854, 5858, 5859, 5876

No 85 Squadron *Debden, June 1938 to September 1938*
Very briefly, before re-equipping with Hurricanes, this squadron had a few Gladiators (ex-No 87 Sqn) on strength but it never became operational and carried no distinctive markings

Right *Gloster Gladiator Is of No 72 Sqn with second production aircraft K6130 in the foreground. This Gladiator later transferred to No 112 Sqn and hit a hill obscured by a cloud at Qaret el Naga on 18 July 1940. The other aircraft in this formation are K6142, K6144, K6131 and K6134. Every single one had been lost in crashes by the end of 1940*

Above left *With their silver paint replaced with dark earth and green, a line up of No 615 'County of Surrey' Sqn Gladiator Is sit chocked at Kenley in August 1939. Formed in December 1938 on Gauntlets, the squadron moved to Croydon once war was declared, receiving No 605 Sqn's Gladiator Mk IIs in place of their elderly Mk Is in October*

No 87 Squadron *Debden, June 1937 to July 1938*

Markings: A black bar through which a green undulating line was threaded. This appeared alongside the fuselage ahead and aft of the roundel but not on the wings

Serials: K7966, 7967, 7968, 7969, 7970, 7971, 7972, 7973, 7974, 7975, 7977, 7978, 7979, 7980, 7981, 8026, 8027, 8028, 8033

No 94 Squadron *Khormaksar, March 1939 to May 1941*

Markings: Desert camouflage and the code letters 'GO' in grey

Serials: K7899
L7616, 7617
N2278, 2279, 2283, 2284, 2285, 2288, 2289, 2290, 2291, 2292, 2293, 2294, 2295, 5627, 5777, 5778, 5780, 5787, 5857, 5887, 5889, 5892, 5895, 5896 (N2278 to 2295 were in fact sea Gladiators)

No 112 Squadron *Helwan, June 1939 to February 1941*
Gladiators were supplemented by a few Gauntlets between March and July 1940

Markings: Desert camouflage, initially with the code letters 'XO', later 'RT', in grey
Serials: K6134, 6135, 6136, 6143, 7948, 7969, 7974, 7977, 7986
L7612, 7619

No 123 Squadron *Abadan, October 1942 to November 1942*
While awaiting re-equipment with Hurricanes, one flight was equipped with Gladiators for Army Co-operation duties

Markings: Desert camouflage. It is doubtful if the assigned code letters 'XE' were actually used

Serials: N5857

No 127 Squadron *Iraq and Syria, June 1941 to July 1941*
Operated one flight of Gladiators (the other flight had Hurricanes) mainly in Syria

Markings: Desert camouflage

Serials: K7899, 7907, 8048
N5857

No 141 Squadron *Turnhouse, October 1939 to November 1939*

Markings: Camouflaged, but it is not known whether the officially allocated code letters 'TW' were ever applied to the Gladiators

Serials: K7918, 7921, 7925, 7926, 7928, 7936, 7938, 7990
N5626, 5893, 5902, 5903

No 152 Squadron *Acklington (with detachments at Leconfield and Sumburgh), October 1939 to January 1940*

Markings: Camouflaged, with the code letters 'UM' in grey

Serials: K7894, 7920, 7924, 7927, 7932, 7935, 7972
N5579, 5588, 5589, 5623, 5624, 5638, 5640, 5642, 5643, 5645, 5646

No 247 Squadron *Roborough (with detachments to Exeter), August 1940 to January 1941*

Markings : Camouflaged, with code letters 'HP' in grey

Serials: K8049
N2308, 2306, 5576, 5585, 5622, 5631, 5644, 5648, 5649, 5684, 5685, 5702, 5897, 5901

Above An anonymous Gladiator patrolling the Suez Canal, Egypt, in typically oppressive heat

No 261 Squadron *Malta, August 1940 to January 1941*
Habbaniyah, July 1941 to September 1941
This squadron took over the remains of the Hal Far Fighter Flight, but later added other Gladiators, though it was primarily a Hurricane unit

Markings: Desert camouflage with individual aircraft indentification letters

Serials: K6147, 7928, 7984, 7989, 7990
N5780

Hal Far Fighter Flight *Malta, April to June 1940*
Sea Gladiators taken over from Royal Navy reserves at Kalafrana and operated by the RAF

Markings: Retained Fleet Air Arm camouflage. No individual unit insignia, but carried single identification letter after of roundel

Serials: N5519, 5520, 5523, 5524, 5528, 5529, 5531
Also assigned as spares were N5518, 5521, 5522, 5525, 5527, 5528, 5530

No 263 Squadron *Filton, October 1939 to April 1940*
Norway, April 1940 to June 1940

Markings: Camouflaged, with code letters 'HE' in grey

Serials: K6145, 7917, 7946, 7942, 7952, 7961, 7965, 7979, 7985, 8004
8020, 8032, 8044
N5579, 5588, 5589, 5624, 5628, 5632, 5633, 5634, 5635, 5639, 5641,
5644, 5647, 5681, 5690, 5695, 5697, 5698, 5699, 5705, 5894, 5898,
5905, 5906, 5907, 5908

No 274 Squadron *Amriya, August 1940 to November 1940*
Gladiators equipped one flight of this squadron, before it became wholly
equipped with Hurricanes

Markings: Desert camouflage. It is not certain whether the officially
allocated code letters 'YK' were used on the Gladiators

Serials: N5750, 5756, 5810, 5829

No 520 Squadron *Gibraltar, September 1943 to August 1944*
Gladiators formed part of the mixed equipment (which included Hudsons,
Halifaxes and Hurricanes) used by this meteorological reconnaissance
unit

Markings: Camouflaged, but it is not certain whether the Gladiators used
the official code letters '2M'

Serials: N5630

No 521 Squadron *Bircham Newton, July 1942 to March 1943*
Docking, September 1943 to March 1945

*Below Lacking No 72 Sqn's fuselage markings, K8004 still
boasts flight commander's colours. This Gladiator was later
lost in Norway in April 1940 whilst serving with No 263 Sqn*

Gladiators were used as part of the mixed equipment of this meteorological unit (which included Blenheims, Hudsons, Spitfires and Mosquitoes)

Markings: Camouflaged, but no code letters were used

Serials: K7972, 8043
N2307, 2309, 2310, 5594, 5621, 5897, 5900, 5902

No 603 Squadron *Turnhouse, March 1939 to October 1939*

Markings: Camouflaged, with the code letters 'RL' in grey. These were
changed to 'XT' in September 1939

Serials: K7894, 7917, 7918, 7920, 7921, 7924, 7925, 7926, 7927, 7928,
7929, 7931, 7932, 7935, 7936, 7938, 7972, 7990

No 604 Squadron *Northolt and Manston, May 1940*

Markings: Camouflaged, but unlikely to have carried the code letters 'NG'
used by the Blenheim night fighters to which they quickly reverted

Serials: K7943, 7970, 7990, 8033

No 605 Squadron *Castle Bromwich, April 1939 to August 1939*
Tangmere, August 1939 to November 1939

Markings: Camouflaged, with the code letters 'HE' in grey

Serials: K6145, 7917, 7942, 7946, 7951, 7952, 7961, 7965, 8044
N2303, 2304, 2305, 2306, 2310, 2311, 2312, 2313, 2314

No 607 Squadron *Usworth, December 1938 to October 1939*
Acklington, October 1939 to November 1939
Croydon, November 1939
France, December 1939 to March 1940

Markings: Camouflaged, with the code letters 'LW' in grey. These were
changed to 'AF' in September 1939

Left The Gladiator's generous amount of flap caught new pilots napping and minor accidents were very common during the type's introductory period into service – damaged wingtips reached almost epidemic proportions

Serials: K6137, 6147, 6149, 7931, 7965, 7967, 7980, 7982, 7983, 7988, 7989, 7992, 7995, 7996, 7997, 7998, 7999, 8000, 8020, 8026, 8030

No 615 Squadron *Kenley, June 1939 to September 1939*
Croydon, September 1939 to October 1939
France, November 1939 to May 1940

Markings: Camouflaged, with the code letters 'RR' in grey. These were changed to 'KW' in September 1939

Serials: K7938, 7946, 7948 7957, 7961, 7976, 8004, 8044
N2302, 2303, 2304, 2306, 2308, 2309, 2310, 2312, 5577, 5578, 5580, 5581, 5582, 5583, 5585, 5586, 5587, 5900

No 3 RAAF Squadron *Helwan and Gambut, September 1940 to January 1941*
Operated under RAF control using mainly ex-No 112, 33 and 80 Sqn Gladiators. Until December 1940, was mixed with one flight of Lysanders and four Gauntlets.

Markings: Desert camouflage, with the code letters 'NW'

Serials: K6142, 7615, 7616, 7617, 7893, 7901, 7922, 7947, 7963, 8008, 8009, 8022, 8048
L7615, 7616, 7617, 8008, 8009
N5750, 5753, 5754, 5756, 5763, 5764, 5765, 7566, 5768, 5769, 5776, 5779, 5780, 5782, 5786, 5810, 5856

Miscellaneous units using Gladiators

No 16 Squadron
N2306 (coded 'UG-R') for Army Co-operation

No 239 Squadron
N2304 (coded 'HB-G') for anti-aircraft gun calibration

Prestwick Fighter Flight
N5912, 5914

Turnhouse Station Flight
N5693, 5714, 5719, 5720, 5894

Shetland Fighter Flight
N2266, 5642, 5643, 5701, 5716, 5901

Aden Station Flight
N5910, 5911, 5913, 5916, 5917, 5918

No 1401 (Met) Flight *(Bircham Newton)*
N2307, 2309, 2310, 5594, 5621

No 1402 (Met) Flight *(Aldergrove)*
N5575, 5576, 5590, 5591, 5592, 5593, 5687, 5900

No 1403 (Met) Flight *(Mildenhall)*
N5594, 5620, 5621, 5630

No 1411 (Met) Flight *(Heliopolis)*
K6138, 7893, 7925, 7963, 8003, 8008

No 1412 (Met) Flight *(Khartoum)*
K6140, 8001

No 1413 (Met) Flight *(Nicosia)*
K7914, 7919, 7926, 7949, 7978, 7983, 7999

No 1414 (Met) Flight *(Eastleigh, East Africa)*
K8037

No 1415 (Met) Flight *(Habbaniyah)*
K6147

No 1560 (Met) Flight *(West Afica)*
N5622, 5625, 5682

No 1561 (Met) Flight *(West Africa)*
N5648, 5693, 5703

No 1562 (Met) Flight *(West Africa)*
N5625, 5637, 5684, 5702

No 1563 (Met) Flight *(Cyrenaica)*
K8003, 8027

'X' Flight Abadan
K7928, 7989
N5780, 5857

'X' Flight Amman
K6140, 6141, 7907, 7914, 7947, 7954, 7978
N5777, 5780

No 1 Anti-Aircraft School
K7933

No 2 AACU
K7920, 8041

Nos 2, 7 and 10 FTS
K8040

No 9 FTS
N6131

CFS
K7898

No 5 OTU
K7926, 7945, 7970, 8001, 8033, 8052

No 6 OTU
K8020, 8027, 8052

No 8 OTU
K8041

No 41 OTU
N5636

No 60 OTU
K8044, 8045

No 61 OTU
K7898, 7927, 8004
L8032
N5903

No 237 Squadron
N5815, 5820, 5824, 5830, 5853, 5856

Footnote
From the time of the Munich Crisis in September 1938, all Fighter Command Gladiators (in common with other silver-painted biplanes) were camouflaged in green and brown and ultimately received grey code letters identifying the squadron. The codes allocated were 'OP' (No 3 Sqn), 'RX' (No 25 Sqn), 'DL' (No 54 Sqn), 'FZ' (No 65 Sqn), and 'RN' (No 72 Sqn). There is some doubt whether Nos 25 and 54 Sqns actually used their codes on Gladiators.

Gloster Gladiator I data

Engine: Bristol Mercury IX, 830 hp, 2750 rpm, +3 lb/in² boost, 14,250 ft

Dimensions
Span	32 ft 3 in
Length	27 ft 5 in
Height	10 ft 4 in
Wing Area	313 ft²

Weights
Empty	3217 lbs
Loaded	4594 lbs

Performance
Max Speed	254 mph, 12,400 ft
Stalling Speed	53 mph
Time to 10,000 ft	4.75 minutes
Ceiling	32,800 ft
Fuel	83 gallons, in 20 gal reserve and 63 gal main tanks, 87 octane

Armament: Four belt-fed 0.303 in Colt-Browning machine guns, two mounted in the fuselage, each with 600 rounds and two in the lower wings, each with 400 rounds

---

Below *Photographed on 12 December 1939, just a month after arriving in France, a clutch of optimistic No 615 Sqn pilots share a joke prior to flying a patrol. Six months later, these men were locked in mortal combat with Messerschmitt Bf 109s and Bf 110s during the May Blitzkrieg*

INDEX

Aircraft types are indexed under
manufacturers, not individual names, eg
Sopwith Snipe, not Snipe, whilst figures in
italics denote photographs.